A CULTURAL HISTORY
OF IDEAS

VOLUME 5

A Cultural History of Ideas
General Editors: Sophia Rosenfeld and Peter T. Struck

Volume 1
A Cultural History of Ideas in Classical Antiquity
Edited by Clifford Ando, Thomas Habinek and Giulia Sissa

Volume 2
A Cultural History of Ideas in the Medieval Age
Edited by Dallas G. Denery II

Volume 3
A Cultural History of Ideas in the Renaissance
Edited by Jill Kraye

Volume 4
A Cultural History of Ideas in the Age of Enlightenment
Edited by Jack R. Censer

Volume 5
A Cultural History of Ideas in the Age of Empire
Edited by James H. Johnson

Volume 6
A Cultural History of Ideas in the Modern Age
Edited by Stefanos Geroulanos

A CULTURAL HISTORY
OF IDEAS

IN THE AGE
OF EMPIRE

Edited by James H. Johnson

BLOOMSBURY ACADEMIC
LONDON • NEW YORK • OXFORD • NEW DELHI • SYDNEY

BLOOMSBURY ACADEMIC
Bloomsbury Publishing Plc
50 Bedford Square, London, WC1B 3DP, UK
1385 Broadway, New York, NY 10018, USA
29 Earlsfort Terrace, Dublin 2, Ireland

BLOOMSBURY, BLOOMSBURY ACADEMIC and the Diana logo are trademarks
of Bloomsbury Publishing Plc

First published in Great Britain 2022

Cover image: *The Artist's Father, Reading "L'Événement"*, 1866 by Paul Cézanne/Collection
of Mr. and Mrs. Paul Mellon/National Gallery of Art

A catalogue record for this book is available from the British Library.

A catalog record for this book is available from the Library of Congress.

ISBN: HB: 978-1-3500-0748-2
        Set: 978-1-3500-0755-0

Series: The Cultural Histories Series

Typeset by Integra Software Services Pvt. Ltd.
Printed and bound in Great Britain

To find out more about our authors and books visit www.bloomsbury.com
and sign up for our newsletters.

CONTENTS

ILLUSTRATIONS

GENERAL EDITORS' PREFACE

When Arthur Lovejoy introduced the field of the history of ideas to his listeners in the 1933 William James lectures, later published as *The Great Chain of Being*, he compared ideas to molecules. As he explained it, molecules combine and recombine to make compounds that vary over time. Yet the underlying stuff abides. The comparison gave him a way to capture the dynamic properties of ideas themselves and to forestall this or that thinker's eagerness to claim novelty. Further, since the periodic table has only so many elements, Lovejoy's conceit suggested that a person could, retroactively, make sensible statements about the whole.

In this book series devoted to the history of ideas, we hope to be able to make sensible judgements about the whole, but we are also convinced that the analogy needs rethinking. When Lovejoy accorded agency to the elements, with their pent-up interactive energies, he left out of focus the solution or medium in which those chemicals do their interacting. The non-noetic factors for which Lovejoy allowed come only from thinkers' internal dispositions, personal habits and preferences that might vary from person to person or from time to time. These volumes aim to widen considerably the intellectual historian's conception of how ideas emerge and move through the world.

A Cultural History of Ideas sweeps over 2,800 years of evidence. It proceeds on the premise that certain broad areas of inquiry have held humans' collective attention across a segment of the globe over all of this time. These nine topics are not presented as ideas in any simple sense. G. E. R. Lloyd's treatment of "Nature" in antiquity in volume 1 will already belie any confidence in a singular, perduring core even in this one-ninth of the terrain these volumes lay out. We propose this taxonomy instead as a set of general areas of investigation focused on comparable subjects across the ages. As historians of ideas, we aim to trace in this book series prominent lines of thought in each of these various realms—chapter by chapter, in the same order across volumes, from antiquity to the present—with close attention to constancy, change, and variation alike.

The first of these areas is "Knowledge" itself: what are we to make of the immaterial notions stored in our minds? Which ones count as true? How are such truths found, divided into new categories, conveyed, and used? After all, it is only in the twentieth century that anyone could speak meaningfully of the humanistic, social, biological, and physical sciences as distinct branches of knowledge. Many other systems came before. From "Knowledge," we turn to one of its central foci and the other starting point of this series: "The Human Self" in all its dimensions, physical, intellectual, emotional, and more. For it is the self that is the knower.

Then, moving outward from the singular self, we shift to "Ethics and Social Relations," or humans in concert with one another, and "Politics and Economies," or systems for organizing that collective existence legally and materially. "Nature" follows, including the human body, but also encompassing the earth that humans share with other animals, plants, and minerals, as well as the atmosphere and celestial bodies. Continuing to widen our lens, "Religion and the Divine" then takes the focus to the world beyond nature and to thinking about our origins, our afterlives, and our beliefs, which also means at times the limits of human knowledge.

The final categories take up, in close conversation with all of these previous domains, the realm of representation. "Language, Poetry, Rhetoric" concerns thinking about words in their many forms and uses. "The Arts" expands those questions into other symbolic systems employed in music, dance, theatre, fashion, architecture, design, and especially the visual arts, with a focus too on conceptions of beauty. Finally, "History" draws our attention to the representation of time itself, including notions of past, present, and future that simultaneously bring us full circle back to the understandings of knowledge and the self where we began.

Some specific ideas or concepts—freedom, dreams, power, difference, the environment, anger, to pick a random assortment—cross these many areas of inquiry and will appear more than once. But we take these nine broad categories to be proxies for some of the most fundamental areas to which humans in the domains of our focus—from so-called great thinkers like Plato or Locke or Einstein, to political leaders from Augustus to Charlemagne to Catherine the Great or Gandhi, to now-nameless scribes or teachers or midwives or bricklayers—have, over the centuries, applied their minds, alone and together.

But what is a *cultural* history of ideas? There are two distinguishing features of this approach, and both begin from the premise that the history of ideas is not, as some earlier historians including Lovejoy would have it, best understood as the record of a perennial conversation that largely transcends the specifics of space and time. Rather, we posit that just as the answers to big questions change depending on where and when we look, so do the questions themselves along with their stakes. "What is freedom?" means something very different to an enslaved Celt living in ancient Rome, a twelfth-century French monk, an aspiring merchant involved in transatlantic trade in seventeenth-century London, and a political theorist working in a US university in the era of late capitalism.

A cultural history of ideas is thus imagined, first, as a way to demonstrate the proposition that even the most innovative ideas to emerge from such queries, as well as the uses and impact of those ideas, have varied enormously depending on a host of contingent and contextual features extrinsic to the intellects that gave birth to them. These external features go well beyond other, competing ideas, or even competing texts in which other ideas are housed, despite the arguments of Quentin Skinner and much of what is thought of today as contextualized intellectual history. Cultural historians of ideas, to understand the thought of the past, necessarily look considerably more widely at a range of different domains of human life—or culture in the broadest sense.

Those cultural factors include changes in technology, media, and the economics of production and distribution; the authors in these volumes consider the evolution of ideas in relation to the emergence of alphabetic script and scribal culture, the printing press, photography, the computer, and other methods of communication that shaped their respective eras, as well as the commerce established around them. Our list also includes differing social structures and kinds of hierarchies and status markers, from race and gender, to estate, wealth, patronage, and credentialing, that have brought new kinds of thinkers to the fore and turned others into enemies or nonentities. In these pages we will meet, and also identify the support systems behind, philosophers, physicians, librarians, clerics, writers, artists, state officials, and only from the nineteenth century onward, "scientists," "experts," and, indeed, "intellectuals," as well as those denied these appellations. Other factors shaping ideas—including those of the most influential thinkers of every era—have been changes to laws; to religious practice and identity; to the distribution of resources; to patterns of migration, settlement, and urbanization; to notions of taste and manners; and to literacy rates, education, and intellectual life itself. So, too, do we need to study encounters between different peoples, whether through war, conquest, travel and exploration, exploitation, or peaceful cultural and commercial exchange. Then there is space in another sense. Historically specific settings, whether they be market places, monasteries, universities, salons, courts, coffee houses, medical clinics, port city docks, or think tanks, have inflected how ideas have been forged, disseminated, and debated and, ultimately, the form they have taken. So have modes of sociability. How can we understand the power of the ideas of Demosthenes or Horace or Lord Byron or Sarah Bernhardt without accounting for the social practices in which they were embedded, be that public oration, letter writing, listening to sermons or novels read out loud, or attending public performances, but also the material infrastructure behind those endeavors, from road construction to the microphone? And scaffolding everything else in the realm of ideas have, of course, always been geopolitics and the apparatuses of power: empires, nations, regions, city states, kingdoms, dioceses, and villages, but also competition about and between ideologies, factions and parties, and policies, whether established by vote, by decree, or by physical coercion.

In approaching ideas in this deeply contextual way, the cultural history of ideas could be said to be borrowing from the subfield known as the sociology of knowledge. Both share an interest in uncovering the structures, including practices and institutions, that allow for the varied means by which knowledge has been invented, organized, kept secret, exchanged, transformed, and weaponized to accomplish various goals, from acts of radical imagination and liberation to keeping people in their place. Equally, though, the approach employed in these volumes could be said to draw on histories of reading, of looking, and of hearing, that is, of interpretation and reinterpretation, or hermeneutics and textual exegesis, across genres, languages, and eras—all modes long associated with histories of the arts and literature and philosophy. Moreover, a cultural history of ideas should equally be a history of dissent and of forms of censorship and repression instituted in response. Historians also need to establish the evolving boundaries between the sayable and the unsayable, the representable and the unrepresentable, and why and how they have been enforced or not. That means paying attention to conflicts and forms of violence over just these questions as well as networks and modes of intellectual collaboration. Part of the interest in looking at the history of thought embedded in ever-shifting contexts over such a long period of time is discovering how some ideas—say, ideas about gender difference or modes of seeing others—persist across moments of social and political fracture, such as major wars. Another part is discovering how ideas are transformed by—or help transform—larger movements in the worlds that produced them; consider, for example, how much the ideas of Jean-Jacques Rousseau shaped political and religious practice in the context of the French Revolution, from republicanism to the institution of a civil religion, but also how his conceptual innovations were blamed for the revolution's excesses and thus delegitimized afterward. Some ideas, of course, fail to create any kind of traction until long after their moment of invention. Or they never do. All this is of interest to the historian of ideas too.

Yet there is a second sense in which these volumes function as a *cultural* history of ideas. Grasping this aspect requires looking more to anthropology than to sociology or literary theory. It also demands taking seriously the ideas and representations that animate everyday life, which is another meaning of culture. This approach turns our attention at least partly away from the ideas associated with philosophers, famous thinkers, or even major social movements or modern "isms" like nationalism or communism in their larger contexts. It does so in favor of a focus on collective habits, rituals, patterns of speech and behavior, and customary forms of representation operative in social, political, and economic experience, seeing them as imbued with, and productive of, a vital, culturally specific landscape of ideas. Some scholars call these ideas, taken together, folk knowledge or folk logic. From the Annaliste tradition of history writing in France, others have adopted the term *mentalité*. Included under its purview are, potentially, studies of the history of collective memory, of values, of popular and mass culture, and of the senses and emotions and decision-making in all their historical particularity.

Importantly for our purposes, sometimes the realm or realms of *mentalité* have operated to uphold the dominant ideology of the moment or to boost an ascendant one; Jack Censer and Gary Kates's introduction to the volume on the Enlightenment, for example, highlights the way eighteenth-century advertising circulars, the so-called *Affiches*, subtly bolstered the intellectual currents associated with Enlightenment philosophy without ever drawing directly on the work of any of its key thinkers. But other times folk knowledge has worked to undergird marginalized people's efforts to resist, circumvent, or revise dominant thinking, whether that has been in order to preserve traditions under pressure or to try to break free of various forms of repression. Consider craftworkers or Black revolutionaries of various eras deploying vernacular notions and forms of protest to challenge those with political and material power, including those who own the means of production. Often these commonplace and quotidian ideas, even as they structure collective life, are so routine and taken-for-granted within the culture where they exist that they go largely unremarked upon in any of the standard modes of conveying thought that are the focus of most histories of ideas. It is only when such everyday ideas collapse or get deployed in new ways that we tend to see that they belong to history too—and bear some relationship to the better-known history of explicit ideas.

What this means is that a cultural history of ideas in the second sense must extend its source base well beyond great books or texts of any kind; relevant ideas are just as likely to be embedded in visual, material, or somatic forms as they are in writing. Coin collections, garden designs, bits of code, temple complex plans, dance patterns, even habits of greeting: all become potential sites for uncovering foundational ideas in past moments and varied places. It also means thinking beyond traditional notions of thinker or audience to encompass the voices, eyes, and ears of those traditionally excluded from the tribe of "intellectuals," including women, people of color, and the nonliterate, as they can be unearthed from these varied sources. The volumes and individual chapters of this series will have succeeded if readers come away with an ability to take recognizable ideas or ideologies (i.e., those of Karl Marx and, subsequently, Marxism) or recognizable moments in intellectual history (i.e., "the Middle Ages") and see them as doubly imbricated in culture as ideational context and culture as the realm of everyday meaning-making and representation.

One risk, of course, is that this collection, with its cultural approach to ideas, ends up reinforcing an obsolete ideological construction paid lavish attention, particularly in the last century: that of "Western Civilization." The primary focus of these volumes is indeed the part of the globe, the temporal range, and much of the subject matter that scholars have inconsistently labeled and identified with "the West." But not content just to reject this terminology, we aim in these volumes to avoid the trap of its logic too, and we do so in several ways. The authors of these chapters do not take their geography to be bounded in any *a priori* way; their terrain stretches variously beyond Europe to the Near East, to China and other parts of Asia, to Russia, to Africa, and, unevenly over the last half millennium to North, Central, and South America. It is also important that every volume pushes back on the idea that the subject at hand can be described as constituting some unified cultural ethos. Radical intellectual pluralism exists in every era, and links of commonality also reach across whatever temporal and geographical boundaries we might construct. At the same time, we advocate a kind of geographical awareness that keeps us from losing sight of the fact that the histories under primary scrutiny here have been both carefully constructed and profoundly shaped by fantasies about, as well as dehumanizations of, varieties of others, whether labeled barbarians, foreigners, exotics, or heathens, whether near or far. This kind of thinking, in turn, is inseparable from an often violent history of the extraction of resources and commercial practices around the globe, of missionary activity and evangelization within and well beyond Christendom, of the enslavement of, particularly, African peoples, and of the conquest and colonization of various Indigenous peoples from the Americas to the South Seas. Advocacy for social justice is a distinct project from this one, but exposing the blinding legacies of injustice stemming from every era is very much a part of it. These volumes embrace the idea that a cultural history of ideas is necessarily a "connected history," with a focus on circulation and hybridity, along with serious attention to disparities of power.

But even more, perhaps, a cultural history of ideas potentially offers a conceptual way out of the trap of Western Civilization precisely because it historicizes, indeed "provincializes" (to borrow Dipesh Chakrabarty's term), the very categories long used to bolster it. Of particular pertinence here is "progress." Rather than treat techno-scientific or moral-political progress across time as a given, this series sees conceptions of progress, as well as those of newness and modernity, as polemical claims invented to serve different purposes at different moments (see especially the introductions to the volumes on the Enlightenment and the Age of Empire, but also the Middle Ages). The same could be said for periodization, including the very terms into which these volumes are carved up; Jill Kraye, in her volume on "the Renaissance," starts off not by guiding a tour of this arena but by showing us how this category was invented in the first place and then exposing its retrospective ideological functions. Indeed, the authors in this collection uniformly work hard to take up the intellectual pillars of standard accounts of what has been called Western Civilization and embed them, as ideas, in history. In addition to the notion of progress, these include the idea of the individual genius thinker, the advent of intellectual tolerance, the mastery of nature, secularization or the ultimate triumph of scientific reason over the enchantment of the world, and a firm distinction between past and present.

Moreover, despite the fact that this set of volumes ties ways of thinking to particular circumstances in the past, it is also designed to make the case that no one era or people or place owns those ideas going forward. Even the pointed anxieties of today, which Stefanos Geroulanos lists in the introduction to the final volume as including "dehumanization, species extinction, climate catastrophe, economic indifference to individual suffering, and artificial [forms of] intelligence," are in some sense variants of old concerns. We can thus treat previous responses to them as a storehouse from which people anywhere can continue to build new answers even as those ideas' initial relationship to particular conditions and situations remains important to understanding their full complexity. If this collection of the work of sixty-two scholars from multiple humanistic disciplines has a central goal, it is to remind us that inherited ways of thinking and our ever-changing lived experiences are constantly pushing against one another in productive ways, generating refreshed responses or, indeed, ideas as a result. We all aim to continue this endeavor.

Sophia Rosenfeld and Peter T. Struck,
General Editors

Introduction

JAMES H. JOHNSON

A Cultural History of Ideas in the Age of Empire shares the same nine topics with the other volumes in this series, which together reach from antiquity to the twentieth century. Over the course of the nineteenth century, the complexion of these fields—Knowledge, the Human Self, Politics and Economies, Nature, Ethics and Social Relations, Language, Poetry, Rhetoric, the Arts, and History—underwent such fundamental change that the thinkers who shaped them regularly proclaimed their work to be epoch-making. Successive generations of social visionaries announced plans for a new order founded for the first time on the true nature of humanity. Philosophers elaborated encompassing systems of thought that stretched beyond the field's accustomed subjects to include wider realms of history, art, and religion. Self-described revolutionaries included not only political writers but also scientists, poets, and composers. The watchword of the age was progress, a restless, confident, forward-looking impatience with the current state of affairs.

The span of this volume is the long nineteenth century, loosely construed as the period that began with the taking of the Bastille and ended with the First World War. The ideas most fully treated in the pages that follow are European, although important voices from other cultures also appear. The ideas of Black abolitionists and Haitian revolutionaries, for instance, are considered in their European reception. Historical works by Native Americans and women are set alongside those of the century's more familiar figures. Well-known political and philosophical programs appear in unexpected settings, including Brazil, Argentina, Japan, and on the Indian subcontinent. In this period, European ideas exerted a far greater impact on the rest of the world than at any time before or since. This global impact, for good and for ill, is reflected in these chapters.

What does it mean to write a cultural history of ideas in "the age of empire"? Empires frame the nineteenth century, and their features carried the defining ideals and faults of their founding myths. Napoleon's "civilizing mission" exported rights, the rule of law, and high ideals of freedom throughout his continental empire. Its liberation was delivered by means of conquest, confiscation, and terror. At the end of the century, public figures promoting overseas colonies extolled the particular benefits their nations' benevolence brought to subject territories and peoples. The stark difference in the breakup of empires at the start and close of the period is worth noting as well. The demise of Napoleonic Europe inaugurated an extended period of international stability among nations that permitted their unprecedented intellectual and cultural flourishing. The catastrophe of the First World War, fueled in part by the militarized competition for colonies, spread international turmoil that continued for much of the twentieth century.

It is a striking fact that few major European intellectuals wrote systematically about imperialism. The word itself appeared in English only at mid-century, with a strongly negative inflection.[1] Yet the elements of empire—ideological, economic, technological, military—were not absent from the work of thinkers and creators. On the contrary, the imperial project's assumptions drew from the works of social and political theorists, philosophers, religious leaders, artists, and educators. The ideals of the French Revolution would spread "downward" from Europe to Asia and Africa. Political figures who called themselves liberal wrote favorably about imposing despotism to elevate "barbarians" from a state of infancy. Historians adapted the narrative of civilizational progress to describe their own countries' inheritance from ancient empires: it was a duty now to disseminate this glory worldwide. Portrayals of "exotic" non-Europeans in paintings, novels, and works for the stage more typically revealed the predilections of their creators than an earnest effort to depict other cultures.

The aim of Bloomsbury's *Cultural History of Ideas* is to consider anew its nine defining topics. These broad themes were once the study of a discipline largely indifferent to context, as though their carriers were participants in a timeless, ongoing conversation. With the advent of cultural history, the exchange has been reframed to acknowledge a clamor of voices speaking all at once and in different languages. Tracing these contexts of ideas once thought timeless—the study of their production and dissemination, for instance, of how contemporaries understood their terms and of the uses to which they were put—are now essential concerns. Understanding the reasons for which authors were deemed significant or excluded has opened the field to figures formerly neglected. Grasping the place of institutions in promoting or silencing ideas has provoked an awareness of curricula, scientific networks, and spaces of elite or popular sociability. The ways in which cultural history has deepened our understanding of large ideas in particular settings are on ample display in this volume.

Particular examples from this volume illustrate the exciting variety of approaches. Reception history, for instance, which was once devoted to describing the social makeup of readers, listeners, or spectators, has increasingly drawn attention to the influence of works of literature, music, and art in shaping the inner life. Where scholars might once have plucked illustrative details from a novel to give a feel for the period, or cited an evocative musical passage to illustrate a presumed *Zeitgeist*, some have begun to study the effects of particular forms works on experience. In the nineteenth century, when individuality became more intentional and the conviction of one's own uniqueness grew widespread, these influences were central. Writing about the Arts, Julian Johnson identifies the self-portraits of Eugène Delacroix and Vincent Van Gogh and performances by Frédéric Chopin as formative in the spread of a self-conscious subjectivity. Such artists' self-presentation, he notes, "speaks on behalf" of its witnesses, giving expression to, and in so doing opening a space for, one's inner experiences and those of others.[2]

With the spread of literacy and new technologies of publication, the means of receiving knowledge changed dramatically in the nineteenth century. Educational initiatives, publishers' freedoms or limits, and particular practices of reading—in a private salon or public library, aloud in a workshop before a gathered circle of craftsmen or alone in absorbed silence—are all part of this story. Cheap magazines and newspapers were a prominent feature of daily life in Paris, Berlin, and London, not to mention New York, Buenos Aires, and Beirut, and they quickly became a vehicle for the dissemination of ideas. In his chapter on "The Human Self," Jerrold Siegel returns to the well-known guide for personal advancement, Samuel Smiles's *Self-Help*, to recover an essential social role in self-formation: the "life-education given daily in our homes," as Smiles writes, "in the streets, behind counters, in workshops, at the loom and plough." The process of "self-making," Siegel writes, was not individualistic.[3]

Just as important was the spread of secondary and university education for unprecedented numbers of students. In her chapter, "Knowledge," Jan Goldstein details the policies and procedures intended to enshrine particular thinkers in private and public school curricula. In so doing, she draws attention to the institutionalization of particular strands of thought and the cultural and political ends they aimed to achieve among students. She also describes how the settings and pedagogical styles of celebrated professors helped to shape how their words were heard and understood. Jerrold Seigel describes the means undertaken by clubs and organizations—"an archipelago of associational life," as he calls them—to promote self-improvement among the German working classes. These included volunteer choruses, gyms, literary societies, and discussion forums.

In each chapter of this volume, the range of voices is refreshingly wide, with unfamiliar figures in revealing proximity to those much better known. Writing on Politics and Economies, Brian Vick discusses Frederick Douglass alongside Rommohan Roy, a Bengali reformer who advanced political and social reform in England, and Dadabhai Naoroji, who was the first South Asian elected to the British Parliament. In their chapter "History," Donald R. Kelley and Bonnie G. Smith evoke the singular historical perspectives of voices worldwide, including neglected national histories by Finnish, Swedish, Danish, Latvian, and Lithuanian scholars. Krishan Kumar, in his chapter, "Ethics and Social Relations," includes the work of "scholar-administrators" and "scholar-generals" who, unlike the age's major thinkers, wrote with authority about colonialism from their experiences in Egypt, Russia, Persia, and the Far East.

Because *A Cultural History of Ideas in the Age of Empire* treats the same topics as other volumes, which stretch from antiquity through the twentieth century, the series offers an extraordinary perspective that is at once panoramic and focused. Consulting multiple volumes, a single topic might be traced across centuries for its continuities and deviations. Within a single volume, the shared settings of diverse fields of knowledge may reveal unexpected kinship. What were the common influences and areas of convergence among ideas in the age of empire? The following sections offer three headings under which the work of artists, writers, scientists, and other intellectuals in the nineteenth century might be profitably gathered. Their concerns are the steady expansion of science into worlds of thought and belief endowed with metaphysical significance; effects of the growth of cities and appearance of the masses; and the contours and eventual demise of ideas of progress. Readers of the volume will find connections of their own.

METAPHYSICS AND ITS DISCONTENTS

The role and place of speculative thinking underwent considerable change between the French Revolution and the First World War. At the start of the nineteenth century, speculative thinkers constructed vast metaphysical systems intended to comprehend all human history and thought, as well as achievements and institutions, within a single conception. Over the course of the century, these comprehensive systems gave way to more limited aims. The pursuit of convergent truths was questioned or set aside, and universal abstractions receded before the practical applications of science.

Efforts to describe this meaning apart from customary religious categories were widespread early in the century. One such vision dates from 1805, when William Wordsworth published the book-length poem *The Prelude*, narrating the growth of his own mind. Its culmination comes as the English poet stands on the summit of Mount Snowdon. He has climbed through the night in a thick fog. Near the top, the atmosphere clears and a full moon emerges, causing the reflection of distant peaks to shimmer in the water below. The poet suddenly perceives a "mighty mind" that feeds upon infinity. Its all-pervading unity overspreads the human, natural, and spiritual worlds:

The sense of God, or whatsoe'er is dim
Or vast in its own being, above all
One function of such mind had Nature there
Exhibited by putting forth, and that
With circumstance most awful and sublime. (ll. 73–7)

Wordsworth's vision of the whole, fragments of which have accrued over the poem's twelve books, sets the community of humankind within a natural world suffused with divinity. This moral unity connects city- and country-dwellers, beggars and the mighty, ministers and prostitutes. Until this point, the poet's life has been a sequence of half-glimpsed truths and fragmentary, irreconcilable illuminations. He names several modes of knowledge through which the oneness he now grasps has come to him: reason, imagination, and love. Early in the poem he writes:

The mind of man is framed even like the breath
And harmony of music. There is a dark
Invisible workmanship that reconciles
Discordant elements and makes them move
In one society. (ll. 351–55)

The truth of things, seen on the mountaintop, is part discovery and part creation, "an ennobling interchange / Of action from within and from without" (ll. 376–77). This truth reveals to him the near-limitless power of human understanding and an ultimate meaning and coherence that exists beyond the merely human.[4]

Many thinkers in the first half of the century shared some version of Wordsworth's vision. Human faculties were capable of discovering the laws of nature and society while discerning a higher order that underlies existence. This alignment of knowledge with truth, moral virtue, and human contentment found its roots in the Enlightenment. One memorable articulation is the opening sentence of Denis Diderot's essay describing the aims of the *Encyclopédie*, a 21-year project whose first volume appeared in 1751. The practice of collecting and presenting knowledge, Diderot wrote, was useful in the broadest sense: it rendered humans happier, better educated, and more virtuous. To this, Wordsworth's generation brought a metaphysical perspective that confirmed this truth in things unseen.

The most capacious philosophical system of the age was that of G. W. F. Hegel, whose youthful enthusiasm for practical philosophy as a theology student in Tübingen deepened into a considerably more ambitious project. His life's work was to demonstrate the unity of human thought and the world. Hegel's method traced the progression of thought over time, providing a means for ever greater intelligibility of oneself, of one's relationships to others and of the world's institutions, beliefs, and creative expressions. In his mature works of the 1820s and early 1830s, as well as in notes from his university lectures in Jena and Berlin, Hegel drew together the unfolding logic of reason across human history. For Hegel, the unity of human thought and the world assumes concrete expression on multiple levels. Women recognize themselves as wives, for instance, and men as husbands, in the family. Individuals recognize themselves as economic beings in civil society. A nation recognizes itself in its laws, institutions, and artistic forms. The historian recognizes the steady advance of freedom through civilizations over time. "The True is the whole," Hegel declared in the *Phenomenology*.[5]

Versions of such connections linking human pursuits to abiding philosophical or spiritual truths characterized artists, writers, and some scientists in these decades. Bettina Brentano, a German painter, writer, and musician who moved in the highest literary circles, transcribed a conversation with Ludwig van Beethoven on the otherworldly realms to which, he believed, music gave access. The composer spoke of his work as possessing qualities that were infinite, eternal, and not wholly comprehensible. "Speak to Goethe about this," he told Brentano, "tell him to listen to my symphonies, for then he will admit that music is the only entrance to the higher world of knowledge which, though it embraces a man, a man cannot grasp."[6]

The German philosopher F. W. J. Schelling undertook to develop a scientific model to bridge the divide between human powers and a higher world of knowledge. As Frederick Gregory describes in his chapter on Nature, Schelling developed his *Naturphilosophie* (1799) in an effort to build a connection between mind and nature. His approach was organic rather than mechanistic; it declared morality and aesthetics to be essential to cognition. For Schelling, God was the pervasive presence that unified the world and its knowing subjects. Among poets and novelists of this generation, as Patrick McGuinness describes in his chapter, "Language, Poetry, Rhetoric," was a conviction that the immensity of human feeling—intimated in surging lava and raging storms—overran language itself. An essential part of the Romantic project was to discover a means of uniting humans to a greater whole, to which they were manifestly connected.

Yet even during this generation, prominent skeptics questioned such surpassing unity. The Schlegel brothers—Friedrich and his older brother August Wilhelm—found truth in incompleteness, which their published collections of fragments conveyed in both form and content. "In poetry, too, every whole can be a part and every part really a whole." "No occupation is so human as one that simply supplements, joins, fosters." "Morality without a sense for paradox is vulgar." These fragments from Friedrich Schlegel approach the heart of things indirectly, with allusive, subjective, and incomplete expression. "Let anyone who knows the road do likewise in his own way, from his own point of view."[7]

Such reservations grew in the second third of the century. The Danish philosopher Søren Kierkegaard's principal objections to Hegel and his all-embracing systems stemmed from the inescapability of subjectivity, which he believed eclipses and distorts even the most penetrating thought. For Kierkegaard, there was no single path to the heart of things, a claim he illustrated by publishing a sequence of sometimes discrepant books under a series of pseudonyms: Johannes de Silentio, Johannes Climacus, Victor Eremita. The greatest certainty was intense inwardness—the despair of the unbeliever, for instance, that becomes faith—which one can know only through individual experience.

For many, the expanding domain of science in the nineteenth century eroded the need for metaphysical truths. As verifiable law explained an ever-widening range of phenomena, *Naturphilosophie* was replaced by *Naturwissenschaft*, the science of nature. A mechanical view could account for matter in motion, the course of heavenly bodies, the appearance and disappearance of species and perhaps the mind itself. In 1834, the year the word "scientist" was first coined, the German explorer Alexander von Humboldt began work on a book intended to describe the interconnectedness of the natural world as a living whole subject to predictable laws. *Cosmos: A Sketch of the Physical Description of the Universe*, united astronomy, geology, botany, and biology. It also included subjects that ranged from poetry and politics to human migration and the effects of the natural world on the emotions. The word God does not appear in the book. *Cosmos* was by turns called blasphemous and brilliantly comprehensive. It quickly sold out its initial run of 20,000 copies and was translated into English, Dutch, Italian, French, Danish, Polish, Swedish, Spanish, Russian, and Hungarian.[8]

In his 1855 work *Force and Matter*, the German physician and philosopher Ludwig Büchner asserted that the laws of thought were identical to those of matter. Certain that science would one day provide an account of consciousness itself, Büchner dismissed all non-scientific speculation as "theological." Such assurance was not universal. For those devoted to science but faithful to the authority of scripture, discoveries about the natural world could bring anguish. The English author Edmund Gosse describes the humiliation suffered by his father, an author and respected chronicler of the natural world, when he attempted to align science with the Bible. Philip Gosse believed in a six-day creation, the fixity of species, and a young earth. In *Omphalos: An Attempt to Untie the Geological Knot* (1857), he wrote that God had created a world that bore false witness of its antiquity to conform to natural law. Adam, for instance, had a navel but was tied to no mother by an umbilical cord. The response among his peers was ridicule and scorn. The experience broke Philip's spirit and played a part in destroying his son Edmund's faith.[9]

For scholars of religion, a more critical attitude did not always signify the loss of its power to inspire and transform. In his chapter on "Religion and the Divine," for example, Thomas Kselman describes the ways in which the German theologian Friedrich Schleiermacher's wish to "intuit" the universe with childlike passivity was a knowing departure from orthodox views. Schleiermacher went yet further, asserting that a doctrine of immortality and the concept of God were not necessary to religion. A generation later, Ludwig Feuerbach and David Strauss cast doubt on the existence of God and the divinity of Jesus while still affirming the moral and spiritual values of human love, forgiveness, and self-sacrifice.

Some thinkers embraced a humanistic atheism even as they expressed misgivings about what a widespread loss of faith would mean collectively and individually. Many denounced religious rites and institutions while retaining a spiritual impulse that they considered innate. Sully Prudhomme, the French poet and essayist born near the middle of the century, wrote that the doubts of his intellect were an insult to the God of his desires. "We have lost our gods!" the French historian Jules Michelet exclaimed in his sweeping work called *The People* (1846). Yet the people were more than ever in need of a God, he continued, so that they may "recognize and love one another."[10] Among many, the century's "honest unbelief"—a pervasive if not always welcome skepticism of higher powers—still retained a place for the ethical, social, and spiritual teaching of religion. For others, any hint or hope of higher powers in public or private life grew intolerable.

An explicitly earthbound view of religion's limits is on display in the French painter Gustave Courbet's *A Burial at Ornans*, which appeared in the Paris Salon of 1850. Its low sky, distracted clergy, and oddly shuffling mourners, all cast in muted colors, convey little transcendence. A proud gravedigger alone possesses dignity. Only a small handful

FIGURE 0.1 Gustave Courbet, *A Burial at Ornans*, 1849–1850. © DeAgostini / Getty Images.

of women show genuine grief. "I cannot paint an angel because I have never seen one," Courbet stated.[11] His work and that of other Realists mark a change in both subject and style. Artists and novelists of the period depicted recognizable settings peopled by unidealized subjects. The mythological and grand historical scenes favored by earlier Romantics gave way to the ordinary and often grim conditions of life and work. The ugly and unpleasant—out of place in an aesthetic that had praised the unity of goodness, truth, and beauty—now entered works of art, literature, and even music as necessary and fitting.

Instances of this realist sensibility appear in the opening sentences of novels from the 1850s and 1860s. From George Eliot's *Felix Holt, the Radical*: "On the 1st of September, in the memorable year 1832, some one was expected at Transome Court." From Ivan Turgenev's *Fathers and Sons*: "'Well, Peter, do you see nothing yet?' asked, on the 20th of May, 1859, a man of forty odd years, dressed in a rusty overcoat and plaid pantaloons, who stood bare-headed on the threshold of an inn, on the high road of X, in Russia." And from Gustave Flaubert's *Sentimental Education*: "On the 15th of September, 1840, about six o'clock in the morning, the *Ville-de-Montereau*, just on the point of starting, was sending forth great whirlwinds of smoke, in front of the Quai St. Bernard." Implicit in these choices is an awareness of swift change. Such verifiable particularity was a way to establish and fix the action in a place and time. Writing in the 1858 *Westminster Review*, the critic George Henry Lewes claimed that Realism was the basis of all art. Its antithesis, he stated, was "not Idealism but *Falsism*": "Art always aims at the representation of Reality, i.e. of Truth; and no departure from Truth is permissible, except such as inevitably lies in the nature of the medium itself."[12]

On the threshold of the twentieth century, the German biologist and best-selling author Ernest Haeckel surveyed the field of science, which now embraced anatomy, paleontology, anthropology, psychology, and cosmology, to conclude that the soul was a fiction. Christianity, he wrote, was as baseless as witchcraft. His book *The Riddle of the Universe* appeared in 1899. It sold 450,000 copies in Germany alone and was translated into twenty-seven languages, including Sanskrit, Chinese, and Hebrew.[13] The same year, Sigmund Freud finished *The Interpretation of Dreams*. Both authors did little to hide their scorn for metaphysics.

Yet despite such voices, the *fin de siècle* witnessed renewed interest in a kind of transcendence. Claims of science's soullessness, of the journalistic thinness of "realistic" novels, and of the popular taint of art for the masses produced a reaction against militant secularism and, with it, a resurgent concern for matters of the spirit. The wide appeal of Spiritism and its associated phenomena of séances, mysticism, and the use of mediums were among these responses.

In the creative arts, the embrace and cultivation of spiritual elements was in explicit rejection of the Realists' assumptions of previous decades. The 1910 treatise *Concerning the Spiritual in Art* by the Russian painter Wassily Kandinsky described humanity as beginning to awaken from "the nightmare of materialism," which stripped all things of ideals or a higher purpose. It was left to artists to reclaim their centuries-old destiny to revive, nourish, and advance the public's inner life after a long period of neglect. While this vision in certain ways recalled the views of poets, painters, and philosophers from one hundred years earlier, there was no implied connection to divinity or embracing moral wholeness among all living beings. The spiritual element artists were summoned to revive was experiential and individual, an effect of varied combinations of colors bounded by abstract forms. Kandinsky decried his contemporaries' announcements of the death of God, but the renewed spiritual life he heralded was wholly the work of humans.

THE CONTAGION OF NUMBERS

Thanks to the French poet Charles Baudelaire, a Dutch artist who would have likely been forgotten is now widely known as the Painter of Modern Life. Constantin Guys was a journalist who spent most of his career between England and the Near East sketching military scenes for the British press. He settled in Paris in the 1850s, where he became a sensation for his watercolors of women in high and low society, at the theatre, in carriages and cafes, at the races and in the streets, sidewalks, doorways, and bordellos. Two features characterize him: a body of work shaped by the city and an artistic temperament untouched by Romanticism. His canvas was the new metropolis of Napoleon III's urban architect Baron Haussmann, with its teeming, often rootless residents. He was a "great lover of the crowd and of incognito," Baudelaire writes, "which he rendered into images more alive than life itself, forever fugitive and unstable."[14]

A defining feature of the nineteenth century was the urban experience, which by definition meant living amidst crowds. In sixteenth- and seventeenth-century Europe, the average annual growth rate had been stable at roughly 2 percent. In the eighteenth century, it edged up to 4 percent. By the 1820s, thanks largely to a decline in premature death from malnutrition, it shot up to 9 percent, where it stayed for the rest of the century.[15] The effect was dramatic. In 1800, the population of Europe was 200 million; by 1900, it had more than doubled, to 430 million, as methods spread for treating and preventing communicable disease. The growth occurred principally in cities, where unprecedented migration from the countryside also increased numbers. Their transformed physical features—the stark contrasts of opulence and squalor, public spaces populated by strangers, and new modes of transport that shuttled thousands in and out every day—refashioned the inner life as well, giving rise to terms that have become associated with the age: alienation, aloneness, atomization. The effects of urban life and its masses touched virtually every domain of experience, from politics and social theory, to literature and painting, to the very notion of selfhood.

Writers began to assess the effects of the masses on politics and society well before the full extent of their influence was known. There was unease even among those who embraced the spread of democracy. Alexis de Tocqueville, a visitor to the New World from France, described having written *Democracy in America* (1835) "under the impression of a sort of religious terror." His immediate reference was to the inescapable advance of equality, but behind this anxiety was also the impact of sheer numbers on an individual's thinking. While he marveled at the fact that a single newspaper could put the same thought at the same moment into a thousand minds, Tocqueville feared its consequences. This, too, bred conformity. Tocqueville's English admirer John Stuart Mill was of much the same mind. Two decades after *Democracy in America* appeared, Mill described yet more pervasive threats to independent thought. The masses now "read the same things, listen to the same things, see the same things, [and] go to the same places," he wrote.[16] Tocqueville worried about social fragmentation in the democratic order and employed a new word to describe it: *individualism*, the self-pursuit, heedless of others' well-being, that comes from citizens living without a common purpose to unite them.

Late in the century, the French sociologist Émile Durkheim described how a dense and varied population might become more interdependent. As Jan Goldstein discusses in her chapter, "Knowledge," this shift from "mechanical" to "organic" solidarity fractured formerly shared beliefs and convictions into the multiple perspectives of a diverse body. At the same time, however, specialization in commercial societies drew their members into mutually dependent relationships. For Durkheim, the psychologically dangerous aspect of such societies was a tendency to raise expectations for material and emotional comfort far beyond their capacity to meet them. To strive infinitely for satisfaction—to be reminded daily of the luxuries possessed by others—with no prospect of finding it was for him one of the central afflictions of modernity. These conditions, which were especially pronounced in cities, produced a fundamentally new kind of suffering, to which Durkheim gave the name *anomie*. To him, the word's literal meaning—"lawlessness"—conveyed the absence of any shared set of standards or values.

The roots of *anomie*, which drew attention to individuality in its aloneness, were complex. As Jerrold Seigel describes in his chapter, "The Self," the French Revolution and industrialization had the dual effect of promising individuals greater freedom to shape their own destiny and making them more aware of powerful formative influences over which they had no control. The consequence was at once a deepening sense of selfhood and a more acute feeling of solitude. "What consoles me a little for the impertinence of writing so many *Is* and *mes*," Stendhal wrote in his autobiographical *Life of Henry Brulard*, "is that I assume that many very ordinary people in this nineteenth century are doing as I am."[17] New expressions of the autonomous self's importance ranged widely, from political movements for self-determination, to social initiatives encouraging self-help, to the assertion of originality as an artistic value in its own right. There were just as many new sources of isolation.

Henri Bergson, a professor at the Collège de France, provided a philosophical foundation for the subjectivity of inner experience in what he called duration. Bergson was part of the late century reaction against positivism, which, he believed, had falsified experience through its exclusive reliance on reason. He instead emphasized intuitive and imaginative knowledge. Duration was an ever-rolling stream containing encounters, experiences, memories, and moods unique to each individual. For Bergson, the inner life was continuously creative, an inexhaustible source of freedom.

Yet the very forces that nourished these convictions brought unsettling questions. If one was truly free to shape one's identity, what was the authentic self? In the years before and just after the First World War, writers and artists described an unknown inner world in which reliable reference-points became blurred or dissolved altogether. The erotic, subliminal dreamscapes of the Austrian painter Gustav Klimt, or the early musical works of the Austrian composer Arnold Schoenberg that teeter on the far edge of tonality, convey an inner life that is foreign and often menacing. In a letter from 1914, the Czech-born novelist Franz Kafka described the self as remote and perhaps unfathomable: "What I write is different from what I say, what I say is different from what I think, what I think is different from what I ought to think and so it goes on further into the deepest darkness."[18] Several years earlier, the Viennese writer Hugo von Hofmannsthal detailed the breakup of the self in a fictional letter dated 1603. In it, Lord Chandos does not recognize himself as the author of his own books and letters. "I feel bound to reveal to you my innermost self," he writes, "the peculiarity, the freakishness, if you like, the disease of my mind."[19]

The city and its crowds offered proximity to those of vastly different circumstances, which furnished exalted expressions of the brotherhood of humanity with graphic and sometimes frightening detail. Wishing to observe the "human document" for a novel that he and his brother Jules had begun, Edmond de Goncourt visited working-class neighborhoods in Paris to engage in what he called "*spying* for the truth." What he discovered was both thrilling and disgusting, a "horror of the *canaille*" alongside a strange feeling of euphoria.[20] Similar responses rippled through political and social thought, both late and early in the century. In his chapter, "Political and Economies," Brian Vick observes that many liberals professed support for universal rights and self-government but resisted any dramatic expansion of the franchise. The Great Reform Act of 1832—passed after riots against electoral restrictions raged throughout England and one after another English reformer called for dramatic change—widened the franchise by only 18 percent. The proportion of eligible voters in England after 1832 was nevertheless still larger than those who qualified to vote in France after its 1830 revolution.

Widespread ambivalence among liberals over political rights for women persisted as well, despite the pioneering work of Mary Wollstonecraft, Olympe de Gouges, Harriet Taylor Mill, and others. Unvarnished elitism characterized politics and culture throughout the century. Where it prevailed, democracy remained fragile and incomplete. In Southern, Central, and Eastern Europe, governments acknowledged popular political expressions while retaining the dominance of the landed and aristocratic classes in the diplomatic corps, the military, and the government offices. Even in countries where democracy took firm root, resistance to it remained strong.

Where some saw social and political peril in the masses, however, others grasped opportunity. A pioneering work by the French social theorist Gustave Le Bon, *The Crowd: A Study of the Popular Mind* (1895), drew from the nascent field of psychology to describe techniques that would-be leaders could use to move the masses. Le Bon's fundamental insight was that crowds assume characteristics that few of their members would show individually. Crowds take on a collective spirit, he wrote, exulting in a speaker's passion, verbal violence, and obvious falsehood. The effective orator makes "abusive use" of memorable phrases and repeats slogans until they become identified with him. He avoids giving proof for his claims and instead simplifies and exaggerates. He is not shy about stirring the "bad sentiments" of a population. In the crowd, Le Bon writes, individuals are "freed from the sense of their insignificance and powerlessness, and are possessed instead by the notion of brutal and temporary but immense strength."[21]

The Crowd was both a guide and a confirmation. Before its publication, demagogues had already begun to hone its techniques to demonize, divide, and, for the those caught up in the message, engender a uniquely modern kind of solidarity. Hatred for an internal enemy, now amplified by the institutions of democracy, was a new way to transform the masses' estrangement into purposeful action. The turn was to have its brutal apotheosis in the twentieth century.

CERTITUDE AND LOSS

No age was more convinced of its historical destiny than the nineteenth century. Its early decades brought expectant claims of living on the threshold of a new era. Successive generations provided fresh evidence for this faith. Time's arrow sped toward a future destined to outstrip the past in every realm. Rebirth had come to politics, the social order, education, industry, and transportation. The familiar terms of the conviction were widespread. This observation comes from an 1851 book by Auguste Javary, a *lycée* instructor in the French city of Poitiers: "If there is an idea that belongs properly to our century, at least for the importance accorded to it, and which, whether accepted or not, is foreign to no one and employed to excess by most, it is the idea of Progress, a general law of both history and the future of humanity."[22]

Javary's hymn to progress was but the most recent variant of a vision put forth in the late eighteenth century, when the marquis de Condorcet, a mathematician, economist, and public figure, described an ineluctable advance of knowledge that would encompass the individual and society in waves of illumination. "The time will come," Condorcet wrote, "when the sun will shine only on free men who know no other master but their reason."[23] Those who know the circumstances of Condorcet's last work might view such certainty with unease. His words were written as he fled certain arrest and execution by revolutionary political opponents who claimed to embody the very notion of progress he praised. His death, possibly by suicide, deprived his pursuers of the opportunity.

Economic historians point to the 1820s as a turning point, when the remnants of merchant capitalism gave way to economies built on domestic productivity. Beggar-thy-neighbor policies—the sorts of mercantilist strategies by which England and France, for instance, had stifled Dutch trade in the eighteenth century—shifted to production based on an emergent workforce, mechanization, and economies of scale. The expansion of technical knowledge was met by a willingness to invest in untried inventions. Profits could be sudden and substantial. James Hargreaves's eight-spindle "Spinning Jenny," for example, invented in 1764, increased productivity by some sixteenfold.

Other indices point to dramatic shifts in European economies in the late 1820s and early 1830s. Among them were changes in transportation and communications. The world sped up and grew smaller. Rail came to England in 1829. Tracks were laid in the United States in 1830, Belgium and the German lands in 1835, France in 1837, and Russia in 1838. In 1848, the steam-powered *Antelope* of the Boston and Maine Railroad reached 60 mph. Six years later, a train on the Bristol & Exeter line touched 81 mph.[24] Early passengers feared that traveling at such speeds would be fatal. The German poet Heinrich Heine claimed that space had been annihilated, adding that, with enough money, time might also be killed.[25]

Those who hailed these advances were gratified, but for others they induced a kind of vertigo. In his *Confession of a Child of the Century* (1836), Alfred de Musset described the present as a passage between two worlds, as though drifting on a sea of wreckage. The past was irretrievably destroyed, he wrote, but the future was still far on the horizon. "At each step, one cannot know whether one treads on living matter or dead refuse."[26] Warnings about the human toll of the forces of change came early, most notably from Adam Smith, who cautioned in *The Wealth of Nations* (1776) that the repetitive work required of factory laborers debased the mind. A worker may well have the native intelligence of a philosopher, he observed, but if he is deprived of rational conversation and subject to relentless manual repetition he will grow "as stupid and ignorant as it is possible for a human creature to become." Smith concluded that it was the moral obligation of governments to soften and ameliorate labor's effects. He recommended public schools in every parish and a graduated tax of which the rich would pay the greatest share.[27]

Writing with a different aim two decades later, the German philosopher Friedrich Schiller expressed similar concerns about the effects of industry on the worker. *On the Aesthetic Education of Man* (1795) is haunted by the French Revolution's darkest phase, when close to 20,000 people were executed in the name of liberty. Schiller believed that government by the people was the future of Europe, but he was also convinced that nations were not yet prepared for the responsibilities this entailed. On the one hand, he feared the violence of a mob driven by blind impulse; on the other, he worried that "enlightened" political programs could too easily become a nightmare of reason. An explicitly aesthetic education, Schiller believed, would restore human completeness, which specialization and growing state power now threatened. An example of their distortions was the narrowing effects of labor on the worker. "With the monotonous noise of the wheel he drives everlastingly in his ears, he never develops the harmony of his being, and instead of imprinting humanity upon his nature he becomes merely the imprint of his occupation, of his science."[28]

Some attributed a more encompassing malaise to these large cultural shifts. The French novelist George Sand wrote in 1833 that the age was distinguished chiefly by its "moral maladies," which she called contagious and fatal.[29] Many who came of age after Waterloo believed that the military glories of an earlier generation were being replaced by the crass rivalries of commerce. The response was dejection and withdrawal. A review of French female poets suggests that the affliction, often associated with such writers as François-René de Chateaubriand and Alfred de Musset, was not limited to men. "What is this *mal du siècle* that casts a shadow on the gentle thoughts of women?" its author asks. "It is the sickness of all eras in transition, of all ages when society is transformed."[30] Thomas Carlyle, an English contemporary of Sand, diagnosed the age as destitute of faith but terrified of skepticism.[31] In his chapter, "The Arts," Julian Johnson identifies expressions of this climate in the appeal of landscape paintings by such artists as Philipp Otto Runge, Samuel Palmer, and Caspar David Friedrich. The critic John Ruskin, Johnson notes, viewed such works an as effort to restore a spiritual element to places in the countryside disfigured by industry.

The number of reformers who discussed the emotional effects of capitalism is striking, with Karl Marx's account perhaps the most familiar. The system deprives workers of their work, turns them against their fellows, and strips them of their humanity. However sweeping his and other critiques were, their tone was more resolute than despairing. The world was at a historic pivot, and improvement was near. Socialists sketched a future free of present depravities in the same confident tones that capitalists also used. Such was the power and appeal of progress, whose deviations were merely temporary.

The manufacturer Robert Owen, who brought shorter hours and better working conditions to his textile mills in Scotland, spoke of the evils that ignorance, lack of education, and relentless toil produced among children. When human truths are attained, he wrote, every person will promote the happiness of every other. The eccentric French visionary Charles Fourier described a society grown mistrustful, spiteful, and vicious. His imagined "phalanteries" would bring a utopia of social and sexual bliss.[32] The social theorist Henri de Saint-Simon wrote of an imminent "golden age of humanity" inaugurated by a class of social managers working with industry to achieve the goals of socialism.[33] For Marx and Friedrich Engels, the revolution would not only produce decent work and livable wages but also inspire meaningful pastimes, widespread knowledge of art and poetry, and satisfying intimate relationships.

Is it possible to pinpoint the moment when such hopes were defeated by events? To generalize is to falsify; many reformers held firm to an unsullied vision of society remade throughout the century and into the next. Perhaps a turn to fiction can nevertheless suggest a turning. Gustave Flaubert's *Sentimental Education* (1869) ends with Frédéric Moreau and his friend Deslauriers reliving their days as students, a time before the compromises, betrayals, and spoiled ambitions both have endured. Each has failed in the thing he dreamed of possessing, love for one and power for the other. They recall a visit to a house by the river, where prostitutes hummed in low voices to men as they passed. Frédéric had brought flowers and stood petrified before the women, who burst out laughing at his embarrassment. He turned and fled, and since he had the money for both of them, Deslauriers ran out of the house too. "That was the best time we ever had," says Frédéric. "Yes, perhaps you're right. That was the best time we ever had," says Deslauriers.[34]

As dreams of change across Europe were crushed by the "forces of order" in 1848 (the revolutionary backdrop for Frédéric and Deslauriers's ruined hopes), and incremental improvements in wages, hours, and working conditions smothered the spirit of insurrection, the terms of progress also shifted. Some who enumerated its costs found no obvious solution, in part because political and social institutions seemed more firmly entrenched than ever. In 1904, the German theorist Max Weber wrote of economic structures that determined a rigid style of life for all, including those not engaged in earning a living. Weber closes *The Protestant Ethic and the Spirit of Capitalism* with an ominous prediction: the coercive demands of capitalism—self-denial, iron discipline, and a religious attachment to one's work however meaningless—would remain "until the last ton of fossil fuel is burnt to ashes." Convinced of their own superb accomplishments, humans will become "specialists without minds, pleasure-seekers without heart."[35] Weber's contemporary, the Austrian sociologist Georg Simmel, described modern work in similarly spiritless terms. An increasing number of occupations, engendered uniquely by large cities, possess only one aim: "Money, the absolute entity, is for them the fixed point around which their activity circulates with unlimited scope."[36] In 1900, the novelty of this fact was worth noting.

In the last third of the century, the notion of progress narrowed and turned strident as its chief carrier became the nation. The Enlightenment's cool authority of universal reason gave way to the fervid call of blood and soil. One indication of this shift came in the focus and tone of historians. In their chapter, "History," Donald R. Kelley and Bonnie G. Smith describe the intellectual trajectory of those who once followed Leopold von

Ranke's credo of depicting the past "as it truly was." The task was now to reveal the spirit of a nation in terms of race and terrain. As the German Heinrich von Treitschke moved away from the liberalism of his youth, he took exception to what he called the Rankean School's "bloodless objectivity." Since the state is the expression of its people's inner life, he wrote, its "personality" is the source of its authority.[37]

Nationalist histories grafted the notion of progress onto a global struggle for dominance. The process by which the British East India Company grew from a commercial enterprise to become a lawgiver in nineteenth-century India became a model for European colonization in North and West Africa, South America, and Indonesia. A substantial gap in weapons technology between the West and other regions of the world opened in the 1850s and persisted until the turn of the century. This meant that European forces could conquer local armies many times their size. In Sudan, for instance, French forces subdued a population of some 15 million against an army whose men outnumbered them by 50 to 1. The British did roughly the same in Nigeria.[38] In 1862, European powers and the US controlled 28 percent of the globe; in 1912, the figure was 62 percent.[39]

Since the Enlightenment, when Condorcet declared human progress to be limited only by the globe itself, Europeans had regularly furnished lofty reasons for colonial ventures. Near the end of the eighteenth century, Edward Gibbon concluded the third volume of his *History of the Decline and Fall of the Roman Empire* with an account of how war, commerce, and religion had diffused civilization's inestimable gifts "among the savages of the Old and New World." Such "savages," he specified, were the common enemies of civilized society. "We may therefore acquiesce in the pleasing conclusion, that every age of the world has increased, and still increases, the real wealth, the happiness, the knowledge and perhaps the virtue, of the human race."[40] The nineteenth century added a scientific footing to Gibbon's "pleasing conclusion." A willful misreading of Charles Darwin identified its mechanism in natural selection. The English mathematician Karl Pearson, for instance, declared that the path of progress was "strewn with the wreck of nations" and "the hecatombs of inferior races." These deaths, he continued, were the stepping-stones by which humanity had achieved its "higher intellectual and deeper emotional life."[41] Nathaniel Barnaby, Director of Construction for the British Royal Navy, was more precise in describing the means of improvement: "the sword, the rifled breechloader, and the torpedo boat become part of the world's evolutionary machinery."[42]

The course of the First World War—when the thrill of those who cheered its declaration turned to horror at the unending savagery—was the greatest conceivable repudiation of the age's certitudes. The very forces that Europeans had championed as evidence of progress—including exponential growth in industrial output, expanding networks of transportation and communications, and the "scientific" roots of national uniqueness— now combined to prolong the killing. The trauma of unfathomable loss—an average of 147 soldiers from Great Britain, 1,303 from Germany, and 1,459 from Russia *each day* between 1914 and 1918—endured well beyond the war's end.[43]

The instability of democracies after 1918 owed in part to prophets from both the Left and Right who promised a redemptive future. In *The Revolt of the Masses*, which appeared in 1929, the Spanish writer Ortega y Gasset described the appeal of Bolshevism and Italian Fascism as a distorted legacy of the nineteenth century. These movements were in some ways products of the very things the masses now rejected: compromise and reasoned disagreement, a tolerance for political and ethnic minorities, the recognition of and respect for extraordinary achievement. The achievements of nineteenth-century progress, Gasset wrote, widely disseminated by technical advance and market economies, had succeeded in producing indolent, self-contented, and fatally complacent populations, whom he likened to spoiled children. His diagnosis captured the dilemma of his own day and restated the previous century's unease with its accomplishments. "[W]e live at a time when man believes himself fabulously capable of creation, but he does not know what to create. Lord of all things, he is not lord of himself .... Hence the strange combination of a sense of power and a sense of insecurity which has taken up its abode in the soul of modern man."[44] The revolt of the masses, Gasset concluded, was a rejection of history itself, which had, over the course of the nineteenth century, provided the learning in science, the wisdom in political thought and philosophy, and the means through economic development to bring comfort to all. If so, the roots of that rebellion had been long foreseen.

CHAPTER ONE

Knowledge

JAN GOLDSTEIN

An examination of the production and circulation of knowledge in nineteenth-century Europe can profitably begin on the Left Bank of Paris in an upper-floor apartment on the rue Servandoni, off the Luxembourg Gardens, during the French Revolutionary Terror. For some months in 1793, this abode served as the hiding-place of the famous mathematician and social theorist, the marquis de Condorcet. A Girondin by political persuasion, outspoken about his preference for a decentralized, liberal government for France, he had fallen afoul of the ruling Jacobins, who consequently issued a warrant for his arrest. In this situation of extreme duress, Condorcet calmed his nerves, it would appear, by writing a philosophical treatise. Without access to a library, and keeping dark thoughts at bay, he nonetheless completed during his confinement the manuscript of the resolutely optimistic *Sketch for a Historical Picture of the Progress of the Human Mind*. "Nature has set no term to the perfection of the human faculties," he confidently proclaimed. In light of the continual improvement of human reason and the expansion of the store of knowledge it generated, "the progress of this perfectibility [of man] ... has no other limit than the duration of the globe upon which nature cast us."[1] Condorcet's capture by the Jacobins and his death in prison soon followed; the manuscript was published posthumously in 1795.

Condorcet's *Sketch* recommends itself not only because of its specific content—it is widely viewed as an epitome of the High Enlightenment, the ground zero of the period under consideration here—but also because of the categories of analysis that Condorcet employed in his meditation on the vicissitudes and eventual triumph of human knowledge. He declared a position on epistemology: how we know, and, by extension, what counts as knowledge and what must be excluded. His interest in knowledge extended to many collateral areas as well: how knowledge is related to the development of society; which institutions have a stake in obstructing it; how it is transmitted to the laity—that is, to people who do not participate in its production—both within Europe and in Europe's colonial possessions. In other words, Condorcet saw knowledge as simultaneously shaped by abstract philosophical commitments and thoroughly imbricated in concrete social practices. His approach thus provides us with both a background in the High Enlightenment and a template for considering regimes of European knowledge in the long nineteenth century.

The *Sketch* begins with an epistemological credo. "Man is born with the ability to receive sensations ... to remember, recognize and combine them, to attach signs to them all in order to recognize them more easily and to allow for the ready production of new combinations." Condorcet adhered to the theory, often called sensationalist psychology, that the mind is a *tabula rasa* at birth, subsequently inscribed by "the action of external objects" as well as by man's "communication with other beings like himself." By mentioning, in his opening sentence, the production of *new combinations* of ideas as a common occurrence in mental life, he highlighted an inbuilt mechanism of intellectual progress that provided a narrative line for the whole text. Furthermore, in the pain or pleasure that attends sensation, and in man's capacity to impute these same negative or positive feelings to "other sentient beings," Condorcet located the source of human morality—those "ties of interest and duty" that "arise between him and his fellow-creatures."[2]

A few brief paragraphs later, Condorcet introduced another basic principle: the development of the mental faculties of the individual, starting from the first sensory impingement, obeyed "general laws." So, too, did the collective "progress of the human mind" over historical time, which was, after all, "no more than the sum of that development in a large number of individuals joined together in society."[3] Condorcet thus conceptualized society as produced through addition, with each atomistic individual bringing to the group an iteration of that same, law-governed mental apparatus that all possessed. The logic of society-making was for him much like that of mind-making, since in the latter, too, atomistic entities—sensations, perceptions, ideas—were accumulated and combined. This additive or combinatory logic was characteristic of much Enlightenment knowledge.

The ten "stages" into which Condorcet divided the *Sketch* were a familiar Enlightenment conceptual device, discrete portions of a supposedly universal and basically linear developmental sequence through which all societies were said to pass. After positing a First Stage of hunters and fishermen, Condorcet once again displayed his overriding concern with knowledge formation by observing, "The uncertainty of life, [man's] difficulty in providing for his needs ... do not allow him the leisure in which he can indulge in thought and enrich his understanding with new combinations of ideas." With the sum total of knowledge more or less static, "the progress of the human species was necessarily very slow." But the pace quickened once agriculture and inherited property made surplus possible. At that point, the principle of the division of labor reorganized social life, turning some people away from manual labor and to the business of exchange. By that same principle, the time left over for the production of new knowledge increased: "A life that was less hazardous and more leisured gave opportunities for meditation or, at least, for sustained observation."[4]

Eventually a whole class of specialists in thinking called philosophers came into existence. As the primary (if not infallible) agents in the production of knowledge, they ultimately propelled the progress of mankind. They could not, however, act alone. At every moment they might be stymied by two groups: first the laity, or in Cordorcet's terminology, "the less enlightened classes," whose "prejudices retard the propagation of truth"; and second "certain eminent and powerful professions"—most notably the Church hierarchy and the officialdom of despotic governments—that "deliberately place obstacles in truth's way." History was thus a struggle without respite between "reason" and its "enemies."[5]

Condorcet's model of knowledge was diffusionist. From the philosophers it spread downward to the less knowledgeable classes within the same country. And from the most "civilized" of those countries—those, such as France, that had traversed the Ninth Stage—it similarly spread downward to the "uncivilized" parts of the world, for instance

Africa and Asia, that were unaccountably developmentally arrested. If a magnanimous, civilized country were to colonize one of these "savage nations," and if it responsibly shunned the familiar tactics of exploitation, for example, setting up a trade monopoly, it could deliberately accelerate the progress of the benighted population. "The progress of these peoples is likely to be more rapid and certain than our own because they can receive from us everything that we have had to find out for ourselves."[6] Condorcet's worldview thus included advocacy of what would later be labeled "liberal imperialism."[7]

What, then, was the Ninth Stage, so critical to the attainment of "civilization"—a keyword in modernity's self-understanding that Condorcet helped to establish in the European vocabulary? Chronologically, it stretched from about 1650 to the foundation of the First French Republic in 1792; metaphorically, it saw mankind's reason definitively throw off the "chains" of superstition and tyranny. The emancipation of reason from the double oppression of religious authority and unjust political authority occurred because philosophers had conclusively demonstrated the individual's capacity for autonomy. Condorcet provided the core of that demonstration in a pithy, underlined formulation that recalled the opening sentences of his text: "man is a sentient being, capable of reasoning and acquiring moral ideas." In his view, a firm grounding in sensationalism conduced, by necessary logical deduction, to the "true rights of man." These included the right to be informed about politics, to fashion one's political opinions through the use of one's reason, and to participate in democratic government (here Condorcet primarily credited Rousseau). They also included the right to pursue one's economic interests free of government interference, secure in the knowledge—supplied by Adam Smith and the French Physiocrats—that the unhindered pursuit of self-interest would automatically result in the general social interest, even "in the remotest corner of the globe" touched by far-flung European commercial activity.[8]

But if philosophers had reached the critical point of finding freedom through reason, how would they get the laity to follow them? Condorcet's answer hinged on division of labor *within* the intellectual class. To the philosophers were added "a class of men ... concerned less with the discovery ... of the truth than with its propagation," who "made it their life-work to destroy popular errors." Condorcet was referring to those supporters of Enlightenment such as the Encyclopedists whose mission was to deploy an expanding print culture to expose laymen to the "new philosophy." Their success in doing so was proven by the sheer fact of the French Revolution. The Revolution, which Condorcet apparently viewed as the apogee of human history, occurred—indeed, was "inevitable"—because "the people" compared the existing political reality with "the reasonable and natural principles that philosophy had taught them to admire" and hastened to do all they could, even to use violence, to bring reality and ideals into alignment.[9]

With the Revolution accomplished, Condorcet claimed to be able to predict the future, the Tenth Stage of the *Sketch*. He grounded his predictive capacity in a strict analogy between the natural sciences and those branches of knowledge treating human affairs. "The sole foundation for belief in the natural sciences is this idea, that the general laws directing the phenomena of the universe ... are necessary and constant. Why should this principle be any less true for the development of the intellectual and moral faculties of man than for the other operations of nature?"[10] We can now appreciate Condorcet's care and purposefulness when, in his introductory account of sensationalist psychology, he described its findings in terms of "general laws." He was preparing the way to assert the scientific status of the properly conducted study of history.

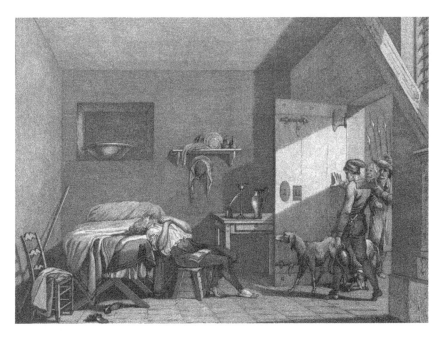

FIGURE 1.1 Condorcet found dead in his cell. Paris, engraving of 1802. © Bettman / Getty Images.

Condorcet proved remarkably prescient about the future. He had a global perspective, predicting a homogenization of the world through European imperialism and international commerce. He foresaw a growing equality within nations: laissez-faire policy would smooth out disparities in wealth between the most and least fortunate classes. Mass education would raise the intellectual level as much as innate endowments allowed. Condorcet was confident that everyone could learn enough to be intellectually independent—that is, in his eighteenth-century idiom, to cease being a "dupe" preyed upon by "charlatans." Moreover, such education would be extended to women. Medical discoveries would extend life expectancy. The mathematical discovery of the "calculus of probabilities"—one of Condorcet's specialties as a mathematician—would enable insurance schemes to provide pensions for the elderly. And so on.[11]

The regime of High Enlightenment knowledge instantiated in the *Sketch* may be summed up as follows. (1) It was grounded in a sensationalist epistemology and typically operated by an additive or combinatory logic. (2) It had a natural-scientific model based on the observation of phenomena and the discernment of the general laws that regulate them. In extending this model to history, it denied any epistemological difference between natural and human phenomena—a position termed "positivist" in the nineteenth century. (3) It took seriously public opinion and the print culture that helped form and disseminate it. Put differently, it addressed a public. (4) It took into account the world outside Europe, seeing it primarily as a field for European colonization and commercial endeavor. It regarded the non-European world (with the possible exception of the new United States of America) as occupying stages of human development long ago abandoned by Europeans and stunted by inferior forms of knowledge, but capable of catching up quickly if instructed by benevolent Europeans.

Much to Condorcet's credit as a prognosticator, his picture of the contours of human knowledge at the end of the eighteenth century retained a good deal of its relevance in the century that followed, a century faced with absorbing the shock-waves of the French Revolution and the First and Second Industrial Revolutions. But he did not, of course, predict perfectly. This chapter will take up the configuration of nineteenth-century European knowledge under each of Condorcet's four headings.

EPISTEMOLOGICAL OPTIONS

The Epistemological Creativity of the Early Nineteenth-Century Germans

Despite Condorcet's certitude on epistemological matters, the sensationalism that undergirded his whole system had already been put into question on the other side of the Rhine. In his *Critique of Pure Reason* (1781), Immanuel Kant held that the process of knowing required more than receptivity to sense data. The activity of consciousness was needed to construct the categories of space and time and impose them on inchoate sense data. Such activity set the so-called sensuous manifold in conceptual form, thus making rational thought possible.

The incommensurability of sensationalist and Kantian views about how the mind produced knowledge can be vividly seen in the account by the young Prussian savant Wilhelm von Humboldt of his visit to Paris in 1797–1799. Readily insinuating himself into the philosophical circles of the French capital, he found that the transnational dialogue he sought was all but foreclosed. "I fear your imagination works overtime and embroiders nature," Antoine Destutt de Tracy told the eager Kantian emissary. The Abbé Sieyès added that "German metaphysics was to true metaphysics as astrology was to astronomy." Getting to the heart of the matter, Pierre Laromiguière "affirmed a total *passivity* (Humboldt's emphasis) of the mind in the production of representations."[12] That Humboldt advocated not only for Kant but also for Kant's unruly disciple Johann Fichte did not help matters. In an effort to seize the thing-in-itself that Kant judged inaccessible to human reason, Fichte had by the time of Humboldt's Paris sojourn projected the active consciousness theorized by his master onto the metaphysical stage in the form of a self-positing, absolute "I" (*Ich*) that grounded his system. Replete with strange neologisms— the external world became the "Not-I" (*Nicht-Ich*)—Fichte's doctrine of knowledge laid "the foundation stone of the immense edifice known as German idealism" that culminated in the work of G. W. F. Hegel.[13] It also marked a parting of the ways between the French, who, in the early decades of the nineteenth century, still clung to a minimally revised and biologically accented sensationalism called *Idéologie*, and the Germans, who moved on to pyrotechnic feats of philosophical speculation far removed from the flux of sensory data.

The Hegelian version of German idealism had the greatest impact, both in its own era and subsequently. Hegel's vast philosophical system traced the path of Absolute Spirit as it came to full knowledge of itself through its encounter with a series of concrete domains, like civil society, the state, history, art, religion, and philosophy. Its development adhered to the rational procedure that Hegel believed characterized all thought and that he called the dialectic. Often simplified as a three-part sequence whereby a "thesis" generated its own negation or "antithesis," and the opposition between the two was then resolved through a "synthesis," or *Aufhebung*, that preserved the contradictory elements by raising them to a higher plane, Hegel's dialectic was actually less rigid. He regarded it as an effort to capture the fluid movement of thought and, by extension, of becoming.[14]

Epistemology was never far from politics in this era. Just as Condorcet saw sensationalism as leading inexorably to the French Revolution, so too did German commentators perceive a connection between the new German epistemologies and that world-historical event. Recognizing that the insufficient development of civil society in the German lands precluded French-style political emancipation, some regarded Kant's epistemological upheaval as a compensatory revolution in the realm of thought.[15] The young Hegel believed that the French revolutionaries had failed to grasp the import of their actions; it fell to German idealism to provide in thought what they had accomplished in practice, explicating the nature of a self-determining agent capable of realizing freedom in the modern world.[16]

Hegel's death in 1831 left his many German disciples with the task of determining the relative status of religion and philosophy in his system: had Hegelian philosophy replaced religion as mankind's locus of ontological security, or had it shored up the traditional faith by demonstrating its truth? The most progressive of these disciples, called Young (or Left) Hegelians, chose the first option and in the 1830s and early 1840s turned Hegel's dialectical reasoning to radically new ends. They included Ludwig Feuerbach, who argued that religion was a form of self-alienation in which human beings depleted themselves by ascribing their best qualities to gods they created, and Karl Marx, who began his long career by arguing that human self-alienation primarily occurred not in religion but in labor under capitalism.[17]

A modified—and decidedly non-radical—Hegelianism crossed the Rhine in the 1820s with the influential French philosophy professor, Victor Cousin, who had traveled to Germany and met with its principal philosophers. Interested in fostering political stability, Cousin faulted sensationalism for accommodating revolutionary impulses. Sensationalism eroded moral responsibility, he believed, because it constructed the human self as a composite of sensory impingements, thus effectively consigning it to fragmentation and passivity. Inspired by the tripartite structure of the Hegelian dialectic, Cousin endowed human consciousness with "triplicity." It included sensation, now recognized as merely a single component; reason, identical in all human beings; and will, the personal, active component and locus of a unified, *a priori* self.[18] Cousin's watered-down Hegelianism led the German writer Heinrich Heine to refer sardonically to him as "your great eclectic, who … was desirous of giving you instruction in German philosophy, [and] had not the slightest comprehension of the subject."[19]

Romanticism as Epistemological Mood

Another rupture with Enlightenment sensationalism that came out of Germany developed more or less in tandem with the new idealist philosophy but proved far more malleable, transmissible, and influential. This was Romanticism. The definition of the term bedeviled contemporaries from the early nineteenth century. Already in 1836, a letter appeared in the *Revue des Deux Mondes* from two subscribers, Messieurs Dupuis and Cotonet, concerned citizens of the provincial town of La Ferté-sous-Jouarre, who had conducted a harrowing and inconclusive twelve-year inquiry into its meaning. Possibilities ranged from a new form of drama to a certain disheveled style of dress. Scholars ever since have shared the helplessness of this pair, who were in fact the satirical creation of the Romantic poet Alfred de Musset.[20] But the difficulty of defining Romanticism was in a sense foreordained by the Romantics themselves—at least in their original incarnation as a circle of writers and philosophers, including the Schlegel brothers and the poet Novalis, who congregated in the university town of Jena in the 1790s. They were opposed to definitions, boundaries, and limits of all sorts, inclining instead to appeal to the "infinite."[21] In its disdain for pedantic precision, Romanticism might better be seen as an epistemological mood than as an epistemology.

That mood revolved around three concepts, each constituting an anti-Enlightenment protest: the Romantics extolled *das Ganze*, connoting holism or organicism; *Streben*, or striving, which connoted voluntarism; and *Eigentümlichkeit*, or individuality and diversity. Thus, while Enlightenment thinkers such as Condorcet typically viewed the whole as an aggregate, Romantics regarded it as prior to its parts. Thus, too, while Enlightenment thinkers prized reason above all, Romantics prized will—a restless and even titanic faculty depicted as striving infinitely. Process or becoming—and the continual self-transcendence it implied—mattered more than any static result. Finally, while Enlightenment thinkers valued reason as a universal human capacity, Romantics valued human difference, be it the linguistic and cultural singularity of nations and ethnic groups that Herder championed or the originality of the artistic genius who defied rule-governed classicism.[22]

The figure of the Romantic genius—who might be an artist or philosopher or that extraordinary politician, Napoleon—deserves examination, for it derived not only from the Romantic valorization of *Eigentümlichkeit* but also from a salient aspect of the movement's historical context: the literary marketplace. Writers had long chafed under the regime of patronage, which made their livelihood dependent on the favor of a high-born, flesh-and-blood benefactor. But, as Raymond Williams showed with respect to the early nineteenth-century English Romantics, writers nonetheless reacted with great ambivalence to the advent of commercial publishing and the possibility of earning their keep through the sale of their works to anonymous consumers. This new economic basis for their career certainly offered them much-desired independence; yet at the same time it demoted their works to the status of commodities and, especially when sales were tepid, diminished their personal status accordingly. The concept of genius salvaged their self-respect, raising them to lofty heights from which they could look down on the market and condemn as philistines the book-buyers who spurned them.[23]

A similar conceptual shift occurred in the domain of the sciences, especially in the German lands, where the Baroque experimenter, said to possess "ingenuity"—that is, cleverness and craft skill—gave way to the Romantic natural philosopher as a "genius" of nearly divine powers. "So the Experimenter is also simply the Genius," observed the German Romantic poet Novalis. Here, too, shifting institutional structures played their part: the attack on corporate institutions that culminated in the French Revolution led scientific practitioners to seek new marks of legitimation beyond membership in the now suspect academic faculties, royal academies, and established savant societies.[24]

The Romantic concept of genius contrasted sharply with Condorcet's Enlightenment approach. Arguing on sensationalist grounds, Condorcet opposed granting authors proprietary rights over their works. Knowledge, he believed, inhered in the world rather than in the mind, and the author—far from engaging in the godlike creation that Romantics ascribed to the genius—was merely a midwife to its disclosure.[25]

The Romantic suspicion of reason was epitomized in a line of verse by the English Romantic poet William Wordsworth. "Our meddling intellect / Mis-shapes the beauteous form of things: / We murder to dissect," he declared in "The Tables Turned," the first poem of his path-breaking collection, *Lyrical Ballads* (1798). In other words, rational analysis was death-dealing. Taken together, Romantic preferences bespoke a horror of the accumulation and propagation of rational knowledge on which Enlightenment thinkers premised human progress and happiness. The kinds of knowledge the Romantics sought were not necessarily useful.[26] Fichte, for instance, explicitly distanced himself from what he and other idealists called the "utility message" of the Enlightenment.[27]

A Nineteenth-Century Culture War

Although Romanticism reshaped many fields of intellectual and artistic endeavor during the first half of the nineteenth century, it never fully displaced sensationalism and its concomitant Enlightenment values. Rather the two coexisted uneasily and were often reified as poles of a kind of culture war, with the Enlightenment representing the "useful" forces of progress, science, and industry and Romanticism giving voice to the feelingful subject oppressed by the exigencies of modern life. The utilitarian philosophy that flourished in Britain was identified with the first pole—and as such was mercilessly caricatured by Charles Dickens in the person of the fictive school superintendent, Gradgrind, in *Hard Times* (1854). The brainchild of Jeremy Bentham (later elaborated by James Mill and his son John Stuart Mill), utilitarianism was grounded in that same human sentience that Condorcet regarded as foundational: it turned the supposedly innate human tendency to maximize pleasure and minimize pain into an exclusive criterion of morals, legislation, and social policy. And just as Condorcet had declared history a science by ascertaining its general law, so, too, Bentham declared morality a science by quantifying it—that is, roughly calculating the balance of pleasure and pain that would attend the likely consequences of any action. "Moral arithmetic," Bentham dubbed his theory, and his contemporaries frequently referred to it as the "felicific calculus."

Even closer to the spirit of Condorcet was the system of "positive philosophy" that Auguste Comte constructed in France in the 1830s and 1840s. Comte hypothesized that three successive epistemologies had governed the production of knowledge. During the theological stage, people explained the world by the actions of divine beings; during the metaphysical stage, they explained it by the operation of abstract entities akin to gods stripped of their anthropomorphic properties. These two epistemologies, comparable to those spontaneously devised by children and adolescents respectively, erroneously assumed that human beings could attain absolute knowledge. The third, "positivist" epistemology corresponded to the adulthood of the species. Opting for epistemological modesty, positive thinkers relinquished the quest for absolute knowledge and recognized that, as knowers, human beings were limited to the observation of phenomena and "the study of their laws—that is, their invariable relations of succession and resemblance."[28]

Both the natural and human worlds could be known by this method. Moreover, the different branches of knowledge crossed the threshold of positivity in a strict order, with the most simple, general, and independent leading the pack: thus mathematics, astronomy, physics, chemistry, and physiology. Comte believed that the science of psychology—a word he deliberately avoided—was becoming positive under his very eyes. Construed as the physiology of the brain and nervous system, it replaced the futile, metaphysical effort of introspection with the sober observation of the physical organs that made human mental life possible.[29] Comte predicted the imminent arrival of the science of society and, while vague about its contents, named it "sociology." His system-building was as much politically as philosophically driven. The "anarchical" state of knowledge in his own lifetime, a hodgepodge of bits and pieces from all three stages, seemed to him to have produced an incoherent, potentially revolutionary world-picture. He wished to purge all but positive knowledge from public consciousness and expected sociology to be the master science, the one that would expressly safeguard social order.[30]

An embodiment of the nineteenth-century culture war, Comte eventually felt compelled to temper the positivism he had created with Romantic elements. Even before he completed his *Course of Positive Philosophy* (1830–1842) or met the fabled love of his life, Clotilde de Vaux, he sensed the inadequacy of an exclusive reliance on reason.[31] Hence his *System of Positive Philosophy* (1851–1854) recommended establishing a religion of humanity, replete with a ritual calendar of holidays and a special cult of women as bearers of sympathy and members of the "philosophic priesthood."[32]

Many of his contemporaries, including John Stuart Mill, separated the "good," scientific Comte of the *Course* from the "bad," apparently addled theorist of the *System*, and subsequent commentators have often followed suit. But his impulse to end the prevailing culture war was actually widespread. In France, at least, a group of left-leaning utopians including both natural scientists (Alexander von Humboldt, A.-M. Ampère, François Arago) and scientific theorists of society (Comte, the Saint-Simonians, Pierre Leroux), propounded what the historian of science John Tresch calls "mechanical romanticism," seeing machines not as unnatural contrivances but as nature's self-expression. They eventually lost out to their mainstream competitors—Comte was pitted against himself in this contest—by dint of the failure of the Revolution of 1848. The road they charted but failed to take was a conception of science that resonates with the environmentalist concerns of the twenty-first century. It rejected a thoroughgoing human mastery over nature in favor of a strictly limited mastery coupled with a harmonious and ultimately sustainable coexistence.[33]

After 1848, the way was more or less clear for a triumphant positivism to reign over the latter half of the nineteenth century. But it never reigned uncontested. In his great work of liberal theory, *On Liberty* (1859), J. S. Mill modulated his commitment to utilitarianism in a chapter on individuality, construed like Romantic *Eigentümlichkeit*, where he defended eccentric "experiments of living." He chose as the book's epigraph a quotation from Wilhelm von Humboldt on the "absolute and essential importance of human development in its richest diversity."[34]

Positivism was also beset by new, Romantic-tinged currents. Toward the end of the century the French philosopher Henri Bergson restored intuition—defined as "the kind of *intellectual sympathy* by which one places oneself within an object in order to coincide with what is unique in it"—as a privileged mode of attaining knowledge.[35] He famously demoted the Kantian category of time, which organized its units spatially like beads on a string, to a mere social utility or scheduling device. He contrasted it with pure duration (*la durée*), which he likened to the interpenetrating notes of a tune, each successive addition altering the rest. In its unpredictability, pure duration was the medium of human freedom, and only by learning to inhabit the "deep-seated self" could an individual apprehend it.[36] Bergson's conception of time inspired the stylistic innovations of stream-of-consciousness novelists such as Marcel Proust and Virginia Woolf, who joined him in suggesting the impoverishment of ordinary everyday awareness.

POSITIVISM OR HERMENEUTICS?
THE NINETEENTH-CENTURY SOCIAL SCIENCES

Tantalized by the prospect of creating a science of society—Comte's unfinished business—the French novelist Émile Zola pioneered the literary genre of naturalism based on his own detailed research in working-class ateliers and wine shops, the Paris department store and stock exchange, and the nation's railroads and coal mines. Modeling his argument on an 1865 treatise about experimentation on living organisms by the physiologist Claude Bernard, he set forth the ideal of an "experimental novel" in which the author's creative genius would be expressed in the choice and treatment of a particular social problem; once set in motion, the plot would unfold on its own, without authorial control, according to the general laws of heredity and environment that Zola believed determined human action. For example, a family history of alcoholism coupled with daily life in a working-class neighborhood where drinking was the norm and "the air of the Paris streets [was] polluted by fumes of wine and spirits" made it difficult to avoid alcoholism, especially under stress—a hypothesis that an appropriately constructed novel such as Zola's *L'Assommoir* could prove.[37] Nor was Zola the only European writer to propose turning literature into the privileged medium of sociological knowledge.[38]

Whether or not Zola meant his ingenious theory to be taken literally, the mantle of the founder of French sociology fell instead to the brilliant young philosophy professor Émile Durkheim. Throughout his career, Durkheim openly acknowledged his debt to Comte.[39] The preface to *The Division of Labour in Society*, the published version of Durkheim's dissertation, described the book as "an attempt to treat the facts of the moral life according to the methods of the positive sciences" and to "seek out the laws that explain them."[40] To this end, Durkheim postulated two types of social solidarity. In the first, which he called "mechanical," fundamentally similar individuals were joined together through participation in a "collective consciousness" that spoke with one voice to reprove transgressions such as murder and demand punishment. In the second, called "organic," increased population density and competition produced a division of labor that sharply differentiated people, rendering them at once more individuated and more interdependent. That dual social reality translated into a moral injunction to respect the dignity of the human person and to "equip [oneself] to fulfil usefully a specific function."[41] Durkheim discerned a general sociological law that societies moved from mechanical to organic solidarity, adducing, in good Comtean fashion, quantifiable empirical evidence in its support: ancient legal codes contained a preponderance of repressive penal law, modern ones a preponderance of restitutive civil law.[42] He concluded from his investigation that "what is moral is everything that is a source of solidarity." Morality hence varied historically according to the prevailing type of solidarity.[43]

Like the would-be sociology of Zola's experimental novel, Durkheim's sociology adhered to the positivist program of grounding the study of human society in the same epistemology as that of natural science. "Consider social facts as things," Durkheim admonished in *The Rules of Sociological Method*.[44] But the sociology that arose in Germany at about the same time broke sharply with this pattern.

At the hands of its founder, Max Weber, German sociology was the by-product of the epistemological turmoil called the *Methodenstreit*. In the 1880s that controversy concerned the proper methodology of the new discipline of economics: was it abstract-theoretical or historical? Weber, originally an economics professor, supported a historical approach—or, in the terminology popularized in German academic circles by the neo-Kantian Wilhelm Windelband, an idiographic rather than a nomothetic economics, one imbricated in the unique particularities of cultural life as opposed to one assumed to operate, like the natural sciences, through timeless laws. When Weber turned his attention to sociology, he displayed the same epistemological preference, highlighting the term *Verstehen* (interpretive understanding) and calling for an "interpretive sociology" (*verstehende Soziologie*). By this he meant a sociology focused on outward courses of action that could be understood only in terms of the inner motives of the agents. Often empathetically inferred, those motives also had to be validated by formal argument.[45]

Hence Weber's sociological classic, *The Protestant Ethic and the Spirit of Capitalism* (1905), foregrounded the inner mental states of the agents who first manifested the "spirit of capitalism," defined as a systematic and basically abstinent approach to entrepreneurial activity, a relentless accumulation of profit achieved by reinvestment rather than spending for personal enjoyment. Calvin's doctrine of predestination had, Weber argued, provoked intolerable anxiety and an "unprecedented inner loneliness" in believers less sure of their election than was Calvin himself. Following the advice of their pastors, they threw themselves into hard and sustained work in their occupational calling—not to guarantee salvation, which was theologically impossible, but to buoy self-confidence and manage daily distress. These inner motives produced a generalized outward behavior: the "worldly asceticism" of capitalist practice.[46]

The different epistemological choices of Durkheim and Weber resulted in two distinctive styles of sociological knowledge during the founding period of the discipline. These choices presaged a persistent feature of the human and social sciences. When, in 1904, Weber relayed the complaint of a "despairing examinee in Vienna" who said he had been forced to learn two sciences of economics, one abstract-theoretical, the other historical, he described one form of an epistemological fissure that has continued to mark twenty-first-century academic departments of anthropology, sociology, psychology, political science, and sometimes even economics.[47]

And while nineteenth-century Europe is often regarded as the positivist era par excellence, it is arguable that its two most influential thinkers, Karl Marx and Sigmund Freud, belong in the hermeneutic camp. The twentieth-century philosopher Paul Ricoeur lumped them together as masters of "the hermeneutics of suspicion."[48] A half-century apart, each devised a type of interpretive knowledge that required the unmasking of accepted surface realities and located the truth of things in a deeper level thereby revealed: economic developments for the neo-Hegelian Marx, unconscious psychic forces for Freud, the clinician of middle-class Viennese "nervousness." This modality of unmasking and bringing occluded depths to light was subsequently identified as intrinsic to cultural modernism—only to be rejected by the late twentieth-century movement of postmodernism in favor of a conception of the "flatness" of reality.[49]

PUBLICS

It was a legacy of the Enlightenment that, in the nineteenth century, knowledge could rarely be imagined without considering its public. Not all publics were alike. Condorcet envisioned one composed of the unenlightened classes awaiting instruction. This public of pupils and students ensconced in educational institutions might be resistant and cling to its old errors, or it might be receptive, but it would not intervene in the knowledge-making process itself. Very different was the "bourgeois public sphere" of eighteenth-century origin theorized in the mid-twentieth century by the German philosopher Jürgen Habermas, which took upon itself the critique of dominant ways of thinking about politics, society, and the arts and thus created a force called public opinion.[50] A public of this sort flourished in the nineteenth century, though perhaps in not such an idealized fashion, nourished by the expansion of the newspaper and periodical press. So prominent a feature had the newspaper become in nineteenth-century European life that Hegel called his morning reading of it "the realist's daily prayer," and a French psychiatrist feared that the exposure of thousands of people to the same news articles would promote not rational discussion but epidemics of "moral contagion."[51]

These publics were intertwined: the Habermasian public sphere depended on the public of educational institutions. In the long nineteenth century, that latter public grew markedly and in tandem with the wide variety of educational settings, both formal and informal, on offer. Moreover, the university student was even endowed with knowledge-making capacity.

Formal Educational Institutions

Enrollment in primary schools increased dramatically. In the late eighteenth and early nineteenth centuries, a movement for school reform swept Western Europe, its advocates bent on improving the competence of teachers and making school attendance a childhood norm to ensure the literacy and numeracy of the population. The movement was generally the work of government officials and local notables motivated by some combination of the Enlightenment belief in progress through knowledge and the conviction that the popular classes required discipline for participation in the modern state and labor force. The statistics are impressive, especially in the German lands. Between 1820 and 1900, the number of boys aged six to fourteen enrolled in primary schools in Prussia rose from 59 percent to 97 percent; between 1850 and 1900, it rose from 83 percent to 96 percent in Bavaria, 60 percent to 94 percent in France, and 66 percent to 90 percent in England and Wales.[52] Schooling rates for girls, while always below those for boys, showed a similarly steady rise. The enrollment trends in both secondary and higher education increased as well but far less strikingly than in primary education. As late as 1870, no more than 3 percent of the relevant cohort attended secondary school, and less than 1 percent received a higher education, though these rates improved in the last third of the century.[53] After 1870, new types of secondary schools specializing in technical and business education further expanded the student population; they catered to the upwardly mobile children of the people, who were thus deliberately kept away from the elite institutions of classical learning.[54]

In the area of university education, Germany was again the leader. The general crisis produced by Napoleon's military victory over Prussia in 1806 prompted Prussian bureaucrats to call for the modernization of the university, an institution often regarded as a medieval relic. Wilhelm von Humboldt is credited with having conceptualized the new university, though he drew his ideas from the gamut of German idealist philosophers.[55] His vision centered on the unification of teaching and research. In an essay of 1809, Humboldt underscored the different function of secondary schools and universities, appealing to the latter to "treat the problem of knowledge as one that has not yet been fully solved." At the research university he championed, professors would no longer be vehicles for transmission of existing, agreed-upon knowledge to students; rather, teachers and students would both serve knowledge and work together in its intrinsically endless pursuit.[56]

The first institution constructed on this plan was the University of Berlin, founded in 1810. It pioneered the seminar, "a site of intellectual apprenticeship" where a master teacher guided the research efforts of some fifteen students, teaching by personal example.[57] The state-funded German research university—of which there were twenty-one by 1914—grew handsomely, especially after 1850, in the areas of student enrollment and faculty appointments. It adhered to the seminar system, later adding specialized institutes based on the same principle of faculty-student collaboration.[58] Already in 1798 Kant had envisioned the German university as a sort of factory implementing the division of labor to produce knowledge.[59] That model eventually inspired emulation in other countries, especially the United States, where its chief exemplars were Johns Hopkins University (1876) and the University of Chicago (1893). French bureaucrats warmed to it after 1870 when, shocked by their defeat in the Franco-Prussian War, they hypothesized that scientific superiority explained German success in battle. In the period before the First World War, nationalist students in Paris decried the "German methods" adopted at the "new Sorbonne," where literature classes had been recast as "laboratories of French philology" run by "teams of workers."[60]

The extremely centralized system of higher education in nineteenth-century France—which, contrary to the ideal of the German research university, administratively encompassed the secondary schools, or *lycées*— well illustrates the power of educational institutionalization in validating particular bodies of knowledge and amplifying their influence by ensuring them a captive public. Thus, the psychology and metaphysics of Victor Cousin were, under the aegis of Cousin himself as Minister of Education, installed in the philosophy curriculum of every *lycée* in France in 1832. The material on psychology remained there in many essentials through the opening years of the twentieth century, encouraging generations of bourgeois males—though, significantly, neither their female nor working-class counterparts—to see themselves as possessors of a unified and willful self.[61] Durkheim's version of sociology, strongly inflected with Third Republic values such as *laïcité* (secularism) and social solidarity, decisively beat out its competitors when it was institutionalized at the Sorbonne by his 1902 appointment to the chair of "Science of Education and Sociology." In 1906, Durkheim's course on pedagogy became required for all aspirants to professorships in the humanistic disciplines at either the *lycées* or faculties of letters. Durkheimian sociology penetrated still deeper into the social fabric, reaching even schoolchildren, when in 1920 it was incorporated into the curriculum of all the teacher-training schools in France, remaining there throughout the interwar period. Wrote one Catholic critic, "The obligation of teaching the sociology of M. Durkheim in the 200 *écoles normales* of France is the gravest national peril our country has faced in a long time."[62]

Despite an expanding print culture, the university lecture remained an important site of the communication of knowledge in the nineteenth century. That oral medium even saw a resurgence in Germany around 1800, where, in the context of the ideals of the new research university, it was reconceptualized as a performance in which the professor, rather than declaring finished results, initiated students into his process of thinking.[63] Appointed to the Chair of Philosophy at the new University of Berlin in 1818, Hegel gained additional celebrity when his awkward lecture style—gasps and coughs, uncomfortable pauses and hand-waving, rifling through papers and taking snuff—seemed to contemporaries to be evidence of the actual working out of a thought, of a monologue that Hegel converted into a dialogue with himself.[64] At the Sorbonne, too, professorial lectures could be notable events. Cousin's original fame derived from impassioned lectures delivered to an overflow crowd after 1815, when he belonged to the liberal opposition, and again in 1828, when he was returned to his chair after being silenced by the Restoration monarchy. The same was true of his colleague, the future politician

FIGURE 1.2 Hegel at the lectern. Lithograph of 1828. © Time Life Pictures /
Mansell / The LIFE Picture Collection / Getty Images.

François Guizot, who made a name for himself as a defiant history professor who, against
the Restoration's royalist tide, narrated the accomplishments of a heroic bourgeoisie. The
general public flocked to these lectures. In 1828, one of Cousin's rare female disciples
bristled at the conventions that prevented members of her sex from being admitted to
the amphitheatre.[65]

Informal, Alternate Education

The boundary between state-sponsored and informal education was straddled by the
anomalous and extremely prestigious Collège de France, a government foundation in
the Latin Quarter dating back to Francis I in 1610. Designed as a scholarly research
institute, enrolling no students and granting no degrees, it was a kind of anti-Sorbonne.
But because its professors were obliged to give free annual lecture courses to the general
public, the Collège served as a powerful point of transmission of knowledge. In 1838 and
1841, respectively, the Romantic anticlerical and republican historians Jules Michelet and
Edgar Quinet were appointed to the Collège, where their lectures attracted like-minded
crowds until the newly crowned Emperor Napoleon III removed them from their posts
in 1852.[66] The philologist Ernest Renan was appointed to the Chair of Hebrew in 1862,
where his inaugural lecture, delivered to an overflow audience, constituted a *succès de
scandale*. He was suspended immediately afterward for having depicted Jesus as merely
"an incomparable man."[67] The long tenure at the Collège (1900–1920) of Henri Bergson
was less controversial; the vast popularity of his message of finding freedom through
expanded consciousness presented only the logistical problem of seating an excess of
auditors, including women.

Modes of informal education usually lacked the establishment imprimatur afforded
by the Collège de France and could, in many parts of Europe, assume an alternate,
oppositional character. Thus, for example, Comte, repeatedly rebuffed in his efforts
to secure an official academic appointment, resorted to alternate venues to advance his
social vision for positivism.[68] He addressed his inaugural "Course on Positive Philosophy"
to scientists and other educated elites assembled in his Paris apartment; it later moved to

the Paris Athénée, a private institution funded by subscription. Comte put more stock in another audience: the Paris workers, whose sparse education in pre-positive knowledge left them, he believed, more open to his message. Between 1831 and 1848, he provided them with free instruction in astronomy in the town hall of the third district of Paris on Sunday afternoons.[69]

In a less oppositional vein was the public of workingmen brought into existence by the evening educational program mounted in England in the so-called mechanics' institutes. Voluntary associations of middle-class foundation, they numbered some 700 before declining around mid-century. Whatever their ultimate purpose in the minds of the founders—reconciling workers to the new industrial system or encouraging upward social mobility—they served to disseminate new forms of knowledge, such as political economy and phrenology. The latter, the would-be science of human behavioral propensities based on "reading" bumps on the skull to discern the size of the brain organs they housed, failed to achieve respectability in Europe's scientific communities and found its most avid audience among the popular classes, especially in Britain and the United States. Its vogue left behind for today's antique stores piles of white porcelain models of the human head showing the cerebral region divided into twenty or so labeled parts.[70]

The equation of knowledge with progress that was the Enlightenment's legacy to the nineteenth century placed great, if informal, pressure on individuals for intellectual

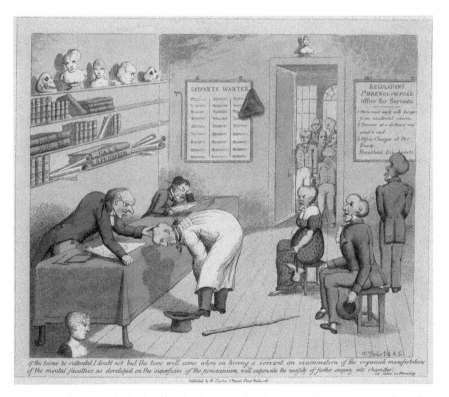

FIGURE 1.3 *Phrenological Office for Servants*, 1805–1830. The presumed utility of phrenology to bourgeois life: hiring a servant of good character. British cartoon, early nineteenth century. © Science and Society Picture Library / Getty Images.

self-improvement. The publishing industry both met and further stoked this consumer demand by producing reference books where knowledge, boiled down to its essentials, could be easily accessed. "The century of dictionaries," Pierre Larousse, one of the publishers responsible for the trend, called it.[71] Dictionaries here denoted not merely lexicons but alphabetically organized compendia of knowledge more generally. The century featured multi-volume reference works designed to facilitate serious middle-class conversation and enable insecure individuals to show themselves well-informed in polite company: thus the German Brockhaus *Conversations-Lexicon* "for the educated estates" (*für die Gebildete Stände*), which seems to have inspired the French *Dictionnaire de la conversation et de la lecture*, was translated into Russian and emulated in America.[72] Another icon of the era was "the Littré," a historical dictionary of the French language that appeared in 1863 under the imprint of the Hachette publishing company. Compiled by Émile Littré, a self-identified positivist and ex-disciple of Comte, it was marketed to a mass public as a scientific work of lexicography and was wickedly caricatured by the anti-positivist contingent during the Second Empire.[73]

If autodidacticism was encouraged by both the publishing industry and the general culture, it was also satirized by critics. Dubois and Cotonet, Musset's hapless pair trying to define Romanticism, were later joined by Bouvard and Pécuchet in Gustave Flaubert's eponymous novel (1881). The two Parisian clerk-copyists met accidentally on a park bench, discovered their mutual affinity and, when one received an inheritance, retired to the countryside to pursue, in antic fashion, encyclopedic self-cultivation.

FIGURE 1.4 Aid for the Autodictact: the Larousse delivery coach carrying the publisher's dictionaries. Paris, photograph of *c.* 1890. © Bridgeman Images.

KNOWLEDGE OF THE NON-WEST:
ORIENTALISM/PHILOLOGY

Condorcet's *Sketch* predicted a link between Europe and the non-West forged by the knowledge, both philosophical and technological, that colonizing powers would spread to their less advanced colonies. He did not envision another kind of link that in fact marked the nineteenth-century intellectual landscape: a European impulse to develop knowledge *about* the non-West and especially about the intertwined linguistic heritage of these two parts of the globe.

An "Oriental Renaissance" many called it at the time—a flood of new manuscript sources into Europe from outside likened in intellectual impact to the Italian Renaissance.[74] At its zenith in the last third of the nineteenth century, the discipline most associated with this effort—philology—had an epistemological solidity that surprises us today. It was one of "the hardest sciences on offer," even furnishing the paradigm of evolutionary biology.[75]

The importance of this effort was brought home to scholars in the late twentieth century by Edward Said's *Orientalism*. Said argued that the nineteenth-century knowledge generated under the broad rubric of Oriental studies was an effort by the West to define its own identity in contradistinction to the inferior identity it imposed on the non-West. Thus, to cite one of his examples from the 1850s, Ernest Renan's pioneering philological investigation of the Semitic languages (Aramaic, Hebrew, and Arabic) concluded on a grossly comparative note: while the Indo-European languages were supple and had repeatedly shown themselves capable of renewal, their stolid Semitic counterparts had barely changed over time; the former served as a vehicle for philosophy, science, and the imagination, all of which were foreign to the latter. Said further argued that scholarly curiosity about the non-West was born of the impulse to justify imperialism.[76]

In the years following the absorption of Said's message, scholars began to explore problematic areas in his argument. Most striking was the apparent counter-example of Germany, a country Said had barely addressed. Although Germany had no overseas empire until the 1880s, Germans pursued Orientalist scholarship even more intensively than their imperialist European neighbors. Their labors began early: Romantics such as Friedrich Schlegel were enthralled by the spirituality of ancient Sanskrit texts; in 1816 Franz Bopp established a rule-governed practice of comparative grammar demonstrating the historical relationships between languages. Eventually the Germans achieved pre-eminence in the field by putting the full power of their research universities behind it. Some three decades after Said's book appeared, Suzanne Marchand published a detailed study devoted exclusively to German *Orientalistik*, persuasively arguing that the concern most consistently driving and shaping that discipline in the nineteenth century was religion, not imperial conquest. Liberal Protestant scholars, engaged in historical criticism of the Bible and grappling with its consequences for religious faith, wanted to know how the teachings of Jesus had articulated with Judaism and with the culture of the larger geographical region surrounding the Holy Land. Pointing beyond Said, Marchand's revisionist research showed that, even if colonial ventures piqued Europeans' curiosity and enabled them to acquire manuscript sources crucial to opening up this terrain to their scholarly investigation, their cultural stake in the project transcended colonial domination.[77]

The figure of William Jones, regarded as the originator of Orientalism, has been a magnet to scholars, and the new directions of that scholarship are likewise instructive. Jones's quasi-mythic fame resides in his "Third Anniversary Discourse" as founder and president of the Asiatick Society of Bengal in 1786. In the middle of that speech, he casually announced a startling hypothesis. The Sanskrit language, he said, possessed "a wonderful structure," in some ways superior to Greek and Latin, "yet bearing to both of them a stronger affinity, both in the roots of verbs, and in the forms of grammar, than could possibly have been produced by accident; so strong, indeed, that no philologer could examine them all three without believing them to have sprung from some common source ..."[78] This hypothesis, which Bopp's 1816 treatise would systematically prove and which spurred the conceptualization of an Indo-European language family, connected the cultures of the West and the so-called Orient in ways almost unimaginable earlier. It is credited with launching the nineteenth-century Orientalist movement.

Who was William Jones, and what made his discovery possible? The historian of science Kapil Raj has painstakingly restored him to his historical context. A London-born parvenu aspiring to gentlemanly status, Jones studied classics at Oxford, as well as learning Arabic and Persian there, and then acquired a law degree; still in quest of a respectable fortune, he found the high salary scale of the East India Company irresistible and accepted a position as junior judge on the court of Calcutta. Once there, Jones assembled a group of indigenous savants to help him discharge his judicial responsibilities and to foster his linguistic interests; it was within this entourage—and especially in the company of one pandit who introduced him to a text on Sanskrit grammar dating back to the fifth century BCE—that he had his celebrated insight. Though he acknowledged this debt only in private, he demonstrated his appreciation of indigenous scholars by publishing their papers in the proceedings of the Asiatick Society.[79]

Jones, to be sure, partly fit Said's model: the colonial situation precipitated his knowledge-making. But what is also significant is that he departed sharply from Condorcet's model in his non-participation in the colonial transfer of fully formed Western knowledge to passive indigenous peoples. Rather, drawing on sources and traditions in the custody of Occident *and* Orient, he collaborated with native savants to produce new knowledge relevant to both cultures. The extent of Jones's reliance on indigenous scholarship seems to have been even greater than Raj realized. He was likely familiar with a rudimentary theory of linguistic kinship developed by an Indian lexicographer who was the first to identify the affinity between Persian and Sanskrit—an affinity on which Jones might well have modeled the one he so momentously proposed.[80]

CONCLUSION

Asking where Condorcet's predictions proved accurate and where they fell short is a good way to sum up the career of nineteenth-century European knowledge outlined in this chapter.

On the positive side of the ledger, Condorcet was certainly correct about the power that the mode of knowledge-making later named positivism—the discernment of lawful regularities among observable phenomena—would exercise in the long nineteenth century. He was correct, too, that the vast project of disseminating knowledge to ever greater numbers of people would be viewed as a major key to human well-being, though

FIGURE 1.5 The collaboration of West and non-West in making philological knowledge: "An European gentleman with his moonshee, or professor of native languages." Aquatint of 1813. © Corbis Historical / Historical Picture Archive / Getty Images.

his cosmopolitanism probably led him to underestimate how routinely that project would be harnessed to the competition among nation-states. But on the other side of the ledger, he did not foresee the range of epistemological options that would arise at least partly in reaction against the anticipated or actual dominance of positive science. Early nineteenth-century Romantics and late nineteenth-century proponents of *Verstehen* regarded a mode of knowledge-making geared to non-human objects incapable of grasping human feeling or the human need to impose meaning on the world. In both its Kantian and idealist guises, nineteenth-century German philosophy found Condorcet's vaunted sensationalism a blunt instrument for seizing human consciousness. And, as a thinker who saw his own epistemology vindicated by the fact of the French Revolution, Condorcet did not anticipate how many systems of knowledge put forth in the nineteenth century—including, ironically, Comtean positivism—would be designed to prevent renewed socio-political revolution. Finally, while well aware of the links that commerce and colonization forged between Europe and the non-European world, Condorcet had no inkling of the depth of nineteenth-century European curiosity about the non-Western world, inspired not only by imperialist calculation but by unsuspected linguistic ties and by the location of Europe's Holy Land outside Europe.

CHAPTER TWO

The Human Self

JERROLD SEIGEL

Central as the idea of the self has long been in thinking about our individual and collective lives, trying to say just what it means opens a Pandora's box of uncertainties. Is the self a real entity or a mere notion? Ought it be singular or plural? Stable or fluid? A source of autonomy or of domination? Taking the self in the "long nineteenth century" as our subject adds a second source of perplexity, namely modernity. In what does it consist? When did it begin? Is it still with us? To avoid getting too tangled in these questions at the start, we limit ourselves to simple answers for now. By "self" we mean whatever it is that makes each of us be the particular creatures we are, distinguishes us from others, persists through our changes, or gives a particular shape to the relations between the parts of our being. And we take "modernity" to be the complex of historical alterations (however they may be related to each other) that made nineteenth-century people highly conscious of living in a world their ancestors would not have recognized.

Although considering people as selves has a long history (when Shakespeare had Polonius tell Hamlet "to thine own self be true," he expected the advice to seem commonplace), the later seventeenth century marked a new moment in thinking about the notion, as people sought to understand both themselves and their surroundings in ways modeled on the transformed world picture built up by Copernicus, Galileo, and Newton. The new cosmology replaced a conception of the universe oriented around spiritual powers and teleological processes with one based on the material and measurable forces of gravity and inertia. Trying to understand the self in the same spirit, the English philosopher John Locke put aside earlier attempts to grasp the self as some kind of compound of soul and body. As a Christian, Locke did not reject that conception, but because no one could understand how such a union could be effected, he proposed to replace it with an account of how people actually acquired and developed their personal identities.

This they did, Locke proposed, primarily in two ways, "as a man," and "as a person." As a "man" (the gendered language went unquestioned in Locke's time), any individual had an identity much like that of plants or animals, grounded in "the same continued life … vitally united to the same organized body." One aspect of the self was thus corporeal. But the other, giving every individual an identity "as a person," was mental, resting on the power that "a thinking intelligent being" possesses to "consider itself as itself, the same thinking thing, in different times and places." It was this conscious sense for the connection among all the parts of one's being "that makes a man be himself to himself," or the self be "*self to itself.*" This personal self exists "as far as this consciousness can be extended backwards to any past action or thought." The being any of us is in the present is the product of our past ideas and actions, to which we are connected by memory, and which remain central to our identity, even if we have sought to forget, replace, or repent for some of them.[1]

This somewhat commonsensical understanding of the self as at once bodily and mental, a coexistence of two separate modes of being, was not the only seventeenth-century account that would be a point of reference for later thinking. Probably its chief competitor was René Descartes' famous formulation *cogito ergo sum*, "I think, therefore I am." In contrast to Locke's two-sided account, Descartes's formula was resolutely singular, equating the core of what defined human existence wholly with consciousness. (In fact, Descartes did not always treat problems of morality or epistemology so one-sidedly as this suggests, but we must leave that aside here.) The contrast between them points to a central issue in modern debates about the self, namely the question of how its parts are related to each other. These parts include features impressed on us by having a particular body and a personal temperament of a certain sort, but equally (an aspect to which we have not yet come but that will loom large in what follows) those that derive from the social world (or worlds) any given person inhabits, the human environments or cultures from which we all absorb ideas, preconceptions, linguistic habits and abilities, and ways of acting toward ourselves and others. Questions about the self are often questions about whether one of these elements dominates the others or how they interact with each other.

Later people would inherit these issues, both in their lives and their thinking, but they would confront them in ways shaped by the atmosphere of their own times and places. In nineteenth-century Europe, two major contributors to this atmosphere were the heritage of the French Revolution and the new conditions of life being created by industrial change and the social transformations it brought. Paradoxically or not, both of these large-scale developments would encourage at once a confidence in the human capacity to give direction to individual and collective life and a belief that people could not escape the control that outside forces exercised over them. The Revolution had this dual effect because its very occurrence (as with American independence, too) encouraged the belief that people had the power to remake both the political structures in which they lived and the personalities of the men and women who interacted within them, while some of its consequences, including the bloody violence of the Terror and the establishment of the Napoleonic dictatorship, instead showed how far the outcomes of human projects were from the intentions of those who acted to realize them. The new forms of industry similarly gave evidence of a previously unrecognized human ability to release new energies and create new forms of social life, but they simultaneously subjected individuals to conditions (overcrowding, sanitary problems, poverty) and large-scale historical forces (economic crises brought on by the spread of distant markets, the breakdown of traditional communities, and the morality they enforced) more powerful than they.

These same developments were also major contributors to an often-remarked characteristic of the nineteenth century with important implications for experiencing and thinking about the self. This was the sense that historical change had never been so rapid, confronting people with fluid and unpredictable situations that called many traditional assumptions and expectations into question. Karl Marx summed up this condition in a famous phrase: "All that is solid melts into air." In such a society, "All fixed, fast-frozen relations, with their train of ancient and venerable prejudices and opinions, are swept away, all new-formed ones become antiquated before they can ossify." If Marx exaggerated somewhat, many others agreed that the world had become a place where the traditional expectations people had about their identities—as family members, workers, constituents of communities—no longer provided the same degree of guidance they once had. With outside direction losing its relevance, people needed to work out for themselves some of the solutions formerly provided by traditional assumptions and guidelines. Some people responded to these new conditions by developing views about the self that made it either highly autonomous or deeply dependent on outside powers, while others attempted to evolve some more moderate position, not unlike the one Locke had proposed more than a century earlier. Often these ideas about the self were put forward on behalf of one or another political position, or some theory about the essence of modern society. There thus developed a wide-ranging discussion about the nature of the self, based on different responses to the challenges of modern existence.

The impact the French Revolution had on thinking about the self can be illustrated by one of its German supporters, the philosopher Johann Gottlieb Fichte. Fichte belonged to the school of German Idealism largely inspired by Immanuel Kant, and which was devoted to advancing the claims of human freedom. Kant himself located the sources of that freedom in rationality, specifically the ability of the mind to find order in nature and predict the behavior of objects. (Newton's cosmology was a prime example.) This capacity fed his belief that the intellect also had the potential to direct the will—in his vocabulary, become "practical"—so that people could act on the basis of the rationality they displayed as knowers. But he was sorely aware that actions were often controlled by feeling and passion instead, and he never quite found a way to prove satisfactorily that reason could supplant them. When the Revolution broke out he welcomed it, not because he fully supported its political aims (he was wary of activism and in his own state of Prussia supported the monarchy), but because in his view the sympathy people outside France showed for the revolutionaries' attempt to remake their country was evidence of a "moral disposition within the human race" to fulfil its inner aptitude for freedom.[2]

Fichte, younger and more radical than his teacher, supported the Revolution even in its more extreme Jacobin phase, seeing in it evidence for the human power actually to introduce freedom into the world. At the core of this power was the self, the ego (*das Ich*), which Fichte theorized as "pure activity," giving it a quality of unalloyed self-directed energy that never stopped flowing, so that it was preserved from ever becoming a mere object in the world, subject to the limitations of material existence. Fichte did not deny that the world chiefly consists of such objects, but he thought that the self or subject was constantly recreating its relationship to them; thus its freedom came to reside not in any identifiable moment of fulfilment, but in its constant striving to realize the spiritual core of its nature. Whether such an account is really an image of a self capable of pure freedom or instead compelled to accept its limitations is at best a moot point, and it may be that in Fichte's thinking, as in the outcomes of the Revolution itself, the visions of radical self-renewal for both individuals and society were never realizable. Later he would recast his views of the self in a very different mold, to which we will return shortly.[3]

However problematic Fichte's thinking may appear to us, his example is important here because it illustrates a widespread impulse in the nineteenth century to identify the

FIGURE 2.1 Johann Gottlieb Fichte. © Hulton Archive / Heritage Images / Getty Images.

self with some kind of inner freedom. Like other thinkers in his time, he was engaged in seeking an alternative to a widespread pre-Revolutionary materialism, rooted in natural-scientific forms of explanation and in Locke's emphasis on the power of sense-experience to form the mind. People affected by such materialism emphasized the capacity of both bodily temperament and environmental circumstances to impose a kind of existence on individuals far removed from what they wanted to believe possible for themselves. One such person was the prominent eighteenth-century *philosophe* Denis Diderot, one of the editors of the famous *Encylopédie*, who in some writings advanced a radical fatalism that made no place for free will, and who ascribed the capacity to rise above circumstances only to those people accidentally gifted with strong constitutions, which made their power over themselves merely a matter of innate disposition, not the kind of moral direction Kant cared about. A second was Diderot's sometime friend Jean-Jacques Rousseau, who, despite his belief that human beings possessed a core capacity for freedom, saw himself and others as denatured and whirled about by the changing circumstances of the worlds they inhabited. In place of this post-Lockean pessimism about the self, Fichte and others like him, for instance the early nineteenth-century French liberals Germaine de Staël and Benjamin Constant, were engaged in what George Armstrong Kelly calls a "respiritualization" of the world, hoping thereby to support "a more idealized and voluntaristic version of human freedom."[4]

The other major historical turning that encouraged confidence in individuals' abilities to be agents of their own formation was economic and industrial change, which opened up opportunities for people with the right combination of talents, resources, and luck to achieve sometimes striking rises in social status. The label we associate with such people is "the self-made man" (women were seldom envisioned in such terms), an appellation that minimizes what such people owe to others or to the world that sustains them, declaring them to be fashioners of their own social being. Their motto might have been the exhortation that François Guizot, a dominant figure in the French "bourgeois monarchy" (1830–1848), offered as an alternative to extending the franchise by reducing the tax-based requirement for voting: *Enrichissez-vous, par le travail et l'épargne* (enrich yourselves by work and saving). Then, as now, the notion that only personal effort determines the position people come to occupy in society was seen as making untenable claims for the independence of the self, and some of its best illustrations belong to the realm of caricature rather than reality. Of these the most famous remains Josiah Bounderby, the representative of middle-class self-centeredness in Charles Dickens's great novel *Hard Times* (1854). To point up his claim that he owed his success as a manufacturer only to himself, Bounderby maintained he had been born in a ditch, raising himself out of the mire with no aid from family or friends. In (fictional) fact, as Dickens lets us know, he had been lovingly cared for by a mother whose support made his career possible, and whose continuing attempts to maintain her ties to him he shoved aside lest her presence spoil his myth of pure self-creation. As recent historians have emphasized, such family connections remained crucial for nineteenth-century people, one of several reasons for putting aside old fables that nineteenth-century bourgeois were narrow-minded individualists. If Bounderby was a self-made man, so was Dickens himself, who all the same acknowledged the dependence of individuals on both other people and the social institutions that mutually sustain them, metaphorically figuring it in the mutual support by which circus acrobats stayed aloft (there was such a circus in *Hard Times*) and in the Cheeryble brothers, who employed Nicholas Nickleby in the story that bears his name.

Precisely this notion of self-formation, in which individuals realize their potential through interacting with others engaged in the same quest, stands at the center of the most popular nineteenth-century treatise on the virtues of individual self-development, Samuel Smiles's *Self-Help*, published in 1859. Smiles is often presented as a maker of the myth of rags to riches, an individualist who stressed self-reliance to a degree that veiled the dependence of people on social conditions and on others, as well as the class differences that allowed some to succeed through their efforts while others could not. One can quote from his writings in a way to support such a reading. But closer attention reveals that his individualism never lacked a social dimension. The England he loved was a collective product, formed out of the action of great and small, who had "all ... worked together, one generation carrying forward the labours of another, building up the character of the country and establishing its prosperity on solid foundations." Far from resembling the "windowless monads" proposed as a model of individual existence by the seventeenth-century German philosopher Gottfried Wilhelm Leibniz, the individuals pictured by Smiles were permeable to the influence both of others and of the social whole that their efforts built up. Formal education was important in self-formation, but "far higher and more practical is the life-education given daily in our homes, in the streets, behind counters, in workshops, at the loom and plough." Indeed, *Self-Help* was inspired as much by Smiles's awareness of such interactions as by his focus on individual achievement by itself: he attributed the book's origins to his observation of an informal group of young men whose envisioned path to success led through their common participation in a project of mutual self-betterment.[5]

Where a more purely individualistic notion of self-making became operative, it could lead to unexpected and paradoxical results, as illustrated by the remarkable relations between John Stuart Mill and his father James. Because the story of the two Mills has much to tell us about selfhood in the nineteenth century, it deserves considerable attention here. The younger Mill portrayed his father as a remarkable example of personal self-creation. Born to "a petty tradesman and (I believe) small farmer" in Scotland, the boy James was given a boost in life by a wealthy patron, who sent him to the University of Edinburgh to prepare for a career as a clergyman. But rationalist criticism dissolved his religious faith; abandoning the ministry, he supported himself as a tutor and then a writer. Only by virtue of "extraordinary energy" was he able to marry and support a large family on such badly paid foundations (and without ever going into debt), especially since his frankly expressed radical and democratic opinions were "odious to all persons of influence, and to the common run of prosperous Englishmen" in the time. His material situation improved in 1819 (John was then thirteen), when his talents won him an appointment to help manage the correspondence of the East India Company, a post he won despite the fact that his much-noticed history of India, published the year before, was highly critical of the Company's policies.

James Mill's views were much influenced by those of his close friend Jeremy Bentham, and the two cooperated in numerous reform projects. Among these was to rear up a partner in reform who would carry their work into the next generation, and in pursuit of this goal they devised and subjected young John Stuart to a remarkable regime of education, at once intellectual and moral. He was introduced to Greek at age three, Latin at eight, classical logic and political economy before he was twelve, with mathematics and history along the way. He was also taught to question received opinions, examine the weak points in arguments and clarify the expression of his own ideas, all however in the service of the radical democratic and anti-religious ideas of his father and Bentham. (John Stuart later acquired a reputation for being impolitely disputatious.) To prevent him from thinking that this regime was at all unusual, lest he acquire an inflated opinion of himself, and in order to shield him from both "the ordinary corrupting influence which boys exercise over boys" and "the contagion of vulgar modes of thought and feeling," young John was kept from contact with other children (and from unapproved adults as well). Thus he grew up in considerable isolation, his situation managed so as to subject him to the concentrated influence of a narrow range of people and circumstances, and allowing him little chance for spontaneous and undirected interaction with others. His father James had been a self-made man, and proud to be one. But precisely the value James attached to that independent way of being lay behind his attempt to turn his son into a person fabricated by others.

In his remarkable *Autobiography* (1873), John Stuart Mill acknowledged the positive effects of this formation; after all, it produced one of the leading thinkers and progressive reformers of his time, just as his father hoped. But it also had a number of results the elder Mill had not intended, and which opened a distance between father and son. John identified one of these as a certain passivity in his character, a lack of energy he contrasted with his father's never wasting a minute. "The children of energetic parents frequently grow up unenergetic," he wrote, "because they lean on their parents." Especially troubling in his own case was the "absence of moral spontaneity" in his character, "an inactivity of the moral sense and even to a large extent of the intellect, unless roused by the appeal of someone else."[6] Mill saw these features of himself as especially visible at a painful moment in his life that he similarly connected to his youthful circumstances, namely the deep depression or "mental crisis" into which he fell in his twenties, and which threatened to put an end to his career as a reformer. So detached did he feel from the goals to which his life was supposed to be dedicated that when he asked himself whether it would make him happy, were all the changes in "institutions and opinions" sought by himself and those close to him accomplished, "an irrepressible self-consciousness distinctly answered 'No!'," and "the whole foundation on which my life was constructed fell down."[7]

Mill believed that one main contributor to this painful outcome was the sensationalist psychology and severely rationalistic view of human nature that gave the tone to his childhood. Bentham and the elder Mill expressed contempt for passionate emotions, and they regarded feelings of any sort as morally indifferent, since what mattered about people's actions was whether they contributed to happiness or detracted from it, not what motivated them. The identification they hoped to form between young John and radical reform was therefore to be brought about from the outside, through the influence of environment and argument; inner feeling and affect were at best an accidental element in it. Looking back on his crisis, one thing the younger Mill thought it had taught him was that the ties woven out of such treatment were abstract, weak, and easily unraveled by the same habit of argumentation he had been taught as a weapon against prejudice and traditional authority. "The habit of analysis has a tendency to wear away the feelings," and finding that he had no vital connection to the principles around which his identity had been constructed left him without the tie to life that only feeling can sustain. At what seemed his lowest moment, however, a turning point came, when he found himself reduced to tears by reading an account of how a French writer was affected by the death of his father. The discovery that he was not "a stick or a stone," but still capable of feeling, did not resolve things all at once, but it allowed him to begin to reknit his ties to the world and return to something like the role his father had planned for him.[8]

In doing so John Stuart Mill remained broadly loyal to the reform program championed by his father and Bentham, but he simultaneously took on some ideas quite foreign to their way of thinking, including—and most relevant here—notions about selves and their relations to the world. This mix appeared in the younger Mill's most famous work, *On Liberty* (1859). The work was a determined and powerful defense of freedom of thought and expression (both spoken and written) and of the right of individuals to follow any plan of life they chose, however offensive to the opinions of those around them, provided that their actions did no harm to others. This individualism was very much in line with his father's views, and it was partially justified on the core Benthamite grounds

FIGURE 2.2 John Stuart Mill. © DEA Picture Library / Getty Images.

of contributing to "the greatest happiness of the greatest number." But the individuals whose freedom was validated in these terms were no longer envisioned in the mechanical and intellectualistic way that inspired his treatment as a child. To be sure, both the human capacity for rational reflection and the power that environment exercised over personal development remained central notions in Mill's thinking. But two additional elements were now grafted onto these. The first was that the life of every individual resembled that of a plant, seeking to realize the potential contained within the seed from which it springs. A human person was like "a tree," he wrote, "which requires to develop itself on all sides, according to the tendency of the inward forces that make it a living thing."[9] This image had its roots in German thinking, going back to Leibniz's notion of "monads" developing along their separate trajectories, which came to Mill from the great advocate of German philosophy in the England of his time, Samuel Taylor Coleridge. Seen in this way, individuals were bound to be harmed by attempts to impose some exterior model on them, whether founded in custom and social preconception or inspired by some well-meant educational program.

The second element in Mill's new thinking in this area bore the clear marks of his "mental crisis," since it involved a firm recognition of the importance of feeling and emotion in personal formation and moral life. But the views he now adopted also had a history, going back at least to eighteenth-century ideas of a different stripe from the rationalistic environmentalism espoused by Mill's father. Opposed to such a perspective in spirit, but rooted in some of the same Lockean soil, a "cult of sentimentality" grew up, associated with literature and especially novel-reading. Both Diderot and Rousseau were important figures in this current, despite their simultaneous involvement with elements of materialistic determinism. What made such a perspective important in connection with self-formation was the notion that people could build up their powers of self-direction by identifying themselves emotionally with virtuous figures in fiction who somehow triumphed over temptation, such as the heroines of Samuel Richardson's novels *Pamela* (1740) and *Clarissa* (1748), and the Julie of Rousseau's still more popular *La nouvelle Héloïse* (1761). But these hopes were regularly undermined by the fear that such emotional arousal, and the sexual feelings connected with it, would weaken people instead of strengthening them, making them prey to dangerous and uncontrolled emotions.[10] Just such notions about the unreliability of feelings had operated in the indifference or suspicion with which James Mill and Bentham regarded them, but in *On Liberty* the younger Mill took the other side. Passions and feelings were (as his predecessor David Hume had insisted a century before) "the raw material of human nature," and personal strength could not be developed without calling on them. In his *Autobiography* Mill explained that his recovery from his crisis was aided by turning to literature and poetry for examples of virtue and self-command, having learned "by experience that the passive susceptibilities needed to be cultivated as well as the active capacities, and required to be nourished and enriched as well as guided." The mode of self-formation Mill envisioned here, in contrast to the one practiced on him as a child, called on inner feeling from the start, seeing the cultivation of affect as a way of strengthening both the self and its ties to the world.[11]

Such a self is not what the image of the "self-made man" usually called up, but it recognized the need for individuals to be agents in their own self-making, developing their inner potential by drawing on materials from outside themselves. These included literature and culture but also the examples provided by people around them. One reason why people should be free to follow a life plan in harmony with their particular natures, in Mill's view, was that a society whose members had free rein to do so gave itself a broader store of resources for others to call on. Society became more "rich, diversified, and animating, furnishing more abundant aliment to high thoughts and elevating feelings, and strengthening the tie which binds every individual to the race, by making the race infinitely better worth belonging to." What Mill was here providing, even if he never quite put it this way, was a new program of self-formation suited to the same weakening of traditional identities, and the same need for individuals to call more on their personal resources, that gave the notion of the self-made man its relevance. For Mill, however (as for Samuel Smiles), this kind of self-making had nothing to do with any Bounderby-like denial of dependence on others.[12]

To be sure, Mill and Smiles developed their views largely in connection with the experience of middle-class males. Both women and men lower down the social scale had to confront very different circumstances. But this does not mean that the perspective Mill developed was irrelevant to people in these other situations, as both his own support of unions and certain socialist aspirations (albeit without a general transformation of society), and the large contributions his treatises on feminine equality made to the development of the women's movement in the nineteenth century, may suggest. We will return to the question of female self-development at the conclusion of this discussion; first we need to think for a moment about workers.

One major disparity between middle-class and working-class men lay in the resources of wealth and education that each could bring to bear on their lives; the poverty, disruption, and degradation many workers faced in the early phases of modern industrial society was a subject of widespread lament. In face of these privations, some observers expressed doubts that workers had the capacity to participate actively in their own self-formation. One of these was the influential Welsh socialist reformer Robert Owen. A

FIGURE 2.3 Robert Owen. © Pictorial Press Ltd / Alamy Stock Photo.

strong social determinist, Owen pictured individuals in a way that excluded independent self-making altogether. As he put it in one writing, it was a "well-known fact" that "human character is always formed *for* and not *by* the individual." The consequences were especially unfortunate for workers in his time, because "the character of the lower classes in Britain is now formed chiefly by circumstances arising from trade, manufactures and commerce"; taught by the world around them to "buy cheap and sell dear" and thus to "acquire strong powers of deception," they had been rendered incapable of introducing into society the spirit of "open, honest sincerity, without which man cannot make others happy, nor enjoy happiness himself." Unlike the middle classes, however, for whom "buy cheap and sell dear" lay at the core of who they were, workers could develop a different spirit if they were placed in different conditions, given education of the right sort and an actual experience of cooperation in communities set up to exemplify it. Everything depended on how the truth that "character is formed *for* and not *by* individuals" was implemented.[13]

As Marx would point out, there was a worm at the heart of this rosy vision, namely that in order for education to work, those in charge of it had to be free of influence by the social environment that degraded the character of everyone else: the "educator" had first to be "educated." Marx did not contest Owen's assertion that working-class selfhood was wholly formed by conditions, or that its present form could be totally altered in the future. For him, however, what would accomplish this "education" was not cooperative communal life planned by reformers but the active experience of making the revolution to which the proletariat was driven by poverty and oppression. It was the same conditions that rendered workers "completely shut off from all self-activity [*Selbsttätigkeit*]" in the present that put them in "a position to achieve a complete and no longer restricted self-activity in the future." What would give birth to such "unrestricted self-activity" was that revolutionary activity, fed by human consciousness and will, would take over the determining role formerly played by social conditions, a transmutation made permanent by the creation of a society of liberated individuals who shared ownership and control of the productive forces that sustained their common life.[14]

To be sure (and alas), this was a utopian vision of both society and the self, and like some other radical dreams, it saw individual existence as more or less bound to take only the extreme forms of no-self or all-self, total oppression or total liberation, excluding the more moderate and complex alternatives theorized and experienced by figures such as Locke and Mill. Just how many workers may have seen themselves in the negative of the two poles posited by Owen or Marx is a knotty question to which we can only point here. But many behaved in ways that suggest they did not, for example by taking part in the great efflorescence of working-class self-help groups that emerged during the nineteenth century. Such associations were dedicated to individual and group improvement through discussion, education, and mutual intellectual and cultural stimulation, working on the assumption that their members brought some potential for self-development to them. Such groups were prominent in the Owenite movement, whether or not they fit into its founder's notion of how selves were formed, and they became still more significant in working-class efforts as time went on, becoming a central feature of the archipelago of associational life (choruses, gyms, literary societies, discussion forums) sponsored and coordinated by the German Social Democratic Party from the 1880s. Such groups were often modeled on the voluntary associations for self-improvement already prominent in middle-class life in many European countries, and some of these, including the ones described by Samuel Smiles, contained better-off kinds of workers alongside people with middle-class occupations. As Michael Mason has noted, such a social mix reflected the degree to which the idea of self-improvement permeated working-class as well as bourgeois culture, constituting "one of the most challenging points of convergence between working-class and bourgeois moral ideology." Although some historians have pictured this shared ground as a sign of the hegemony of bourgeois attitudes, radical working-class leaders themselves saw the virtues they sought to inculcate—such as temperance and self-control—as important tools in strengthening radical organization and action.[15]

Taking note of such connections is important here because it helps to remind us that concern about the state of workers was not the only motive that encouraged people to regard character or the self as formed for rather than by individuals. Whether or not people shared Owen's view of this question depended less on the social class of the people they had in their sights than on what they hoped to make of them. Among those who proceeded on the assumption that middle-class subjects could be formed by controlling the conditions around them was Fichte, in the German nationalist phase he entered in reaction against the Napoleonic domination of Germany. His vision for his country now included an educational project that sought to form pupils "in such a way that [they] simply cannot will otherwise than what you wish [them] to will." The formula was not so imperious as it may seem, since what Fichte wanted his pupils to will was the freedom that comes from following only the stable precepts of reason, not the winds of impulse or desire; it was the species of will that Kant identified with the moral good as such. Fichte believed that shaping people toward such an end would stimulate their "self-activity" because it would arouse their core potential for freedom, located in the quality of pure activity he had identified with the *Ich*'s essence in his earlier writings. But this stimulation had to take place in an environment totally cut off from outside influences, so that nothing affected by ordinary life could distract the mind from its pure self-referentiality (the German version of the more practical rationality Bentham and James Mill sought to inculcate in the young John Stuart).

A strikingly similar program, also aimed chiefly at middle-class pupils, was pursued in mid-century France by Victor Cousin, then the dominant figure in French education. Cousin, like Fichte, was part of the "respiritualization" of thinking referred to above. He saw the core aim of education as teaching "the intelligence to know itself," that is, recognizing its participation in the quasi-divine power of "thought in itself, ... the substance and cause of the truths that man perceives." Such truths aspired to universality, but individuals could not attain them by themselves, especially in France, where the political divisions inherited from the Revolution led people to identify with partial and limited perspectives, the one-sided ideas that corresponded to one or another party, tradition, or particular interest. To counter the identification of the *moi* with such narrow prospects, the self-discovery education aimed to bring about needed to be directed by the state. Introspection had to be taught and guided; giving proper form to the self required "the tutelary intervention of the state in the education of youth." As a recent student of Cousin puts it, the philosopher's psychological method was intended "not just to discover the truth, but [as Fichte frankly avowed] to impose it on people's minds."[16]

The point of highlighting views such as these is not to suggest that nineteenth-century theories of self-formation were in general intrusive or domineering; some were and some were not. Rather, the common element linking Fichte's and Cousin's programs was that both were responses to the new conditions of self-formation created by the complex of changes Marx summarized as "all that is solid melts into the air," the weakening or dissolution of traditional attachments and the need to evolve substitutes for them. Cousin's approach to shaping the *moi* of French students was self-consciously designed for a world transformed by Revolution, and Fichte believed that Germany was ready for the education he was proposing because its defeat by Napoleon had undermined traditional German particularism and the assumptions on which it rested, weakening the country's attachment to narrow interests and the identities they fostered, and leaving individuals open to more elevated ways of being.[17]

In the later decades of the century, Cousin's successor as chief theorist and practitioner of moral self-formation in France, Émile Durkheim, would evolve a body of theory concerning both social and individual development that rested on the transformation of traditional social relations. Where these had obtained, most people were limited to the experience of their localities and everyone typically engaged in the same—chiefly agrarian—activities. Sharing experiences in this way, they all held the same values, so that neither identity nor social integration was a problem for them. Modern societies, by contrast, were characterized by a more elaborate division of labor, growth in population, and greater communication between distant locales. The diversity of situations provided greater opportunities for individual differentiation and self-development, but it also made individuals aware of being unlike those around them, and unleashed a previously more restrained potential for egotism. Both individual identity and social integration grew more difficult to achieve, and Durkheim looked to society and the state to educate citizens in a new kind of morality, protect the new freedoms they were acquiring, and yet restrain the egotism that threatened to accompany them. It was a difficult assignment, and over time it pushed Durkheim from an early position not far from Mill's sense that individuals liberated to work out their own paths could provide each other with models of personal development, to a conception much closer to Cousin's sense that the narrow and selfish impulses to which individuals were subject on their own meant that they needed some kind of strong direction from outside. Society and the state combined to provide it, first by giving people a sense of collective engagement in moments of moral exaltation such as the Dreyfus Affair, and then by diffusing a new morality by means of educational programs that infused people with a sense of how much their individual development owed to the modern social conditions that made it possible.[18]

By contrast, Durkheim's German contemporary Max Weber saw modern social life only as making individual autonomy more difficult. He famously described the freedom to identify themselves with a calling or vocation that had been open to early modern people (and especially encouraged by English Puritans) as imposed on those in his time by powerful economic and social conditions, rooted in the rigidities (what he called the "iron cage") of industrial and bureaucratic organization. Moreover, he saw the radical pluralism of values that modernity had unleashed (a replay of the polytheism of ancient life, but in purely secular terms) as confronting individuals with unprecedentedly hard moral choices. Only those of exceptional strength could resolve the consequent tensions in satisfying ways; the growing power of society deepened the need for self-reliance.[19] One way to describe the place of Durkheim's and Weber's contemporary Sigmund Freud in relation to them is to say that he was in search of new ways for individuals to strengthen their selfhood (which he identified with the part of the psyche he called the ego) and thus to recover from the wounds both society and their own natures inflicted on them.

But the decline of traditional models of self-formation should by no means be seen only in negative terms. Many of those considered here recognized that the diminished relevance of inherited identities meant the opening up of pathways to independence and self-creation much less available before. One large category for whom this was gradually coming to be true was women, traditionally confined to a narrow sphere largely identified with home and family, and seldom seen before the nineteenth century as able to open up new arenas of personal and social activity. To be sure, we must be careful not to exaggerate the progress they were able to make; many features of life today remind us how painfully distant the goal of equality between men and women remains. But by the end of the century unprecedented opportunities for education were being opened to women in all Western European countries, and the notion that women should have some kind of independent life outside the home, including taking on work previously limited to men, had begun to spread too. From the 1860s, active feminist movements had appeared in many countries, inspired by ideas about feminine equality that strikingly anticipate more recent ones. In their unstinting attack on the notion that women ought to remain in the "separate sphere" of domesticity, John Stuart Mill and his wife Harriet Taylor took sharp aim at the notion that women's traditional role gave them virtues of sympathy and moral concern that allowed them to soften and civilize otherwise harder and rougher men, arguing on the contrary that the subordinate position imposed on women distorted their selfhood, pushing them to develop subtle and harmful forms of domination, based on pretense, deception, and artifice.[20]

This critique shows that the Mills, like others in their time, recognized that the modern reconfiguration of social relations required people to evolve new social identities. Evidence of how particular women experienced this need is hard to come by, given the rarity of published letters or autobiographies that discuss it. But at least one recently studied diary (from the 1860s) suggests that otherwise unexceptional young bourgeois women were open to imagining a life outside the circle of expectations imposed by their families, and to flirting with men who might be their partners, even if they had insufficient courage to move into such uncharted territories.[21] By the 1920s, such possibilities were openly acknowledged and discussed, for instance in the furor over Victor Margueritte's novel of 1922 La Garçonne (The Boy-Girl), about a young woman who rejects traditional gender boundaries, engaging in sexual experimentation and seeking economic independence. Even earlier, however, some open-eyed observers thought they could see women's changed manner of experiencing their selves in the way they looked out on the world, and that the alteration had been discerned and recorded by artists. One of these observers was Camille Mauclair, then a well-known writer and critic who moved from an early radicalism to support a series of reform causes, at once social and aesthetic. In 1899, he published an article on "Women in the Eyes of Modern Painters." Although focused on artists' representations of female subjects, it took the change it chronicled as evidence of a larger shift in the way women appeared to themselves and to men.

Mauclair was fully aware that traditional male ways of gazing at women turned them into passive objects of masculine desire and fantasy, and that the representations painters made of them did the same. In such images, "Her happy face, radiating a virgin brightness ... is devoid of any mental mystery; it waits, like a sheet of blank paper, for the man's feeling to inscribe his dream on it." In the decades before Mauclair's article, however, women had begun to present a different countenance and display a different kind of presence, first in work such as Édouard Manet's famous *Déjeuner sur l'herbe* (1863) and *Olympia* (1865), and Edgar Degas's portraits of women in his own family, then in pictures by lesser artists as well. All these women gave evidence of a developed individuality and a power of expression that testified to independent self-awareness, making viewers aspire to know, no less than with portraits of men, what links tied these surface features to the mental and psychic life beneath their surface. In place of the ideal of a placid beauty, "carnal, radiant and animal," we find ourselves face to face with a being whose enduring magnetism derives from a "psychological expression whose birth is within."

She has broken through the barrier imposed by gallantry and tradition, that isolated her from life and confined her in a narrow domain, by respect as much as by belief in her mental incapacity. She takes part in moral life, she shares the cares and responsibilities of modern man, she adopts the same mental habits, she is acquiring an equivalent personality, and her physiognomy gives evidence of it. This "new woman ... thoughtful and active" will inspire a new painting, where she will be studied and depicted not by lovers but by equals.[22]

Mauclair understood well that feminine opportunities for self-making had not arrived at a point of equality with men's. But he perceived in both the way that the declining power of tradition spawned a need for a new kind of selfhood, one in which people participate in their own self-formation by bringing inner resources to bear on the task of

FIGURE 2.4 Édouard Manet, *Luncheon on the Grass*, *c.* 1863. © Fine Art Images / Heritage Images / Getty Images.

FIGURE 2.5 Edgar Degas, *Portrait of a Young Woman*, *c.* 1885. © Wikimedia Commons (public domain).

working out newly emerging social identities. In earlier conditions female selfhood was formed for and not by individuals; in Mauclair's present external factors had not ceased to play a vital role, but now people—male and female—were at once confronted with the need to become more active in their self-formation and provided with new resources to help them do it.

CHAPTER THREE

Ethics and Social Relations

KRISHAN KUMAR

EUROPE'S CENTURY

The period covered by this chapter is conveniently, if also conventionally, demarcated by two major events, the French Revolution of 1789 and the First World War that began in 1914—the "long nineteenth century." These were events not just of Western but of world history. The French Revolution had a worldwide influence and effect; the First World War inaugurated a period in which all conflicts between the major powers tended to take on global dimensions.

This was also the period in which Western domination of the world, begun in the eighteenth century if not earlier, achieved its greatest extent and impact. "Irresistibly," wrote the great historian Leopold von Ranke in 1879, "armed with weapon and science, the spirit of the Occident subdues the world."[1] By 1914, 85 percent of the world's land surface was occupied or controlled by Europeans. The British Empire alone, the world's largest, occupied a quarter of the world's land surface and incorporated nearly a quarter of the world's population.[2] Europe, and Europe-derived societies such as those of North America, exerted their power and influence over the entire globe, politically, economically, culturally. Non-European powers could compete only by substantially adopting European ways: Japan in the nineteenth century was the most successful in this. Globalization, often discussed as a post-1945 phenomenon, was clearly present in the nineteenth century, then as now mainly in the form of Europeanization or Westernization.

Europe's global hegemony was effected mainly, though by no means entirely, through empire.[3] Mostly this was through the overseas empires of the British, French, Dutch, Portuguese, and Spanish (though in the Spanish case only vestigially by the late nineteenth century). But Russia's land empire extended all the way across Central Asia to the Pacific, where it engaged with the Chinese and Japanese. The Ottoman Empire, too, was firmly Eurasian, despite lacking colonies. The nineteenth century was not just Europe's century, it was also the age of empire, in which the European empires were clearly dominant.[4] Nationalism—also very much a product of this period—might challenge empire, but its successes had to wait mainly until the twentieth century, when it triumphed largely as the result of the destruction of the European land empires in the First World War and the promotion of the national principle by the American President Woodrow Wilson.

To empire, one must add industry. The nineteenth century inaugurated the industrial age, spearheaded by Britain with its Industrial Revolution. Like the French Revolution, the British Industrial Revolution had worldwide repercussions from the start. It led to the industrialization of Europe, on the basis of which Europe developed the technology and military power to overwhelm the rest of the world. Once again, this was a challenge, or threat, to the non-Western world: industrialize or else. Japan was the first to learn the lesson and the first therefore successfully to resist Western pressures (though only with Western means and methods).

Nineteenth-century Europeans were highly conscious that there was something very special about their age, that they were living through an epoch of unprecedented transformation, at unprecedented rates of change. That was bound to produce anxieties, caused especially by the profound impact of industrialization and urbanization on the lives of ordinary people, and of the democratic movement launched by the French Revolution. Thinkers as varied as Thomas Carlyle, Matthew Arnold, Alexis de Tocqueville, and Karl Marx commented incisively on these developments, with varying degrees of hope and confidence. The new social sciences—economics, political science, sociology—were especially prominent in attempting to diagnose and, where possible, suggest remedies for the novel condition of society.[5]

But what was perhaps even more remarkable was that even the sternest social critics, with few exceptions, were supremely confident that the new industrial society could solve its problems. Marx, who wrote some of the most passionate pages denouncing the evils of the new capitalist society, was nevertheless convinced that out of the very materials of that society would come the resources for the building of the new free and egalitarian society of socialism. Nineteenth-century thinkers inherited much of the mental equipment and the optimistic attitudes of the eighteenth-century European Enlightenment. Reason and science would triumph in the end over all obstacles, whatever the travails on the way. That conviction lay at the heart of Auguste Comte's "positivist" philosophy—also known as the new science of sociology—whose slogan was "Order and Progress." The idea of progress, first delineated in the late seventeenth century, and confirmed in the eighteenth, reached its apogee in the nineteenth century. "Progress," as that arch-Victorian thinker Herbert Spencer proclaimed in 1851, "is not an accident, but a necessity."[6]

It is a familiar feature of intellectual history that, at the very moment a society may be thought to have reached its apogee, thinkers begin to discern the signs of decline and decadence, and to express fears for the future of society. Such was also the fate of European society in the later nineteenth century. Many commentators, following French usage, have dubbed the period 1871–1914 "la Belle Époque," and there is plenty of contemporary evidence to sustain this perception of a period of peace, prosperity, and artistic creativity—"the high refinement of civilization," as the American novelist Henry James put it.[7] Europe seemed to be riding high, its global pre-eminence undoubted and unassailable, its rivals competing among themselves to emulate it.

But there were some who were not persuaded, who on the contrary felt they could discern the symptoms of a terrible spiritual emptiness, and all the signs of a looming catastrophe. Such were thinkers like the philosopher Friedrich Nietzsche, the sociologist Georg Simmel, and the cultural critic Max Nordau. Later, before and after the First World War, Sigmund Freud continued this vein of criticism. The First World War itself seemed horrific confirmation of all their fears, with Europe tearing itself apart and dragging the rest of the world into its quarrels. At the end of the war appeared the first volume of Oswald Spengler's deeply pessimistic *The Decline of the West* (1918). Its instant popularity testified eloquently to the somber mood that had succeeded the euphoria and complacency of the Belle Époque.

Any account of European thought in the nineteenth century needs to take note of these fluctuations of mood and opinion. They were present indeed throughout the century, although it is right to stress the generally confident outlook of the first half of the century and the growing doubts in the second half. But at the same time, overriding these particular positions, it is important to stress that all thinkers were aware of the centrality of Europe in the world's development at that time. They might, like the English novelist Jane Austen, choose not to make that fact the subject matter of their work. But it is generally not difficult to find traces of that awareness even in those writers who concentrated on the local or regional (her fellow countryman Thomas Hardy would be another good example of such a wider consciousness). Most thinkers in any case were only too conscious that what happened in Europe, for good or bad, mattered for the world as a whole, as became crystal clear in 1914.

One can recognize thinkers' "Eurocentrism," an intellectually disabling perspective that focuses exclusively on Europe or a European point of view, in whatever period one considers. Europe has always been linked to the rest of the world and should always be seen in a global context (which means, among other things, taking account of the impact of non-European developments, such as Chinese science or the rise of Islam, on Europe). But for the nineteenth century at least, it is not wrong to see Europe as holding center stage, in the sense that the events unfolding there carried greater consequences for the rest of the world than in any other part, or at any other time. That had not been the case in the past, and it was not to be so in the future, in the twentieth century and beyond (though this did not stop Europe from launching humankind into another world war). But, like it or not, the nineteenth century was truly Europe's century, the century in which European thought and power achieved unprecedented heights in the world.

THE DUAL REVOLUTION: CHALLENGE AND RESPONSE

Much nineteenth-century social thought can be seen as a response to the "dual revolution," the French political revolution of 1789 and the British Industrial Revolution that, starting in the late eighteenth century, gathered speed in the nineteenth.[8] The reason is fairly obvious: these are the two events or processes that had the greatest consequence not just for Europe, but for the world. Moreover, what was clear even in the nineteenth century, and is even clearer today, is that these events marked a beginning, not an end or even the beginning of an end. The French Revolution heralded a movement to democracy and popular sovereignty whose victories were partial, often no more than fleeting, and in any case were throughout the world radically incomplete. The Industrial Revolution similarly launched a development in the economies of the world that continues apace today as the global industrialized economy draws in more and more peoples of the world. If "modernity" or "modernization" sums up the global epoch since around 1800, the French and Industrial Revolutions can fairly be taken as its hallmarks.

What this meant was a series of characteristic themes and problems with which nineteenth-century thinkers grappled, seeking to understand and, if possible, control the forces unleashed by these momentous events. The first was the sheer "contagion of numbers," as Europe, then the world, faced a "demographic revolution," a rapid demographic upswing that even today shows scant signs of flattening out. The second was in where most of these people settled: the towns and cities that expanded exponentially throughout the nineteenth century. In 1851, Britain became the first urban society in the world, in the sense that more than half the population lived in large or medium-sized cities. That many of these urban dwellers came from the countryside produced a third problem: the depopulation and alleged "loss of community" that came with the decline of rural life. Urban life was widely thought to lack the resources to re-establish community; rather, it brought a condition of isolation and "anomie," a disabling and disruptive lack of moral regulation.[9]

Then there were the conditions in the new factories, whether in the countryside or the new industrial towns, such as Manchester or Lyons. Industrialism might mean "progress," but if so, it was of a very contradictory kind. The French writer Alexis de Tocqueville, visiting Manchester in 1835, was struck by the contrasts.

> From this foul drain the greatest stream of human industry flows out to fertilize the whole world. From this filthy sewer pure gold flows. Here humanity attains its most complete development and its most brutish; here civilization works its miracles, and civilized man is turned back almost into a savage.[10]

If this was an acute comment on industrialization, Tocqueville was also the thinker who laid out most commandingly the promise and problems associated with democracy and democratization, the legacy of the French Revolution. This he did principally in his observations on what he saw as the world's first mass democracy, the new United States of America. His *Democracy in America* (1835–1840) celebrated America's egalitarianism and civic associationism. But it also portrayed a darker side to democracy, in the stultifying power of mass public opinion and the possibility of "the tyranny of the majority"—concerns that, stimulated by Tocqueville's writings, also creatively preoccupied the British thinker John Stuart Mill. Democracy was slow to advance in nineteenth-century Europe. Most countries still had very restricted franchises—nearly all excluded women—on the eve of the First World War. But it was clear to nearly all thinkers, as it had been to Tocqueville as early as 1835, that democracy was the wave of the future. What to do about "the entry of the masses onto the stage of history," as the Russian revolutionary Leon Trotsky put it—how to incorporate into the political system large numbers of often uneducated people—was a concern to most of the leading thinkers of the century.

It was another French thinker, Henri de Saint-Simon (1760–1825), who gave the earliest sketch of the new "industrial society"—his coinage—in the making. Though an optimist himself, a champion of the new class of "industrialists," there were strands in his rich though unsystematic analysis that allowed for a variety of different interpretations.[11] Thus he was annexed by the Marxists as one of the early forerunners of the socialism they proclaimed and promoted (though he was, said Marx and Engels, unrealistically "utopian" in his beliefs). For liberals, Saint-Simon was one of the founders of "positivistic" social science, the kind of science that his secretary, Auguste Comte, in 1837 labeled "sociology," and which Comte saw as both an intellectual discipline and a program of reconstruction of society along rational, scientific (i.e., Saint-Simonian), lines. Even conservatives, alarmed at what they saw as the subversive and destructive tendencies of both democracy and industrialism, took heart from Saint-Simon's insistence on the need for solid forms of organization to bind individuals to the new society, which included—as his disciples were to proclaim—a new religion, the "religion of humanity." The French sociologist Émile Durkheim developed Saint-Simon's insights into a full-bodied account of the need for a new "civil religion" within industrial society.[12]

FIGURE 3.1 Henri de Saint-Simon. © PHAS / Universal Images Group / Getty Images.

RADICALS, LIBERALS, AND CONSERVATIVES

These indications of Saint-Simon's wide-ranging influence illustrate the extent to which radicals, liberals, and conservatives—the three dominant strands of nineteenth-century political ideology—shared in their understanding of what the age called for. They were, they all felt, living in radically new times, a period in which history itself had abrogated its authority. "The world," as the French historian Alphonse de Lamartine wrote in 1846, "has jumbled its catalogue."[13] Or, as Marx and Engels famously proclaimed in the *Communist Manifesto* (1848), in this new "bourgeois" industrial society "all that is solid melts into air."[14] Here was a world in such a state of flux that no one was sure what terms to use to describe it or where to get a secure intellectual footing. There were naturally disagreements as to what the central problems, causes, and remedies were. The quest linked political activists and intellectuals and scholars, though in many cases

FIGURE 3.2 Max Weber. © Ullstein Bild Dtl. / Getty Images.

such distinctions make little sense. Radicals such as Marx and Engels—who were both scholars and activists—stressed the fact that the new order was capitalist in form, with dehumanizing effects on the working population. Their solution, which they offered through a series of brilliant historical tracts and treatises—of which Marx's *Capital* (1867) stands out—was the abolition of capitalism, if necessary by revolution, and its replacement by a socialist society in which workers ("the proletariat") would be the predominant element.

But one did not necessarily have to be a radical or a revolutionary to regard modern industrial capitalism as the prime focus of analysis. The German sociologist Max Weber (1864–1920) spent much of his working life studying the origins and effects of capitalism, which like Marx he regarded as "the most fateful power of our modern life."[15] But unlike Marx he did not think that capitalism could be abolished, and any attempt to do so—as he noted of the Russian Revolutions of 1905 and 1917—was likely to lead either to social breakdown or to replacement by a form of bureaucratic socialism that merely ran capitalism under different auspices and with a different ideology.[16] For Weber, modern society, whether formally capitalist or socialist, depended fundamentally on the rule of expert bureaucrats, who were indispensable for its effective functioning. Echoing Tocqueville, Weber concluded that such a condition "makes 'revolution', in the sense of the forceful creation of entirely new formations of authority, technically more and more impossible ... In classic fashion, France has demonstrated how this process has substituted *coups d'état* for 'revolutions': all successful transformations [since 1789] in France have amounted to *coups d'état.*"[17]

As a product of Wilhelmine Germany, dominated by the quasi-feudal, aristocratic *Junker* class, Weber saw the problem as one of curbing the power of that class and introducing a political system somewhat akin to Britain's constitutional monarchy. For

FIGURE 3.3 Émile Durkheim. © Bettman / Getty Images.

other liberals, especially in France and Britain, the problem did not lie as much with an entrenched aristocracy at the top of society, though they did battle with conservatives over such matters as free trade, scoring notable victories in the 1840s and 1860s. For liberals such as Tocqueville, Benjamin Constant, John Stuart Mill, and the British historian Lord Acton, the threat came as much from below as above. They accepted the principle of popular sovereignty—the central claim of the French Revolution— but worried about enfranchising masses of the population without the education or experience to make rational choices. They were concerned, too, that "the passion for equality" could lead to a deadening uniformity. The excesses of the *sansculottes* during the period of the Terror of the French Revolution were also in liberals' minds as they contemplated the widening franchise and increasing political involvement of the common people. Works such as Charles Dickens's novels *Barnaby Rudge* (1841) and *A Tale of Two Cities* (1859) vividly portrayed the dangers of an inflamed and active populace bent on revenge against the upper classes. Fear of "the mob," as with the classical Roman republican writers who had such influence on nineteenth-century liberalism, remained a powerful element of liberal thought. In later years, added to the fears of the working-class revolution promoted by the socialists, this was to drive many liberals to make common cause with conservatives.

For their part, conservatives too were galvanized by the French Revolution, but in the opposite direction from radicals and most liberals. European conservatives took their inspiration from the Anglo-Irish statesman and writer Edmund Burke and his great work, *Reflections on the Revolution in France* (1790), with its eloquent attack on the ideas of the Revolution. French writers such as Joseph de Maistre, François Chateaubriand, and Louis de Bonald subsequently denounced the entire ideology and legacy of the French Revolution. In its place they re-stated the values of hierarchy, monarchy, and religious authority. But theirs was not a passive conservatism, content simply to call for a return to traditional ways. This was a new militant and mobilized conservatism, aware of the need to confront the challenges of the age with new weapons and with new arguments. Particularly powerful, and influential in a variety of ways, from politics to art and architecture, was their rehabilitation of an idealized Middle Ages as an organic social order, where all had their valued and fulfilling place. With these thinkers, conservatism obtained a new lease on life, which ensured its survival in the age of democracy and industry.

Especially powerful was the vein of conservatism that developed in Germany, in tandem with German Romanticism.[18] Influenced by Johann Gottfried Herder and G. W. F. Hegel, as well as Burke, it sought to give ideas of community and solidarity new meaning, elaborating concepts of the folk and the nation—but in cultural, not political, terms. A systematic exposition of the leading ideas in this vein was given by the German sociologist Ferdinand Tönnies in his *Gemeinschaft und Gesellschaft* (*Community and Association*) (1887). Here Tönnies did not simply analyze the nature of the face-to-face community of traditional society; he mourned its loss in the face of the increasing power of impersonal, "contractual," *gesellschaftlich* relations between individuals. Leading British conservatives, such as Benjamin Disraeli, discoursed similarly on the loss of community, in Disraeli's case through the vehicles of popular novels such as *Sybil, or the Two Nations* (1845). What was coming into being, with varying degrees of evaluation, was the polarity of "tradition" and "modernity" that structured so much nineteenth-century thought.

Once again, as with radicals and liberals, there could be agreement about the principal problem but divergence on possible remedies. Some liberals also worried about the decline of community, which they traced to the atomizing and individualizing tendencies of democracy, industrialization, and urbanization. The danger, as powerfully analyzed by the French sociologist Émile Durkheim in his study *Suicide* (1897), lay in the condition of *anomie*—"the malady of infinite aspirations"—which he described as a pathological state of society and the individual, brought about when traditional social and moral regulation broke down and individuals found themselves unmoored from the traditional protective institutions of church, neighborhood, and family.[19] One consequence, as Durkheim showed, was a pronounced increase in the suicide rate in modern societies. Unlike the conservatives, however, Durkheim looked for remedies not in the restoration

FIGURE 3.4 Alexis de Tocqueville. © Hulton Fine Art Collection / Heritage Images / Getty Images.

of traditional institutions but in the creation of new organizations, such as trade unions and professional associations, based principally on the individual's place of work. It was this new form of association, which could absorb the individual in his or her social as well as occupational life, that Durkheim thought might provide a substitute for the old medieval guilds and counteract the tendencies toward anomie.

LOOKING EAST: NATIONALISM AND SOCIALISM

The great British historian Sir Lewis Namier wrote of 1848, the year of Europe-wide revolutions, as the "seed-plot of history."[20] He meant by this that it was in the course of these revolutions, and their subsequent outcomes, that many of the leading themes of later nineteenth- (and twentieth-)century history were revealed. It was in these revolutions that, in France especially, socialism first showed itself to be a political force. Even more forcibly, nationalism, in all the revolutions, staked its claims to be one of the most powerful ideologies of the next hundred years.[21] Both socialism and nationalism pitted themselves against the individualism that their defenders felt had established itself to such damaging effect. "The epoch of individuality is concluded," declared the Italian prophet of nationalism, Giuseppe Mazzini, "it has been replaced by the epoch of peoples ... the question of nationalities is destined to give its name to the century."[22]

The failure of the 1848 revolutions everywhere contributed to a change in the character and temper of European thought. It has often been said that 1848 marked a watershed after which intellectual and cultural currents ran in new channels.[23] In France, the revolution was succeeded by the benevolent dictatorship of Napoleon III, who oversaw a massive program of economic and social modernization. In Germany, Otto von Bismarck unified the country on the basis of "blood and iron," not the humanitarian and liberal principle of Mazzinian nationalism. Even Italian unification, as steered by Camillo Cavour and Victor Emmanuel II, had more the character of annexation by Piedmont-Sardinia than a spontaneous movement on the part of all Italians.

The gentle, individualistic liberalism of the first half of the century, the liberalism of Bentham, Mill, and Richard Cobden, gave way to tougher varieties. Liberalism now had to combine with, or at least concede to, nationalism or socialism—"liberty with association," as Mazzini himself had urged. Collectivist doctrines found their way into the liberalism of the later John Stuart Mill, the idealist T. H. Green, and the sociologist L. T. Hobhouse.[24] "We are all socialists now," famously declared the British Liberal statesman Sir William Harcourt in 1887.[25] Liberalism, as Harcourt showed in supporting the Boer War in southern Africa in the 1890s, could now combine not just with "socialism" but also with imperialism: "liberal imperialism" was a significant feature of the "new Liberalism" that developed in late nineteenth-century Britain as well as on the Continent.[26]

Not just nationalism but racism now also found a voice. Though xenophobia and national prejudices had a long history, race and ethnicity, as doctrines, had been minor currents of European thought before the nineteenth century. The Enlightenment had poured scorn on such ideas for the most part. That now changed. Race, in a biological and not simply cultural sense, was added to class, religion, nation, and other markers of distinction and division. The difference, though, was that while those things could be changed through social mobility and migration, one's race could not. Biology was destiny. The new thing was "scientific racism." In the later nineteenth century especially, racial doctrines drew their strength from the interpretation of certain prestigious new scientific theories, particularly those associated with Charles Darwin and evolutionary biology. To these were added some of the works of the new discipline of anthropology. That the associations and derivations were usually spurious did little to damage their popularity.

Racism did not necessarily need the backing of the new sciences, as was shown in one of the most influential publications, Comte Arthur de Gobineau's *Essay on the Inequality of the Races of Man* (1855). Not only was it written before Darwin's work appeared, it drew on a highly eclectic range of sources—German Romantic literature and folklore, medical treatises, travel literature, early ethnography—in advancing its argument of the primacy of the white "Aryan" race.[27] And though its "scientific" status was always crucial to racial theory—hence the elaboration of "social Darwinism" as one variety of racism—its development was not a product of science. Rather, racial doctrine came of the social changes and political developments that brought peoples into increasingly global competition and conflict (not least in the European empires, where racial theories found ample scope for application).

The new ideas and movements made their influence felt throughout Europe in the wake of the defeat of the 1848 revolutions. But it was in Central and Eastern Europe, in the lands of the Habsburg and Russian empires, that their force was greatest. Both of these were multi-ethnic and multinational empires; both struggled to keep up with the more dynamic lands to the West, namely, Britain, France, and Germany. Nationalism, socialism, and even varieties of racism were bound to have an appeal, mostly to the subject peoples but occasionally even to their rulers, who otherwise had most to fear from the new doctrines.

The "nationalities question" was most profound in the far-flung Habsburg lands, with their enormous diversity of populations. Nationalism was strongest among their Hungarian, Polish, and Italian subjects, though it affected also Czechs, Germans, and later the southern Slavs. What was perhaps more remarkable, though, was the emergence of the doctrine of "Austro-Slavism," which, while acknowledging the claims of nationality, did so within the context of the justification of empire.

The founding moment of this doctrine was the response of the Czech historian František Palacký to the invitation to join the German National Assembly meeting in Frankfurt during the 1848 revolution. Palacký astonished the delegates by refusing to attend, declaring that as a Czech he had more to fear from German nationalism than Habsburg rule. He went so far as to offer an eloquent defense of the Habsburg Empire, declaring that "if the Austrian state had not existed for ages, we would be obliged in the interests of Europe and even of mankind to endeavour to create it as fast as possible."[28] Palacký's declaration became the rallying call for Slav nationalists everywhere, concerned about the flanking power of both Germany and Russia. It showed—not just in the context of the Habsburg Empire, but in the European empires more generally—that nationalism was not always in opposition to empire, but that in fact the two could and did collude.[29]

The Habsburg Empire brought forth another unusual but persuasive doctrine that combined nationalism not with empire but with socialism—though once again within the confines of empire. The "Austro-Marxists" of the late nineteenth and early twentieth centuries—notably Karl Renner and Otto Bauer—were alarmed at Marxism's traditional hostility to nationalism, which had been regarded as a bourgeois device to trick and sidetrack the proletariat. For the Austro-Marxists, this was a head-in-the sand position for which Marxists would pay dearly. The claims of nationalism were genuine and should be respected. But this need not, and should not, lead to the triumph of the nation-state, as most nationalists demanded. A world of competing nation-states would be violent and destructive, a regressive move. Nations were first and foremost cultural entities. Their particularities could best be realized in a multi-national federation of communities organized on socialist principles but preserving the specific historical and cultural resources of each nation. The Habsburg Empire—since 1867 the Dual Monarchy of Austria-Hungary—contained the germ of such "a free association of nations." It should not be destroyed but developed, "raised to a higher principle." The task of the Socialist International, urged Bauer, should be "not the levelling of national particularities but the promoting of international unity within national diversity."[30]

Austro-Marxism failed in its mission. In 1914, socialist parties in nearly all the warring countries voted for war credits in support of their governments. Nationalism decisively trumped socialism, a catastrophe from which socialism never fully recovered (1933 was to prove another crucifixion). Oddly enough, it was in the new Soviet Union, reared on the ruins of the Russian Empire, that the nationalities principle was most strongly promoted, making it a kind of socialist federation of the nations that the Austro-Marxists had striven for even though its dictatorial form offended their democratic commitment.[31]

The Russian Empire had faced the same kind of nationalist challenge as the Habsburgs and had dealt with it by similar strategies of suppression and accommodation. But Russia also had an identity problem of a kind that did not afflict the ruling Germans and Hungarians in Austria-Hungary, or at least not in the same way or to the same extent. Russia was a vast Eurasian power, with many Muslim as well as Christian subjects. It looked East as well as West. At the same time, it was, or saw itself as, a country of Slavs and bid to take the leadership of Slavs everywhere, including noticeably those in the Ottoman and Habsburg Empires. How to reconcile these conflicting claims and aspirations?

The Russian Empire did not succeed in this any more than did the Habsburg (or Ottoman). But as with the Habsburgs, the dilemmas gave rise to a vibrant body of thought and writing in the nineteenth century. A principal division was that between Slavophiles and Westerners, between those who believed that there was a special Slav way and culture that Russia should follow and those who thought that Russia's future should lie with an intense effort to learn from and catch up with the West. Thinkers and writers of the caliber of Vessarion Belinsky, Alexander Herzen, Fyodor Dostoevsky, and Ivan Turgenev, in their novels and treatises, took part in the wide-ranging literary debates on these questions from the 1840s to the end of the century.[32] Eventually the First World War stilled these debates, though they were to re-surface in the Soviet era and beyond around the question of how far Russia should consider itself a European and how far a Eurasian nation.

Russia also developed its own influential variety of Marxism. As a country on the periphery of Europe, in which peasants made up over 80 percent of the population and whose degree of industrialization lagged far behind, its Marxists were forced to consider what could precipitate socialism. According to Marxist orthodoxy, it could be built only on a solid base of bourgeois achievement, which was at the time still lacking in Russia with its undeveloped middle class. More orthodox Marxists such as Georgii Plekhanov argued that there would first have to be a democratic-capitalist revolution before Russia could move on to socialism as a later stage. This became the standard Menshevik position, after the break in 1903 with the Bolsheviks, led by Vladimir Lenin and Trotsky.[33]

But the Bolsheviks, arguing on the principle of what Trotsky called "the advantage of backwardness," declared that, so long as revolution in Russia was accompanied by a socialist revolution in the more developed West, Russia could abridge the normal evolutionary process and begin straightaway to construct a socialist society. In 1917, they launched such an effort, and, despite the failure of the revolution in the West to materialize, continued under Stalin to bring about a massive degree of industrialization, under socialist auspices ("socialism in one country"). The Soviet model, and its accompanying theorization, became an inspiration in the twentieth century to many "Third World" societies, such as China, Vietnam, and Cuba. Western Marxism has had no victories; Russian Marxism, in its Leninist form, can claim several.

GOODBYE TO ALL THAT?

It is remarkable that although the nineteenth century was an age of empires—all the leading powers possessed colonies until 1914 and beyond—no systematic treatment of empires ever emerged. There is nothing, for instance, to compare with Edward Gibbon's *Decline and Fall of the Roman Empire* (1776–1788), with its enormous influence on eighteenth-century European thought, nor the many late eighteenth-century writings on empire of Edmund Burke. There were some influential works on particular empires, such as Sir John Seeley's *The Expansion of England* (1883), and many statements of a general kind in the speeches of politicians and statesmen, such as Benjamin Disraeli in England and Jules Ferry in France.[34] But few of the great theorists of the later nineteenth century—the period which saw the "scramble for Africa" and generally an intensified burst of European imperialism—saw fit to make empire a central feature of their analyses of modern society. When Marx, Weber, and Durkheim theorized about "society," they usually meant national society or the nation-state—an aspect (and limitation) of much social thought of the period that has come to be labeled "methodological nationalism."[35]

One interesting genre that did appear—informed by classical models—was the reflections on empire of scholar-administrators and scholar-generals, the practical men who made and governed the empires. A key example was the great *Modern Egypt* (1908) by Evelyn Baring, Lord Cromer, consul-general in Egypt in 1883–1907, following the effective British takeover of Egyptian affairs. Egypt was also the subject of the important and much-reprinted account, *England in Egypt* (1892), by Alfred Viscount Milner, who after a career in Egypt became governor of the Cape Colony and high commissioner for South Africa (1897–1905). Similarly wide-ranging and reflective was the trilogy on the challenges in Asia, *Russia in Central Asia in 1889* (1889), *Persia and the Persian* (1892), and *Problems of the Far East* (1894), by George Lord Curzon, viceroy of India (1898–1905). For the French, there were the many writings on empire by Marshall Louis-Hubert Lyautey, the Resident-General in Morocco (1912–1925), most influentially on the strategy of counter insurgency but also on the traditions and culture of Morocco and the need to preserve them.[36]

It is revealing that the work that came closest—though in rather narrowly economistic terms—to establishing something of a basis for the general study of modern empires came from a passionate anti-imperialist, the British liberal thinker J. A. Hobson, in his *Imperialism* (1902). For Hobson, empire was the necessary result of overproduction and underconsumption, fueled by Western capitalists in search of protected overseas markets for goods that they could not sell at home due to underpaid workers. Echoing the critics of the later Roman Empire, Hobson saw empire as a corrupting and demoralizing force. Hobson's ideas were to have a lasting influence on the study of empire through their more or less wholesale adoption by Marxists, especially Lenin in his *Imperialism: The Highest Stage of Capitalism* (1917).

Hobson's work can also be seen as part of a wide-ranging debate on empire that took place in the press, parliamentary assemblies, and various other public media in the late nineteenth and early twentieth centuries. Despite the fact that this was the period that saw the apogee of empire, in a characteristic pattern it also produced the expression of deep-seated popular anxieties about its moral purpose and its future. How genuine was the "civilizing mission" of empire? Would the European empires, which now spanned the world, survive? Should they? Nationalist and anti-colonial movements were beginning to challenge the legitimacy and resilience of empire, though it would take two world wars to bring them down.

Fears about empire and the moral right to have them echoed a wider movement in thought at this time that questioned European ideas of progress and betterment. Might decline and degeneration, rather than increasing felicity and fulfillment, not also be written into the Western story? Darwin's theory of evolution, announced in the mid-century, had at first been enthusiastically taken up by theorists of progress as providing scientific confirmation of their beliefs. More sober assessments of Darwin's work showed that it carried no such ethical message, no promise of future happiness. Evolution was a story of cosmic indifference. Such was the somber analysis of Darwinism in the Romanes Lecture, "Evolution and Ethics" (1886), delivered with pitiless clarity by the English scientist T. H. Huxley, Darwin's greatest disciple. If humans aimed to achieve perfection, they were on their own; they could not count on nature to do it for them, or even assist them in their endeavors.

The enunciation by Sir William Thompson (Lord Kelvin) in 1852 of the scientific idea of entropy—as popularly understood, that the universe would eventually run down, become inert—added its own melancholy contribution to the assault on progress. It shook that apostle of progress, Herbert Spencer, and forced a fundamental modification of the idea of progressive evolution that had been central to his work for many decades as it gained wide popularity. Entropy was portrayed with consummate literary skill by the novelist H. G. Wells in his popular tale *The Time Machine* (1895), which in its final pages showed a desolate world almost empty of life, under a dying sun.

Reason itself, a cardinal faith both of the eighteenth-century Enlightenment figures and of their nineteenth-century successors, also came under attack in this period. While this did not stop the progressive secularization of thought in the nineteenth century, a result largely of the new geology and biology, it cast doubt on reason's ability to give meaning and value to life. "Rationalization" was the master-theme of Western civilization in modern times, argued the sociologist Max Weber, but its progress led to the "disenchantment of the world," a progressive emptying of meaning. Weber here closely followed the philosopher Friedrich Nietzsche's analysis of our predicament when religion loses its hold, when "God is dead." There is a spiritual void waiting to be filled; only we, by our own unaided effort, can do that (as the later "existentialists" also argued).

The "crisis of reason"[37] could lead to the celebration, or at least recognition, of the power of un-reason, the irrational. Sigmund Freud, in such works as *The Interpretation of Dreams* (1900), was the thinker who did most to popularize the notion of "the

FIGURE 3.5 Friedrich Nietzsche. © Hulton Archive / Stringer / Getty Images.

Unconscious" and the role of irrational forces in the human personality. For Freud, as expressed in later works such as *Civilization and Its Discontents* (1930), the irrational— the forces of the "Id"—was a power to be restrained and tamed in the interest of the higher principle of civilization. For others, artists and poets especially, the irrational might be a source of creativity and vitality. Allied with the discovery of African art and other forms of "'primitivism," dream-states and other manifestations of the unconscious crowded the canvases of painters such as the Norwegian Edvard Munch and the poetry of writers such as the Frenchman Arthur Rimbaud. Modernism, the great cultural movement of the turn of the century, embraced the cult of the irrational and drew from energies that lay below the surface of individual and collective life.

There were other expressions of disillusionment with the promise of reason and the hopes bred by such events as the French Revolution. Toward the end of the century, a group of thinkers, approvingly dubbed later "the Machiavellians" by James Burnham,[38] argued that democracy, as classically defined, was impossible in the conditions of advanced industrial societies. "The people," in whatever sense we define the concept, can never rule. Theorists such as Vilfredo Pareto, Gaetano Mosca, and Robert Michels suggested that, whatever the formal arrangements, elites would always dominate, since they alone had the managerial skills and scientific expertise to run complex societies. Michels, in his *Political Parties* (1911), elaborated an "iron law of oligarchy," expressed in the terse phrase, "Who says organization, says oligarchy." He applied it to the working of modern political parties, such as the German Social Democratic Party, with their pretensions to democratic control.

Max Weber, too, considered democratic rule a myth in modern society. Bureaucracy, the rule of expert officials, was the key institution of modern society, in both public and private organizations. Politicians might pander to the people, but politicians too were dilettanti who had to give way to the superior knowledge and efficiency of the bureaucrats. To this was added the argument, provocatively and powerfully stated in a short book, *The Crowd* (1895) by the French thinker Gustave Le Bon, that the masses were incapable of governing themselves. They would always be led, Le Bon stated, always be willing to hand over power to crowd-pleasing dictators or professional politicians and bureaucrats. Le Bon saw in this condition of the modern populace a reversion to the barbarism of earliest times, before the rise of civilization. "The populace is sovereign, and the tide of barbarism mounts."[39]

Faced with the obvious weaknesses of democratic organization and the limitations of rational persuasion, thinkers turned to other tools. The French socialist thinker Georges Sorel, in his *Reflections on Violence* (1908), urged that not reason but only a powerful "myth"—for instance, the myth of a "General Strike"—could galvanize workers and make them struggle for socialism. For extra measure, he endorsed a necessary degree of violence toward that end, pouring scorn on the hopes that socialists placed in the mechanisms of parliamentary representation. Violence was not always negative; it could be a creative and enabling force. Not surprisingly, Sorel became a hero of later fascist movements—but also of certain twentieth-century anti-colonial thinkers, such as Franz Fanon in *The Wretched of the Earth* (1961).

It was in the Habsburg Empire of the late nineteenth and early twentieth centuries that many of the new ideas and attitudes crystallized. In retrospect, this has cast an elegiac *fin-de-siècle* glow over these years, as the last creative gasp of a doomed empire. At the time, there was no reason to think that the empire would end—it took the cataclysm of the First World War to do that, as happened with the Russian and Ottoman Empires as well. But, certainly, the social and ethnic conflicts, together with the speeded-up rate of change as the empire modernized its institutions, seem to have created an unusually fertile environment for cultural creativity, especially but not only in Vienna.[40]

Freud, of course, belonged to this milieu; so, too, did the philosophers Ludwig Wittgenstein and Ernst Mach, the architects Otto Wagner and Adolf Loos, the painters Gustav Klimt and Egon Schiele, the economists Ludwig von Mises and Joseph Schumpeter, the writers Franz Kafka and Robert Musil, the composers Gustav Mahler and Arnold Schonberg. This was just the tip of a cultural iceberg of monumental proportions, one that laid the groundwork for virtually every important intellectual and cultural development of the twentieth century. How and why this happened, on such a scale and in so many areas of thought, remains something of a mystery and is a fertile field for cultural historians. But of its occurrence there can be no doubt, nor of its significance in showing, in condensed form and in the most vivid colors, some of the most important intellectual and artistic tendencies of the second half of the nineteenth century. Paris might have been, as Walter Benjamin put it, "the capital of the nineteenth century," but Vienna should be called the cultural laboratory of the twentieth century.

The mood of late nineteenth-century Vienna, as of the period more generally, is often described as having been one of cultural pessimism. But this is, as so often, to judge it retrospectively, in view of what came later, in the first half of the twentieth century. It is also to be highly selective. In a more comprehensive view one can find in the cultural products of *fin-de-siècle* Vienna the same mix of hope and despair, confidence and anxiety, as one can find at most points in the nineteenth century. If Freud and Kafka can be said to lean toward a pessimistic view of the world, that is not necessarily true of Wittgenstein or Schumpeter, Otto Wagner or Klimt. "Decadence" was fashionable, as is perhaps only possible in societies, like those of the Belle Époque, where material comforts and personal security can be taken for granted and can even seem cloying.

Nevertheless, in Vienna as elsewhere, it is right to see a much greater degree of questioning, a more relativist view, and even a greater sense of anxiety about the future, than was present at the beginning of the nineteenth century. The century opened in a confident mood. The French and Industrial Revolutions brought war between nations and turmoil in social relations, but they also seemed to provide the resources to overcome the problems they presented. Whatever their political outlooks, with a few exceptions among some conservatives, the analyses offered by thinkers of all kinds suggested remedies for the conditions they encountered. These ranged from reform to revolution. But what was important was the conviction that problems could be solved and that the tools of reason, science, and technology were adequate to the task, formidable as it might seem.

For Europe, the nineteenth century was a period of unaccustomed peace and unprecedented prosperity, however unevenly distributed its fruits. European hegemony in the world was unchallenged. Perhaps these very strengths were the problem, at least in the eyes of artists and intellectuals. For there was bound to come a time—once again the parallels were to hand in classical civilization—when European power was thought to breed a dangerous complacency, an unthinking mood of self-congratulation. Hubris is an ever-present temptation in all successful civilizations. European thinkers toward the end of the century increasingly began to take an anxious stocktaking of the accomplishments and shortcomings of their civilization. They pointed to the dangerous extremes of wealth and poverty, especially evident in such cities as London and Paris. They questioned Europe's continuing predominance in the world, noting America's rapid industrialization and Japan's rise to power. They wondered about the European empires' "civilizing mission," and explored the dark side of imperialism. They speculated on future wars fought with military technology of such power as to bring about unprecedented death and destruction.

All these things were to surface, in one form or another, in the century to come. The fears were prescient and well-founded. The outbreak of the First World War opened an era of mass slaughter, revolution, and dictatorship, much of which could be laid at Europe's door. Europe increasingly lost its hegemonic position in the world. The European century was succeeded by the American century. But the legacy of European nineteenth century thought lived on, even as Europe itself lost its preeminence. Nearly all the significant movements and ideologies of the twentieth-century world—communism, fascism, racism, nationalism, anti-colonialism—had their origins in nineteenth-century European thought.

Many of these, of course, were expressed in Europe itself, which, in the Second World War, hurled up one last convulsive sign of its importance. But increasingly they spread beyond Europe, to influence the lives of peoples the world over. In China, 1.4 billion people today live under Marxism, a system devised in Europe. National states everywhere are run on substantially European principles. For better or worse, the world as we know it today is the world that Europe made in the nineteenth century.

CHAPTER FOUR

Politics and Economies

BRIAN VICK

In searching for the roots of contemporary political debates and traditions, one can certainly look to earlier periods, from ancient Greece to the eighteenth-century European and global Enlightenment. Much of the contours of modern political and economic thought, however, emerged in the nineteenth century in the wake of the French Revolution. By the early 1800s, almost the full modern political spectrum had become visible, from socialism and anarchism to liberalism and conservatism. Perhaps the most striking characteristic of the new political landscape was its sheer diversity, as a rich array of competing ideas and programs rapidly arose within each of the main currents: radical, liberal, and conservative. Variation across national contexts, and regional variation within nations, further added to the mix. Economic thought similarly continued its development after Adam Smith across this political spectrum.

While the primary political camps established themselves early on, they hardly remained static. Nineteenth-century political and economic thought was characterized just as much by change over time, and that of 1900 or 1914 was very different from that of 1800. Not least, the growth of disparate media of political communication and the eruption of new voices and social groups into political culture added to both the multiplicity and the pace of change. Recognizing the full diversity of nineteenth-century political and economic thought enriches our understanding of the period and provides new insights and points of departure in ongoing debates. Studying nineteenth-century actors' recourse to media, interpersonal networks, and political discourses and languages, within specific contexts, helps explain the formation and spread of political ideas in ways that account for both their variety and their family resemblances. Adopting contextualist or network-driven approaches also allows one to incorporate a wider range of voices, including women, lesser-known writers, and non-Europeans alongside the established canon of major political and economic thinkers. Political thought can expand from this perspective to include elements of associational life and visual and material culture or literature, thus further integrating cultural and intellectual history perspectives.

In political and scholarly contexts today, a chief concern is thinking about difference, whether involving race, gender, or nationhood. In analyzing past political speech as well, the treatment of difference and inequality remains a primary focus. The present chapter considers these important matters, but reasons of space prevent making them as central as one could wish. Instead, the chapter concentrates on related but distinct themes of political and economic thought's global dimension, in a nineteenth-century world increasingly, but not solely, shaped by the power of expanding Euro-American empires and colonization.

THE POLITICAL SPECTRUM ACROSS
THE NINETEENTH CENTURY—THE LIBERAL CENTER

Rather than treating the nineteenth-century political spectrum as a bipolar opposition between liberals and conservatives, it is more helpful to think of it as a tripartite spectrum, from various strands of socialist and radical thought on the Left to various stripes of conservatism on the Right, with a range of liberal positions in the center. Integrating the third category adds nuance to the typological analysis of different authors' views, but equally, it helps account for the political dynamics of rhetorical argumentation and alliance-building at any given place and time as well as for the development of political programs and ideologies over time.

In specific situations or conflicts where political figures were forced to choose sides, politics did often turn into a bipolar struggle, but it typically did so on the basis of a prior threefold political spectrum, where the burning question was where the dividing line in the liberal center would fall. This flexibility of political alliances bore important consequences not just for the unfolding of political conflicts on the ground but also for the development of political thought. There was more cross-fertilization, borrowing, and interpersonal contact among liberal, radical, and conservative camps than might at first be expected, as groups interacted and fought over rhetorical ground in the center to win allies and to persuade readers and auditors to their left or right. The influential circle around the liberal Swiss-French thinker Germaine de Staël, for instance, included the Romantic conservative François-René de Chateaubriand and the republican protosocialist political economist Jean-Charles-Léonard Simonde de Sismondi.[1]

To begin with the liberal center as the widest and most dominant segment of nineteenth-century opinion, those in the liberalism camp were notoriously disparate, ranging from more radical democrats to relatively conservative moderates, and incorporating those who drew on older traditions of natural law or the law of reason, as well as those who deployed competing utilitarian, historicist, or even organicist strands of thought. (The presence of historicist or organic frameworks did not characterize conservative political philosophy alone, even before the rise of specifically Darwinian evolutionary ideas after 1859.) Given the frequent association between liberalism and nationalism in the nineteenth century, disagreements also arose about how and how far to pursue nationalist goals such as unification, about the role of national character and diversity in the face of ostensibly universal liberal principles, and about the balance between centralized and federative government. Such debates over nationality particularly affected the linguistically diverse lands of Central, Eastern, and Southern Europe and areas experiencing anti-colonial nationalism, such as Asia and the Americas.

Many liberals focused on questions of civil and political rights and the proper form of government, just as their eighteenth-century predecessors had. In part, this focus reflected the fact that so much of nineteenth-century political debate circled around questions of constitutions, including, for instance, whether to institute them and, if so, what form they should take among emerging alternatives. The French Revolution itself offered a clear choice of constitutions around which different types of liberals might rally. Most notable was the moderate plan for a constitutional monarchy in the French constitution of 1791 compared to the radical unicameral democratic republic of the Jacobin constitution of 1793, but one should not forget the French Directory or Napoleonic constitutions that followed the Jacobin Reign of Terror. As the century wore on, other constitutional models came to the fore, above all the relatively moderate French Charter of the restored Bourbons in 1814–1815 after Napoleon's defeat, or the somewhat more radical Spanish Cádiz constitution of 1812, which was unicameral although not republican. The Charter proved particularly influential in the German states and among moderate constitutional monarchists, while the Cadiz constitution attracted democratic and revolutionary forces, as in the revolutions in Iberia and on the Italian peninsula in 1820–1821.[2] After 1830, the French July Monarchy and the new Belgian and Greek constitutions competed for imitative allegiance and provided litmus tests for constitutional proposals heading into the era of national unifications in the Italian, German, and Habsburg lands. Moreover, throughout the period the British parliamentary model drew both admiration and critique, with questions of the balance between elected Commons and hereditary monarchy central.[3]

Liberals also devoted attention to defining and defending civil and individual rights, not only of political participation but also as a sphere for individuals protected from state power ("protective liberty"). Emphasis on proceduralism and the rule of law could function similarly, particularly in lands with weaker or no constitutions and bills of rights, as in some German states and the Habsburg monarchy. Equality before the law, including the end to feudal ties and serfdom where these still existed, was also a frequent liberal demand.

An influential strand of liberal thought emphasized the distinction between the state and civil society as a means of limiting state power and protecting individuals alike. Such liberals formed the original party of small government in the nineteenth century. A related school of "aristocratic liberals," from Wilhelm von Humboldt to Alexis de Tocqueville, John Stuart Mill, and Cesare Balbo, worried about the "tyranny of the majority," whether through the political will of voters in a constitutional framework or the force of public opinion, in producing social and intellectual conformity in civil society. Tocqueville's *Democracy in America* (1835–1840) and Mill's *On Liberty* (1859) were landmarks in this vein.[4] Concerns about the fate of the individual in the age of the masses continued to shape liberal discourses as well as fuel cultural pessimism later in the century, with state bureaucracy and large corporations figuring alongside democratization as threats to individuality and the autonomy of the self.[5]

Liberal resistance to democratization also featured in the constitutions discussed above, in limiting voting and office-holding rights to those of a certain level of wealth, as in censitary liberalism, named for the use of an electoral census to determine who was qualified to vote or hold office. Some constitutions additionally created complex systems of indirect elections that left the ultimate choice of candidate to a smaller body of elected electors. The British Great Reform Act of 1832 widened the franchise to only about 18 percent of adult males, but this was still much higher than in France after 1815 or even 1830. Wealth was not necessarily meant to be the key to political participation, but it served to mark the qualities demanded of full citizens: that they be independent, educated, and with a clear stake in the existing social order. Full citizenship with political rights was thereby only granted primarily to those of the same lifestyle as middle- and upper-class members of society. These were the right kind of liberal subject, schooled in associational life and exhibiting what the scholar Elaine Hadley terms "liberal cognition." Those from further down or outside the circle of citizens, the urban and rural poor, were not permanently excluded from citizenship, but they had to assimilate to bourgeois lifestyles and acquire the external attributes of that social stratum.[6] It was not until the later decades of the century that successive nations followed the new German Empire in moving toward universal male suffrage.

The case of censitary liberalism points to the larger problem of exclusion and assimilation in liberal thought. As scholars have increasingly emphasized, liberals' supposedly universal rights claims were not only restrictive against men from farther down the social and economic hierarchy but also worked against other categories. Members of minority or even majority religious groups could similarly be excluded from citizenship and subjected to discrimination on grounds of not yet being fit, even where toleration of other religions had been accepted. This was frequently the case for European Jews before the age of emancipation in the 1850s and 1860s, but also for devout Catholics, even in majority Catholic lands such as France or the new Kingdom of Italy after 1859/1870.[7] In the context of colonization, the notion of a "civilizing mission," offered as a legitimation of European imperialism, showed much the same trajectory from exclusion to at least potential inclusion on the basis of education and the eventual assimilation of those perceived as belonging to other races. In this latter case, however, emergent "scientific" racism became increasingly widespread, and moves to expand citizenship proved more limited.

The largest category affected by liberal exclusions was, of course, women. There is considerable disagreement among historians as to how to explain or assess such a marked gender dichotomy and the accompanying public-private divide. For some scholars, the denial of equal rights to women represented a blind spot in the liberal "universalist" program that stemmed from deep-seated cultural beliefs about proper male and female gender and family roles and about female biology. For others, however, liberal ideology was actually predicated upon women's exclusion from citizenship, with the restriction of women to the private domestic sphere being the enabling mechanism for the public political and economic lives of male heads of households. The present author is among those who highlight liberal ambivalence on the so-called Woman Question, whereby continued or even heightened gender distinction played an important role in liberal thought and practice, even as women were increasingly thought to deserve education and partial participation in civil society and public life.

It is significant that when women made incremental gains in civil and political rights over the nineteenth century, it was usually liberals or radicals and socialists who promoted them. This was famously not the case for the Jacobins of the French Revolution, but it was true for figures such as the Marquis de Condorcet, Theodor Gottlieb Hippel, and later John Stuart Mill, who all called for women's political rights, and for those such as Carl Welcker or Léon Richer, who advocated partial improvements in women's conditions and rights status. Just as importantly, most women arguing for women's rights across the period also made use of liberal or radical ideas and "rights talk" as a language of "claim-making," from Olympe de Gouges and Mary Wollstonecraft in the 1790s to Flora Tristan, Louise Otto-Peters, Elizabeth Cady Stanton, Maria Desraismes, Anna Maria Mozzoni, Harriet Taylor, and Emmeline and Christabel Pankhurst in the course of the nineteenth century. Many of the women activists, too, upheld notions of gender difference as an integral part of their campaign for gender equality.[8]

MILL'S LOGIC; OR, FRANCHISE FOR FEMALES.
"PRAY CLEAR THE WAY, THERE, FOR THESE—A—PERSONS."

FIGURE 4.1 *Mill's Logic; Or, Franchise for Females,* caricature from *Punch,* March 30, 1867. © Photo 12 / Universal Images Group / Getty Images.

Liberals of the second half of the nineteenth century increasingly confronted the problem of poverty and the social question as well. Rather than seeing the immiseration that accompanied industrialization as something that would disappear in time with economic progress, or that was fated to exist for all time by the laws of political economy, liberals progressively sought ways to address the issue and at the same time remain true to values of economic freedom and individual autonomy. One can point to the New Liberalism in Britain from the 1880s with T. H. Green or D. G. Ritchie, or to the social liberalism of Germans such as Hermann Schulze-Delitzsch and Karl Biedermann, who, from the 1850s, actively promoted worker cooperatives, credit unions, and liberal trades unions.[9]

At the same time, it is important to avoid the caricature of preceding classic liberals of the early and mid-nineteenth century as hard-hearted Mr. Gradgrinds of Dickensian vintage, concerned solely with economic growth and blind to industrialization's negative consequences. It is true that on balance they prioritized political goals and economic freedoms above social aims, but particularly in Germany they also hoped to ameliorate the condition of the rural and urban poor and to mitigate the harshness of the transition to industrialism. The German political scientist Robert von Mohl, for instance, called in 1838 for an end to guilds, but also supported limits to workers' hours and child labor as well as a minimum wage, profit-sharing schemes, and sanitation improvements.[10]

ECONOMIC THOUGHT

Doctrines of political economy are often presented as direct precursors of the modern discipline of economics, particularly in internal histories of economic thought. For contextualist intellectual historians, however, it is important to avoid teleological or Whiggish interpretations of the discipline's history and to emphasize the origins of political economy within moral philosophy, conjectural history, and politics.[11]

Political economy, as the name suggests, initially pointed as much to politics as to questions of market behavior strictly conceived. As a branch of moral philosophy, questions of justice, the good life, the nature of human motivations, and the relationship between wealth and happiness or wealth and virtue also featured centrally. Thus, the innovator of the field, Adam Smith, in *The Wealth of Nations* (1776) looked not just to individual self-interest to explain human and market behavior but also to notions of sympathy and sociability, as in his earlier work of 1759 *The Theory of Moral Sentiments*. He worried about the deleterious effects on workers of extreme division of labor and supported public education as part of the remedy. Similarly, Thomas Malthus is probably more remembered today in the terms popularized by his Romantic critics: as the founder of an amoral theory that the pressure of population growth always quickly outstrips available resources until the point at which starvation, disease, war, and immoral behavior check its progress, in a grim dynamic equilibrium. But the English clergyman and demographer also stressed the role of divine providence and helped launch a tradition of Christian political economy that emphasized the potential for moral preventative checks on growth and for market-nurtured moral learning— all in competition with the classical and radical political economists who more closely followed the theories of David Ricardo.[12]

Disagreements among early nineteenth-century political economists were rife, with battles over theoretical fundamentals as well as over policy. Among the latter was the pamphlet war over the British Corn Laws at the end of the Napoleonic Wars, in which Ricardo and Malthus disputed whether to follow free trade ideas in pursuit of cheaper bread for urban manufacturing areas or to institute tariffs on grain imports in order to protect landowners and agricultural workers and shore up demand. Other policy debates circulated around banking and monetary policy and poor relief.[13] At the same time, political economists disagreed even about fundamental aspects of economic theory, as for example the source and nature of economic value and related questions of price theory and market behavior. Some followed Ricardo in attributing value on the basis of labor inputs, while others pointed to labor commanded, total costs of production, utility, and use value or to the role of subjectivity and demand in setting exchange values and prices in the market.[14]

Differently from present-day economics, classical political economists tended to think in terms of broader social categories or "classes"—above all landowners, manufacturers/ capitalists, and workers—rather than only individuals.[15] And particularly with Ricardo, some of political economy's lessons were rather bleak. Taking labor as determinant of value and identifying a law of diminishing returns in both agriculture and manufacturing, rent on land and even profits on goods came to seem skimmed off the top at the expense of those who actually did the labor, and in what came to be called the "iron law of wages," some argued that workers' earnings were bound to fall steadily to the level of bare subsistence. Poverty and growing inequalities of wealth thus came to seem like laws of nature, inherent within any market system. Harriet Martineau's fictional popularizations of political economy in the 1830s reiterated such laws while holding out some hope of happy endings for families who accepted them. But working-class and socialist commentators including Karl Marx were not slow to highlight such lessons as damning indictments of capitalist economies, and discontent with the theory increasingly arose among liberal and conservative economists precisely because it provided fuel for social unrest.[16] Environmental historians also note the extent to which nineteenth-century political economists worried about the implications of economic and population growth and resource scarcity for the quality of life in industrializing societies. These included the pillar of classical political economy John Stuart Mill, his sharp critic John Ruskin and the early marginalist William Stanley Jevons.[17]

Liberal political economy was not, however, without its optimistic predictions, as with the economic law of the French political economist Jean-Baptiste Say according to which supply creates its own demand, meaning that it was not possible for a general glut or depression to occur that would not re-equilibrate quickly and avert long-term unemployment. Malthus, the Genevan political economist Jean-Charles-Léonard Simonde de Sismondi and others countered that effective consumer demand could indeed lag behind production and cause a glut or economic downturn in which unemployment might last for years.[18] John Maynard Keynes, with some exaggeration, later claimed Malthus as a precursor for his own demand-centered theories of economic depression and unemployment.[19]

Divisions within economic thought extended still further. Even during the first half of the nineteenth century, there were those who questioned the universalizing assumptions and abstractions of classical political economy and insisted on the significance of differences in economic behavior according to place and time, in different national and historical contexts. Particularly in the second half of the century and above all in Germany, such thinking underpinned the development of a powerful Historical School of Economics focused on empirical observation and historical data, interpreted according to mathematical statistics rather than abstract economic modeling. If statistical evidence suggested, for example, that trades unions could achieve lasting rises in workers' real wages when economic theory said they could not, historical economists were disposed to believe the former over the latter. Prominent historicist professors such as Gustav Schmoller and Lujo Brentano strongly supported social reforms to ameliorate economic conditions in industrializing societies, thus earning the label "socialists of the chair."[20]

By the 1870s, the edifice of classical political economy began to crumble, in what has been termed the "neoclassical" or "marginalist revolution," sparked by William Stanley Jevons in Britain, the Frenchman Léon Walras, and the Austrian Carl Menger. According to marginalist theories, economic behavior was determined by the rational choices of individuals exchanging on the market, with their subjective calculation of a good's utility determining the price they were willing to pay (in particular, the marginal utility of successive purchases of a good, according to a law of diminishing utility—the fifth or sixth automobile or piece of cake likely not delivering the same relative amount of pleasure as the first). The new economics was strongly predicated on methodological individualism rather than social classes, and one of its prime motivations was to avoid the kind of class analysis that led socialists to draw inspiration from Ricardian theories. The new approach was, however, even more abstract and based on simplified market models rather than empirical data; it was the marginalist effort to give economics the status of a science in the mode of classical physics that helped transform it into the heavily mathematical discipline it remains today.[21] In the process of redefining "political economy" as "economics," marginalists more and more divorced the field from its roots in historical, moral, or political science, to leave it based on a narrower range of human psychology and social phenomena, and with its economic laws seemingly true for all times and places, like laws of nature. The pressures of professionalization according to scientific paradigms, and the conflicts between Marxist and non-Marxist politics and social science, each help explain the new approach's rapid acceptance.[22]

Marginalists tended toward free-market thinking, another area in which their methodological individualism could help escape class-based social and economic analysis or policy. There were, however, important exceptions, such as Alfred Marshall in England, the scholar who did as much as anyone to shape the modern discipline of economics and to promote its new mathematized, econometric orientation, but who at the same time advocated government intervention in pursuit of progressive social reform, much like other social liberals of the era in Britain and across the Continent, and, for that matter, like John Stuart Mill before him.[23] Some Austrian marginalists, too, evinced concerns about distributive justice and supported government's role in social reform on behalf of workers. That included two of Austria's most influential theorists, Eugen von Böhm-Bawerk and Friedrich von Wieser.[24]

RADICALISM AND SOCIALISM

Radical doctrines, like liberal and conservative ones, had roots before the French Revolution but took on clearer lines in the course of the 1790s. Radicalism entailed a thoroughgoing attack on established political and religious authorities, coupled with stronger moves toward full participatory democracy. Radicals hoped to replace monarchies with republics or at least introduce strongly parliamentary forms of constitutional monarchy. Radicalism additionally incorporated a strongly social dimension, promoting social and civic equality of all citizens against inherited aristocratic privileges, and at times involving an economic component to support the urban and rural poor. Moreover, radicals often pursued anticlerical and secularizing policies, but could alternatively espouse unorthodox religiosity. It should be stressed that radicalism was also a matter of milieu and lifestyle, with its own world of clubs and associations and a radical press filled with scathing attacks on the political and religious establishment, scurrilous satires, and a visual and material culture to match, sometimes shading into pornography, all in the effort to appeal and politicize as widely across the social scale as possible. Radicals also sometimes adopted conspiratorial methods aiming at violent revolution.[25] While socialism emerged from radical milieus and thought and bore some similarities, radicalism and socialism generally remained distinct movements and traditions.

Socialism itself, like liberalism, saw great diversity of ideas, programs, and movements in the nineteenth century, with the competition among the various groups as fierce as that between socialists and their liberal or conservative foes. As readers of *The Communist Manifesto* (1848) will recall, Marx and Engels had much to say about other strands of socialism, prior and contemporary, and little of it was complimentary. The broadly speaking utopian or Romantic socialist thinkers, such as Count Henri de Saint-Simon, Charles Fourier, Auguste Comte, and Robert Owen, thought of themselves as organizing society along the lines of a new social science, but to Marx and Engels their visions seemed utopian and their tendency simultaneously to promote new religions seemed distasteful. At the same time, it was through the interactions among socialists and radicals around Europe that socialist ideas developed and spread. With Marx and Engels, for instance, their cooperation and sparring with other German radicals in exile or with figures such as the French socialist political economist Pierre-Joseph Proudhon helped them refine their positions during the 1840s and find an audience for their views.[26] Ideas of social leveling and economic equality of course go back much further, to Thomas More's *Utopia* (1516) and earlier, but it was not until the 1830s and after that the terms "communist" and "socialist" came into widespread use with something like their present meanings.[27]

Marx and Engels, from the late 1840s, also aimed to place their Communist brand of socialism on a scientific footing, in ways they thought would distinguish it from utopian socialism, but which could in turn be accused of utopianism by generations of liberal or conservative critics. By setting their materialist theory of history based on revolutionary class conflict within the framework of stadial history and progressive political economy, they sought to show that socialism was not simply a state of things that *should* replace capitalism on grounds of justice, but was rather a new phase of social, economic, and political organization that must and would succeed capitalism for reasons following from the logics of economics and history. The Communist movement would then be present to oversee the transition to the final stage of historical development, where there would be only one class remaining and no remaining form of private property that could lead to competing class interests and conflict.

The thrust of Marx and Engels' thought also displaced the emphasis from constitutional questions and abstract political ideas such as liberty to the sphere of social and economic relations and productive forces. The move can be thought of as a shift from politics to economics as the center of political action; in some ways, however, the transformation was more radical, moving past what one would normally consider economic relations to the level of technology and material life, and with the emphasis on production more than consumption. The notion of the free market in liberal economic thought, whether for goods or for labor, was itself revealed in their view to be a construction, overlaying deeper structuring relations. Marx and Engels achieved this insight through ideological critique, that is, unmasking class interests and relations to reveal putatively universal values, such as political liberty and equality, to be those of the capitalist classes whose interests they served, and to show how what purported to be a socioeconomic and political system predicated on individual liberty and free exchange among contracting parties was actually a smokescreen for relations that were always social, unequal, and unfree.[28]

In the 1860s and 1870s, the German workers' movement was split between the rival ideologies of Marxist revolutionary historical materialism and the more democratic and state-centered socialism of Ferdinand Lassalle. With the merger of the respective parties in the German Social Democratic Gotha program of 1875, the Marxist tendency became dominant, and as the German Socialist Party grew to be the largest in Europe by 1890, Marxism increasingly became the leading ideological direction within the Second International. Even in the decades leading up to the First World War and the Russian Revolution of 1917, however, the ranks of socialists still harbored numerous competing doctrines. In German and European Social Democracy, long-lasting debates pitted reformist revisionists such as Eduard Bernstein against theorists such as Karl Kautsky, who held to the stricter revolutionary line of Marx and Engels, and Rosa Luxemburg, who took the Marxist heritage in a more revolutionary direction that emphasized general strikes and mass violence as necessary to end capitalist liberal and monarchical regimes. For Bernstein in Germany or Filippo Turati and Anna Kuliscioff in Italy, changes in the capitalist order and in the political landscape, including the growth of massive trades unions and universal suffrage, suggested that it was possible to work gradually toward the realization of socialist goals and to achieve incremental benefits for workers in the meantime.[29] More broadly, in Russia, southern Europe, and to an extent France, the so-called anarcho-syndicalist wing of socialism stressed the importance of mass union organization and violence in bringing revolutionary change. The wider anarchist movement also shared anti-capitalist and pro-worker orientations, even as its primary aim was the destruction of the state as such, whether through violent revolution, terrorist attacks, or evolutionary gradualism and cooperative efforts.[30]

FIGURE 4.2 Anna Kuliscioff. © Foundazione Anna Kuliscioff.

FIGURE 4.3 Anna Kuliscioff, Filippo Turati, and other delegates during the 10th Congress of the Italian Socialist Party. Florence, September 1908. Kuliscioff is in the second row on the left. © Mondadori Portfolio Editorial / Getty Images.

CONSERVATISM AND THE RIGHT WING OF THE POLITICAL SPECTRUM

Like radicalism and liberalism, conservative thought was marked as much by diversity as by family resemblances. Even among reactionary monarchists who after 1789 aimed to overturn as much of the revolutionary legacy as possible, some, such as the Savoyard Catholic thinker Joseph de Maistre, supported more absolutist, bureaucratic, and centralized visions of monarchy, while others, quite different, looked instead to a federalist and aristocratic social and political order based on estates-type parliamentary structures and diets, as for example Adam Müller and Friedrich August von Marwitz in the German lands. Rich and intense as the debates among these groups already were, the number of moderate or "reform" conservatives was probably even greater. These figures recognized that there was no going back to the Old Regime before the revolutionary deluge, but they were themselves divided between those who maintained allegiance to a reformist bureaucracy in support of a strong monarchy and those who emphasized more popular input and the role of local self-government and diets.[31]

Conservatives shared some of the liberals' anti-democratic critiques, but the former disagreed about where to draw the line of compromise with popular forces. While liberals worried most about the dangers of too much democracy within constitutional systems, conservatives worried about how much, if any, constitutional concessions one could make without tipping into revolution and chaos. For Maistre, any written constitution was to be resisted. Others, like the German defender of the "monarchical principle" Friedrich Julius Stahl, thought the problem was of constitutional design, as with the need for the ruler rather than the parliament to control the budget.

Conservatives did not, however, offer a solely negative program of opposition to democracy and revolution; many also presented positive visions of the good polity. In his seminal work on the French Revolution, Edmund Burke had lauded what he termed "the real rights of man" over the abstract metaphysical sort he decried among the revolutionaries; he was not about to leave this rhetorical high ground to the opposing side. These rights were in part protective ("Whatever each man can separately do, without trespassing on others, he has a right to do for himself") and in part positive ("and he has a right to a fair portion of all which society, with all its combination of skill and force, can do in his favour"). People did not, however, in his view, have a right to equal shares in government.[32]

Burke and other conservatives also emphasized an organic rather than mechanistic view of society, politics, and historical change, looking to the life sciences rather than physics for metaphors and concepts. By destroying rather than gradually changing existing political and social institutions and relations, they thought, only chaos and violence could result. Social engineering and designing completely new constitutions without roots in a given people's history or habits were deemed recipes for disaster or despotism, and liberals and radicals were faulted as being too abstract in failing to accommodate social realities, or too naïve in positing a one-size-fits-all constitution that could be applied to all peoples without taking into account social, cultural, and historical differences among nations.

Religion also featured centrally in conservative thought, both as motivation and as propaganda, by appealing to an aspect of life that conservatives believed was still important to much of the population despite trends toward secularization in the wake of the Enlightenment. Maistre was again emblematic of those who simply could not imagine a stable and just polity not based on a state religion, in a union of "throne and altar." Emphasis on religion also dovetailed with conservative medievalism, visible even in Burke and Maistre but more characteristic of Romantic writers such as Samuel Taylor Coleridge, François-René de Chateaubriand, and the Germans Novalis and Friedrich Schlegel. Burke's celebration of the age of chivalry in his *Reflections on the Revolution in France* (1790) is notable in this context, while Chateaubriand's *The Genius of Christianity* (1802) and Novalis's *Christianity or Europe* (1799) proved even more trendsetting.

Through religiosity and nostalgia, some conservatives also confronted the problem of poverty in the industrializing era, with early attention to the social question. British Romantics such as William Wordsworth and Robert Southey exemplified the trend through the first half of the century, culminating in Thomas Carlyle's *Past and Present* (1843), with its contrast between the organic social values of the Middle Ages and the individualistic modern age's alienation and immiseration. The Catholic Franz Buß and the evangelical Protestant Victor Aimé Huber typified the same phenomenon in Germany; it is no surprise that the newly unified German Empire of the conservative Otto von Bismarck would be the first nation to introduce state-run social insurance programs in the 1880s. Conservative Catholic social organizations to relieve poverty and industrial exploitation also grew in the later nineteenth century, particularly following Pope Leo XIII's encyclical *Rerum novarum* in 1891.

Conservatives in the early part of the nineteenth century faced a fundamental dilemma regarding both political practice and theory. Should they attempt to politicize the broad mass of the population according to their aims, gambling that most people shared an attachment to traditional ways and dynasties? Or should they instead eschew political propaganda among the common folk so as not to encourage their political consciousness and participation or even their very literacy? British royalists encountered this quandary already in the 1790s. Several thought it best not to stir plebeian waters; others, such as Hannah More, in her widely distributed *Cheap Repository Tracts*, developed a style of political argumentation that would be accessible and compelling to basic readers in affordable formats, even as part of the message was to leave politics to the established elites. In Germany, despite occasional efforts to found conservative newspapers to compete with liberal ones, it was not until the 1848 Revolution that conservatives began to organize politically on a wide scale and to adapt their ideologies to the needs of wider dissemination, as with the founding of the *Kreuzzeitung* newspaper in 1848 in Prussia.[33]

From the 1850s (even earlier in Britain), and particularly by the late nineteenth century, conservative parties were increasingly caught up in the growth of mass politics and grassroots movements in competition with liberal and working-class organizations. A conservative turn to nationalism formed part of this process, in ways that led to the development of a modern type of right-wing radical nationalism, antisemitism, racism, populism and even proto-fascism and "National Socialism." While debates about the origins of fascism and various forms of National Socialism continue, it is clear that in the transition to mass politics, a reshuffling of the political spectrum occurred, as radical and even liberal figures could find their way to the "new right." The historian Heinrich von Treitschke was such a former liberal turned conservative and antisemite in the German context, while the radical democrat Paul Déroulède became a right-radical nationalist leader in the French. As in the Habsburg lands, radical nationalism did not always entail a full rejection of liberalism so much as a decision to prioritize liberalism's exclusionary heritage above its commitment to the rule of law. Along with radical ideologies came a turn to activist, often violent street politics, a component of political thought as well as of political practice. A pronounced masculinist (para)militarism pervaded radical nationalist ranks, whether in a France seeking to recover its national honor after defeat in the Franco-Prussian War of 1870 or in the German Empire that emerged from that conflict.[34]

GLOBAL CONNECTIONS

Liberal political thought tended to promote ideals of humanitarian engagement and the export of freedom to other peoples, both within Europe and beyond. The result could equally be critiques of European involvement overseas or support for a European "civilizing mission." The majority of liberals across Europe opposed the African slave trade, and some even followed Adam Smith and Jeremy Bentham in pointing to the injustice and/or inutility of colonization. As scholars have recently emphasized, however, it is equally important to recognize the prevalence of "liberal imperialism" or "imperial liberalism." Abolitionists, too, often hoped to expand commerce and European "civilization" by ending the slave trade. Even John Stuart Mill, open as he was to then-radical views such as women's suffrage, still had a racialized blind spot when it came to empire. Colonial peoples of more "barbarous or semi-barbarous" type, he thought, were better ruled by Europeans. Such rule was to be in their interests and in pursuit of (European-style) education and eventual self-government, but indigenous peoples were not yet considered worthy of independence. Sometimes, Mill wrote, even "a vigorous despotism" is "the best mode of government ... to render them capable of a higher civilization."[35] Later in the century, amidst mounting racism, liberals such as Jules Ferry in France and Friedrich Naumann in Germany favored colonialism even more strongly, while opponents such as J. A. Hobson formed a decided minority. Socialists were colonialism's main critics.

Historical research also increasingly investigates global flows of ideas, not only from Europe outward but as a series of two-way conversations or networks of global exchanges, especially in the emerging field of "global intellectual history."[36] One should not overlook the growing asymmetries of power and extensions of imperial influence during the nineteenth century that placed European ideas and institutions at a considerable advantage around the globe, but neither should one overstate the dominance of European power and ideas in the face of indigenous concepts and worldviews. Even where European ideas were received and adopted—by choice or by coercion—they were also typically modified and adapted for local use. The ideas of Spanish liberals, British utilitarians, and French Comtean positivists proved influential in Latin America during and after the early nineteenth-century independence movements. But while the utilitarian reformer Bentham was admired by and corresponded with independence leaders such as Simón Bolívar, Bentham's recommendations were not adopted completely anywhere. Positivism in turn was most influential in Brazil, where it informed the ideology of the new republic in 1889 and provided the motto for the Brazilian flag, "Ordem e progresso" or "Order and Progress." Yet Brazilian positivism differed from the French, Mexican, and Argentinian forms.[37] Arab liberal and nationalist thought from the late eighteenth to the twentieth century was similarly less fully a reflection of European trends than previously depicted; local reform ideas, liberal and illiberal, shaped Arab political thought as well.[38]

In the later nineteenth century, students from the United States increasingly populated the lecture halls of Imperial Germany, with effects on the development of American Progressive Era political thought, social science, and economics, as well as social policy. The economists Richard T. Ely and Henry C. Adams, the sociologist Albion W. Small and the African American historian and activist W. E. B. DuBois were but some of the important American thinkers with German educational backgrounds who both built on and redirected German approaches. The scholars and political elites of Meiji Japan also looked to German as to United States ideas and institutions in the second half of the nineteenth century. The influence of German historical economics, for example—coupled with Japanese and Chinese Confucian traditions—helps explain the Meiji government's social reformism.[39]

Translation as a multipolar practice also significantly shaped the reception and hybridization of political thought. In Japan, for instance, there was debate about whether the term "civilization" represented a particular end state or a historical process that might unfold differently in Asia. It is significant that the scholar Fukuzawa Yukichi's *Outline of a Theory of Civilisation* (1875) drew upon the French moderate liberal François Guizot's *The History of Civilisation in Europe* (1828), in British English translation, and using glosses from a North American edition. Notions of "liberty" were also given more communitarian and positive meanings, and less individualist-protective, in the process of translation from English to Japanese, and from the Dutch *"vrijheid"* or German *"Freiheit."*[40] Bentham's aforementioned influence in Latin America was strongly molded by its primary transmission through the French translations of Étienne Dumont, a moderating filter that softened Bentham's radicalism.[41]

FIGURE 4.4 Fukuzawa Yukichi in Utrecht, the Netherlands, 1862.
© The History Collection / Alamy Stock Photo.

While British intellectual influences were the most pervasive in South Asia, thinkers there also sought inspiration in French, Italian, and German texts. Hence references to Comte, Giuseppe Mazzini, or Friedrich List sometimes outweighed those to Bentham or Mill. Figures such as K. T. Telang and Dadabhai Naoroji deployed the tools of political economy and the statistics beloved of colonial administrators to rebut claims that British imperial free trade policies benefited South Asia's economy. And while they drew on List in support of national economic frameworks against free trade ideals, here, too, they modified the German thinker's ideas.[42] Moreover, as in Europe, South Asian liberalism represented not only an ideology but also a lived world of culture and practice, institutionalized in education and the press as well as in a range of clubs and associations in Bengal, Mumbai, and other locations across the subcontinent.[43]

FIGURE 4.5 Dadabhai Naoroji, 1892. © The History Collection / Alamy Stock Photo.

The two-way nature of global exchanges in political thought is also perhaps clearest in the South Asian case. In the early nineteenth century, the Bengali reformer Rammohan Roy became a celebrity in Europe and North America and a correspondent of Bentham and other Europeans. Inspired both by Hindu and Muslim rationalist traditions and by European ideas, Rammohan spoke and wrote in Bengal and on his travels in England against East India Company monopolies and the burning of widows and in favor of parliamentary reform, the extension of jury service to non-Europeans and non-Christians, and the partial emancipation of women in Asia and Britain.[44] Dadabhai Naoroji, for his part, lived and worked in Britain for decades, teaching Gujarati at the University of London, giving evidence to Parliament on Indian affairs and, in 1892, becoming the first South Asian elected Member of Parliament; he was also a three-time President of the Indian National Congress. Both cases helped pave the way for the still greater celebrity of the Indian nationalists Mohandas Gandhi and Nobel Prize winner Rabindranath Tagore in the years after 1900.[45]

Similar examples come from the nineteenth-century Black Atlantic. In addition to inspiring further emancipation and independence movements there, leading figures of the earlier Haitian Revolution and independence struggle such as Toussaint Louverture and Jean-Jacques Dessalines resonated in European political thought in the first half of the nineteenth century, from the writings of revolutionary-era radicals and G. W. F. Hegel to those of the Young Hegelians of 1840s Germany. The prominent profile in nineteenth-century Britain of the Jamaican-born biracial working-class radical Robert Wedderburn and of the African American abolitionist Frederick Douglass also spotlights the role of those of African descent in the political culture of the Atlantic World.[46]

POLITICAL THOUGHT AND CONTEXT
ACROSS THE CENTURY

In addition to stressing the diversity of nineteenth-century political and economic thought, this discussion has emphasized how much that thought changed in the century's course. Political ideas and political culture were very different in the years around 1900 from what they had been a hundred years before. For the most part this chapter has traced the changes within the distinct branches covered: radical and socialist, liberal and conservative, economic thought and global connections. It is worth taking a step back in conclusion to highlight some overarching trends.

At a very basic level, political analysts faced similar challenges at the beginning and end of the century. Following the French Revolution and the wars that carried it across France's borders, observers confronted a seeming dissolution of political and social foundations—inspiring to some, frightening to others—which left many attempting to identify the proper principles that should underpin the life of the polity. At the end of the nineteenth century, too, many observers diagnosed a crisis of values and struggled to establish new foundations and new values for political and economic life. Such thinking is most often associated with the German philosopher Friedrich Nietzsche, but similar doubts and anxieties permeated European intellectual life elsewhere as well. The promise or threat of democracy also remained a dominant theme.[47]

While some of the basic tensions and oppositions endured, however, much of the content and context of opposing political positions and visions had changed substantially over the century's course. There were efforts to make political and economic thought more "scientific" or academic in the early nineteenth century, but the meaning and practice of science was transformed in the intervening years through professionalization, specialization, and university training. Biology-based conceptions of race and ethnic nationhood, for example, played much more central roles in the later period than in the earlier, in both colonial and antisemitic contexts, as did evolutionary thought following Charles Darwin and Herbert Spencer. What one meant by terms like "liberty" or "community" also changed.

As we have seen, one of the driving feedback mechanisms behind political development in the nineteenth century was the growth of political participation (the institutions of mass politics requiring new political rhetoric, practices, and organizations, and the new languages and practices promoting the further expansion of political engagement). All strands of political thought, from radical left to radical right, were strongly altered in the process. Changes in the nature, size, and functions of the state over which political groups competed were also reflected in the development of political and economic thought over the century, even as new political and economic ideas helped spur the growth of the state apparatus. Finally, the related need of states to organize the military might of increasingly industrial and politicized societies in an era of national *and* imperial rivalry also shaped political thought and state power globally in the years before—and during and after—the First World War.

CHAPTER FIVE

Nature

FREDERICK GREGORY

For most people nature is both predictable and mysterious. The sun comes up reliably every day, weather patterns repeat, and objects unfailingly fall to the ground when released. These things happen in a reality apart from humans and appear to be in no way affected by their cares and concerns. While this indifferent nature can be beautiful, it can also be "red in tooth and claw," as Lord Tennyson famously depicted it in Canto 56 of his 1849 poem, "In Memoriam." Nature is also full of hidden forces and strange phenomena. Magnets invisibly pull metals toward them, space and time adjust themselves to accommodate light's constant velocity, butterflies cover vast distances in an annual migration that requires several generations to complete, and animals disguise themselves to escape predators. Such things are closer to the experience of humans because they appear to be less indifferent and more the result of some unseen power or purpose. Purposeful nature can be enticing, but it can also be overpowering.

This chapter is concerned with two grand visions of nature that characterized the West in the nineteenth century. One of these conceptions was inherited from the past, while the other was new with the coming of the century. Among the individuals who embraced each of these general ideas of nature there was often disagreement about its meaning. Finally, the two ideas each changed and developed over the course of the century. The task of this chapter, then, is not only to follow these general conceptions as the century unfolded, but to explain how and why each could mean different things to its adherents.

In order to get at the particulars and variations of these two visions while maintaining the broad perspective necessary to understand their importance in the larger culture, we shall occasionally employ an older notion that has been recently revived as a useful tool for the historian. In his introduction to a 2012 volume on monism, Todd Weir suggests that unpacking the term "worldview" is necessary if one wants to understand how monists dealt with the paradoxes that arose in their philosophy.[1] In our case, the notion of worldview, the larger cause, can help guide us through the levels of meaning that the idea of nature held for those living over a century ago. Our primary concern will be how the idea of nature fit in the greater perspective of what the Germans in the nineteenth century denoted as *Weltanschauung*, the comprehensive conception of the world and humanity's relation to it.[2]

An idea of nature inherited from the eighteenth century and one that persisted throughout the nineteenth was that of a clockwork universe, a gigantic mechanism whose parts could be identified as could the laws governing how the parts worked together. It was joined, as the nineteenth century dawned, by a new vision: a nature that was not static and eternally the same, but one that had a history, one that was alive and evolving. These ideas of nature originated in the relatively narrow boundaries of natural science and philosophy, intellectual realms that most people did not inhabit. They spread beyond these confines to the wider public as individuals, often in the guise of popularizers, attempted to utilize them in a larger cause. The phenomenologist Erazim Kohak confirms that they have endured into our own time when he asks: "Is the Person or is matter in motion the ultimate metaphysical category? There really is no third."[3]

THE IDEA OF NATURE INHERITED
FROM NEWTONIANISM

When Isaac Newton died in 1727 there was no consensus about the meaning of his achievement for natural philosophy. Newton's universe had emerged as a cosmic machinery that ran under the control of God, who, as the divine mechanic, had ordained the laws of motion and gravitational force Newton had described mathematically. Resting content with the quantification of nature's laws, Newton ignored the persistent questions raised by Gottfried Leibniz and followers of René Descartes about how the mysterious gravitational force acted across distances without an intervening medium.

While contention among followers of Newton, Descartes, and Leibniz continued as the eighteenth century unfolded, by the end of the century it was Newton's vision that prevailed. Avoiding the nagging question about how gravitational force was transmitted, French natural philosophers in particular applied Newton's laws of motion to explain complicated movements in the heavens, even devising new mathematical techniques to solve major challenges to Newton's view in the growing science of celestial mechanics. It was a reversible clockwork universe whose machinery could be run backwards as well as forwards.

In 1795 in a lecture to the École normale, the French astronomer Pierre Simon Laplace declared that a being such as God, who could know the positions of all matter from the lightest atoms to the largest bodies, could calculate with certainty the past and future positions of every piece of matter in the universe.[4] In this view, not only the heavens, but all physical nature is completely determined by the forces acting on matter. It is a perfect machinery whose working governs everything that happens with absolute certainty and also reveals whatever purposes its Creator intended. As we will see, this dream, inspired originally by Newton's approach, lingered, reappearing in various contexts over the course of the century.[5]

The Newtonian worldview found another proponent at the end of the eighteenth century. In his *Metaphysical Foundations of Natural Science* of 1786, the German philosopher Immanuel Kant relied on causal law and Newtonian science as the foundation for physical science. He wrote that natural science was only "genuine" (*eigentlich*) to the extent that a description of nature was expressed mathematically, a test that Newton's system clearly met. Some sciences were not genuine; for example, chemistry was an empirical science that did not lend itself to first principles that could be articulated mathematically.[6] Kant also made an exception of biology because he felt that living things supplied their own purpose and did not receive it from outside themselves. The interaction of their parts was more complex than the causality of simple mechanism; hence we must take the fact of purposive organization as an unexplained starting point. While we must recognize that there will not be a strictly mechanical account of organism, however, we have no recourse other than to utilize mechanical explanation in biology as far as we can take it.[7] An acceptable goal when explaining natural phenomena was to identify the blind causal interaction of nature's machinery. This, of course, was separate from the question of the origin of the machinery itself.

This image of nature as a deterministic machinery also lay at the basis of the so-called nebular hypotheses that arose first in Kant's *Universal Natural History of the Heavens* of 1755 and then of Pierre-Simon Laplace's *Exposition of the System of the World* of 1796.[8]

These works represent an important adjustment to Newton's original worldview since each removed God's direct involvement in creating and superintending the cosmos. They wanted, as Peter Gay expressed so succinctly, "Newton's physics without Newton's God."[9] The creation and operation of nature were due to natural law. Later in the century the phrase "creation by law" would capture this deistic revision of Sir Isaac's original vision.[10]

As the nineteenth century began, then, the idea of nature as machine acting in accordance with natural law could allow for a God who intervened or one who did not. Of course, most required God to explain the existence of laws themselves. Further, natural theology, in which knowledge of nature's machinery testified to God's existence, greatness, and wisdom, held appeal for both traditional believer and deist alike. This apologetic enterprise, which has been called "the most characteristic form of thinking, feeling, reading and writing in an enlightened way" during the eighteenth century, continued to flourish throughout the nineteenth century, especially in Britain.[11]

Over the first half of the century, however, the consensus grew among natural philosophers not to resort to explanations of natural phenomena based on God's direct intervention; rather, one should try to identify the causal natural law that lay at the basis of the phenomenon one sought to understand. For example, in a letter to the geologist Charles Lyell from 1836 about "the mystery of mysteries"—how new species had made their appearance to replace extinct ones—the English natural philosopher John Herschel observed that if and when they were accounted for, "it would be found to be a natural in contradistinction to a miraculous process."[12] Such a statement did not discourage those who endorsed it from accepting the existence of a beneficent deity. But after 1850 a more radical variety of the mechanical worldview would make its appearance.

FIGURE 5.1 Laplace's Nebula Hypothesis, 1870. Pierre Laplace postulated a rotating, primitive nebulous fluid that gravitational force congealed into a central sun surrounded by smaller revolving masses. © Universal History Archive / Getty Images.

A NEW VISION OF NATURE

It has long been observed that with the nineteenth century a new idea of nature made its way into Western consciousness. This development has been characterized by scholars in various ways, all with an eye to how nature would eventually be regarded when the dust created by the new vision settled. To be sure, the new idea of nature did not take over completely. Following a brief review of how scholars have depicted the emergence of this view, we will unpack its enduring qualities in debates about nature's meaning.

When R. G. Collingwood wrote his classic 1945 study, *The Idea of Nature*, he suggested that there have been three periods in the history of Western thought in which the idea of nature came into central focus.[13] Among the ancient Greeks nature was alive and infused with mind, whose presence accounted for any orderliness we encounter in our interactions with the natural world. During the second of Collingwood's periods, which he identified as the Renaissance view of nature, mind was imposed upon nature from outside by an all-knowing God in the form of strict causal laws. Nature no longer followed its own purposes; rather, the functions it fulfilled and the intentions it realized came from its creator, whose mechanical laws brought about divine purposes.

Collingwood had more difficulty describing the idea of nature in the third of his three eras, which, he tells us, began at the end of the eighteenth century, developed over the course of the nineteenth, and, as of 1945, was "still young and has not yet had time to ripen its ideas for systematic treatment."[14] In general, he suggested that the modern view is based on treating the natural world studied by natural scientists as analogous to the vicissitudes of human affairs studied by historians. The modern view of nature places the conception of process, change, and development in the center of its picture.[15]

Another lecturer from the 1930s addressed the idea of nature through the concept of the Great Chain of Being. Arthur Lovejoy delivered the second set of William James Lectures at Harvard University in 1933, published three years later as *The Great Chain of Being: A Study of the History of an Idea*.[16] His characterization of the change brought about in the nineteenth century, while depicted even more abstractly than Collingwood's, dovetailed with that of his British counterpart. Lovejoy asserted that in reaction to the Enlightenment assumption that the world (and human activity) should be depicted as nearly as possible in relation to a "standard conceived as universal, uncomplicated, immutable, uniform for every rational being," nineteenth-century thinkers introduced "diversitarianism for uniformitarianism as the ruling preconception in most of the normative provinces of thought."[17] Regarding the new standards of value produced by this departure from the Enlightenment outlook, Lovejoy said that there had been few changes "in the entire history of thought ... more profound and more momentous."[18] This focus on difference as opposed to similarity, and the individual as opposed to the universal, reinforced an understanding of nature that was so radically evolutionary that it would take the entire century and beyond to unfold.

Writing three decades after Collingwood and Lovejoy, the French philosopher Michel Foucault reinforced their perception that a new view of nature had been born near the beginning of the nineteenth century. Foucault focused on natural history, where the emphasis had always been on categorization. He was critical of historians who purported to write histories of biology for the eighteenth century. It was not possible, said Foucault, since biology did not exist then. As he explained, "There was a very simple reason why biology did not exist, for life itself did not exist. All that existed was living beings, which were viewed through a grid of knowledge constituted by natural history."[19] Living things were, in other words, objects in nature like other objects. It is only with the nineteenth century that the idea of life as something constantly changing from an initial state to one more mature was applied to nature itself and became a subject for contemplation.

Of course, just reading the ideas of Collingwood, Lovejoy, and Foucault may give the impression that the new vision of the natural world they describe soon became an established conception. In fact, it would take considerable time for this new view, as opposed to that of nature as a reversible machine acting by strict causal law, to take hold and develop.

BACKGROUND AND EMERGENCE
OF THE EVOLUTIONARY VIEW

The period from the late eighteenth century to the 1830s and 1840s has often been referred to as the Age of Romanticism. In England it was a time when the poetry of Wordsworth, Coleridge, Keats, and Shelley flourished, while on the continent German writers such as Schiller, the Schlegel brothers, Novalis, and others began to turn away from classical thought in favor of an outlook that preferred intuition over analysis, feeling over critical thought, and nature not as a machine but a source of beauty and awe. Some among the German writers in this period, not enamored of Newton's approach to nature, did not wish to abandon natural science so much as to reimagine it. The German poet, playwright, and novelist Johann Wolfgang von Goethe undertook an extended critique of Newtonian optics, urging his readers to avoid Newton's detached analytical approach in favor of the immediate perception and experience of nature. To understand colored light, he urged, hold the prism to the eye and look through it.[20] The young philosopher Friedrich Schelling, who wished to "give wings to physics," thoroughly captured the attention of his age in the first decade of the century with his *Naturphilosophie*. Lovejoy saw the blossoming of the evolutionary view of nature in the works of these early nineteenth-century Romantics.[21] But in order to appreciate the genesis of this view of nature, it is helpful to explore the historical context out of which it emerged.

The waning decades of the eighteenth century was a time of challenge *from within* to a fundamental assumption of the Enlightenment: the capacity of reason to provide an explanation of reality and of our experience of the world. It had begun with thinkers like David Hume, whose skepticism about natural theology had raised a threat of monumental proportions. "Nothing frightens man so much," wrote the philosopher F. H. Jacobi, "nothing darkens his mind to such a degree, as when God disappears from nature … when purpose, wisdom and goodness no longer seem to reign in nature, but only a blind necessity or dumb chance."[22] The young Kant called the prospect "the black abyss," and it along with Hume's philosophy in general jolted him awake from what he called his dogmatic slumber.[23]

Kant attempted to rescue reason from Hume's destruction of traditional metaphysics by limiting its scope to the world of the senses. To Jacobi, the skeptical conclusions of Hume's and Kant's radical restrictions were steps along a path that led ultimately to absurdities like Johann Fichte's efforts to ignore the external world. In Jacobi's mind, this was as ludicrous as believing in nothing: Jacobi labeled it "nihilism."[24] "To the German mind at the end of the eighteenth century," writes Frederick Beiser, "reason seemed to be heading toward the abyss, and no one could see any means of stopping it."[25]

A new view emerged most clearly in the thought of Friedrich Schelling,[26] who rejected Kant's unbridgeable gap between the world in itself and the world we know. Schelling countered Kant's approach by refusing his assumption that the natural philosopher must come to nature as an outsider, analyzing it as machinery operating by means of cause and effect. In his *Naturphilosophie*, Schelling insisted that we know nature not because we stand outside it, but because we are a part of it. Nature is not mechanism. It is organism, and to know it is akin to knowing ourselves. His system was arranged to demonstrate that nature and mind were not forever separated by Kant's famous breech; rather, they were two sides of the same coin. What hovered in the background of his philosophy was the unified Absolute, in which the polarities of nature and mind dissolved. For Schelling,

FIGURE 5.2 Portrait of Friedrich Schelling. With his writings on nature philosophy, the young genius Friedrich Schelling captured the attention of the German states at the turn of the nineteenth century. © DeAgostini / Getty Images.

cognition therefore incorporated elements of aesthetics and morality, not unlike what
Stephen Gaukroger has shown sensibility accomplished for many in the late eighteenth
century.[27]

Schelling's *Naturphilosophie* was intended to preserve nature's integrity by giving it a
primary place alongside mind in a new system. Nature and mind were polarities within
a larger unified view of reality. The world in itself (nature) and the world for us (mind)
were the same world. What was new about the contents of his philosophy of identity was
that they were evolving. This was not a universe that was complete once and for all, but
was instead in process. For Schelling, God represented a pantheistic unity of nature and
mind. He asked:

> Has creation a final goal? And if so, why was it not reached at once? Why was the
> consummation not reached at the beginning? To these questions there is but one
> answer: Because God is *Life*, and not merely being. ... Being is *sensible* only in
> becoming. In being as such, it is true, there is no becoming; in the latter, rather, it is
> itself posited as eternity. But in the actualization (of being) through opposition there
> is necessarily a becoming.[28]

Other thinkers of the late eighteenth and early nineteenth centuries refer to historical
evolution, but none articulates it philosophically as a new idea of nature as well as
Schelling. As Lovejoy declared, "It is ... in this introduction of a radical evolutionism
into metaphysics and theology, and in the attempt to revise even the principles of logic
to make them harmonize with an evolutional conception of reality, that the historical
significance of Schelling chiefly lies."[29]

Elsewhere in Europe the idea of an evolution of living nature was forcing its way clearly
into the minds of the educated public, even though all did not necessarily embrace it. In
England, Charles Darwin's free-thinking grandfather Erasmus believed in a universe that
was self-generated and a living world that was evolving. His three-part *Zoonomia*, which
was published between 1794 and 1796, asserted that various species had been forced
to adapt over time to meet needs of hunger, reproduction, and security. He believed
that monstrosities, which he said could persist over generations, might even become a
permanent variety, if not a new species. It was all part of a cosmic scheme set in motion
by a Great First Cause, a theme developed in his *Temple of Nature* of 1803. There he
speculated about the birth of the planets from exploding suns and the emergence of order
from an original chaos. Here he depicted organic evolution, begun beneath the waves and
ascending to humans, who thus were siblings of lower animal forms. It was too much for
most, although hard to ignore.

Around this same time the first systematic exposition of the evolution of living things
burst on the scene in 1809 in Jean-Baptiste Lamarck's *Zoological Philosophy*. The French
naturalist believed that the Creator had imposed natural laws on nature to bring about
His intent by secondary means. It was an evolution that guaranteed progress because
the Creator, though remote, was in control. Nature, through heat, light, electricity, and
moisture, formed the simplest plants and animals by spontaneous generation. From then
on, the natural tendency of living things to become more complex (the "power of life")
and the law of inheritance of acquired characteristics through use and disuse slowly
modified existing forms over immense time to produce the wondrous diversity of living
things seen all around us today (which God had intended all along). Lamarck's theory
was highly controversial throughout the nineteenth century, although it would persist in
various contexts until the 1930s.

INITIAL RECEPTION OF THE EVOLUTIONARY VIEW

In spite of his acknowledgment of the existence of a Creator, Lamarck, like Laplace, was commonly characterized as a dangerous, godless materialist, mainly because God was the remote absentee landlord of deism. As a result, Lamarck's new evolutionary conception of nature was not taken seriously by many, especially in Britain, throughout the first half of the nineteenth century. This does not mean that the ideas of Erasmus Darwin and Lamarck and the cosmic evolution of Kant and Laplace were unknown to the educated public. Reviews and eventually even popularizations of cosmic and organic evolution, such as the anonymous *Vestiges of the Natural History of Creation* of 1844, created a sensation that was hard to miss. But in Britain at least, the well-entrenched tradition of natural theology, which was no longer matched in France and Germany, made it possible to dismiss evolutionary ideas and relegate them to the status of other "dubious" notions like phrenology, Mesmerism, and the like.[30]

In the German states, by contrast, the romantic mood was widespread as the century began, exemplified in reviews of the new *Naturphilosophie* of the young genius Schelling, in discussions of the latest product from the pen of the revered Goethe, and in the writings reviewed in the plethora of new journals that had exploded on the scene. To Romantic minds, Kant's conclusion that there was no hope of uncovering the ultimate truth of nature fell flat. The young Gotthilf Heinrich Schubert, for example, linked Kant and Fichte together in his mind. In a letter of 1798 to his parents, Schubert referred to "the Kantian-Fichtean egoism," adding, "which I hate." Of his discovery of natural science, he said to a friend: "I have now found something real."[31] Schelling's insistence on nature's fundamental place alongside mind in his philosophy soon drew Schubert and others in.

In the years under French domination and especially after Napoleon's defeat, what was seen as Kant's dualistic outlook became out of synch with the calls for German unification that sounded loud and clear among German youth. By contrast, the Romantic rejection of Kant held great appeal. Dualism became the enemy while "proto-monism"—a unified conception of life and the world—proved more and more irresistible.[32] Schelling's pantheistic version of *Wissenschaft* (systematic knowledge), with its romanticized vision of nature, appeared in popularizations of science and blended with the growing spirit of dissent expressed visibly in the Free Religion movement.[33] For many, the glorification of nature not only challenged older religious ideas but also offered a new context in which to seek new truth.

In what is sometimes referred to as a shift from *Naturphilosophie* to *Naturwissenschaft*, the enthusiasm for Schelling's philosophical nature philosophy gave way by the 1840s to an emphasis on the empirical observation of the natural world and a prescribed method of systematic dispassionate analysis. This shift away from Schelling occurred even though public figures like Alexander von Humboldt in his multi-volume *Cosmos* (1845, English 1846) and Hans Christian Oersted in his two-volume *Soul in Nature* (1850, English 1852) retained strong Romantic elements in their portraits of nature.[34]

As part of the turn away from nature philosophy to empirical research in the years leading to and after 1848, some voices of dissent took on a stridently critical stance of the earlier romanticized evolutionary view of nature. The defenders of the movement later known as scientific materialism, Karl Vogt, Jakob Moleschott, and Ludwig Büchner, appeared to give new voice in the 1850s to the image of nature as a deterministic mechanical machinery.[35] Rejecting nature philosophy and evolution as idealistic speculation, they called for a ban of every kind of supernaturalism and idealism from the explanation of natural events.

There was no thought here that nature's machinery was fulfilling the purposes of an external beneficent Deity, as it earlier had for the orthodox and deist alike. The message of their deliberately strident anti-religious books, essays, and lectures was that humans should grow up and face the unpleasant truth about nature. Vogt declared the world of thoughts was a secretion of the brain just as urine was a secretion of the kidney. Moleschott's book, *The Theory of Nutrition: For the People* (1850), announced that the reliance of the Irish on potatoes condemned them to defeat by their better-fed English overlords. When the book was reviewed just after the revolutions of 1848 by Ludwig Feuerbach, the celebrated materialistic critic of the philosopher G. W. F. Hegel, the world heard proclaimed the ethical and political significance of Moleschott's work in what has become a famous slogan: "Man is what he eats!" (*Der Mensch ist was er isst!*).[36]

Although the scientific materialists banned speculation, idealism, and religion from their worldview, they could not, in spite of themselves, completely eradicate Schelling's earlier conception of nature. Where Schelling's pantheistic worldview, which rested on the unity of the material and ideal, provided him with spiritual meaning, the materialists laid claim to an ethic of a strictly materialistic pantheism that celebrated a higher meaning in the immortality of matter as the foundation of all reality. As Moleschott declared, death was not black and horrible, "for swaying in the air and resting in the mould are the eternally smouldering seeds of blossoms."[37] Once Darwin made the subject of evolution palatable to those who demanded explanation based on causal law, they changed their tune about evolution, although their hesitations about natural selection could challenge the inherent teleology of their worldview.

MECHANIZATION OF THE EVOLUTIONARY VIEW

In the years leading up to Charles Darwin's *Origin of Species* (1859), a wider embrace of the evolutionary idea of nature was hindered by evolution's association with suspect speculative notions such as *Naturphilosophie*, phrenology, Mesmerism, and other claims regarded as outside the established scientific canon. By the middle of the century, an explanation of natural phenomena was considered scientific if it were based on causal laws like those involved in the Newtonian science of mechanics. And, as Herschel had pointed out in 1836, a scientific explanation should not rely on supernatural processes. Should evolution find an explanation based on impersonal causal interactions not supervised by a supernatural agency, it would likely be able to withstand any dismissive charge of pseudo-science.

Darwin did not set out to make evolution scientific. It was true that he was aware of his grandfather's ideas on the subject as well as those of an enthusiastic young radical follower of Lamarck named Robert Grant, with whom he had made excursions as a young student at Edinburgh. But when Darwin left on a voyage around the world in 1831, he, like virtually all his mentors at Cambridge, dismissed the case for evolution. It was strictly hypothetical, not something that could be observed or proven. Furthermore, it challenged socially respected religious norms, not something a young man out to make a name for himself should sanction.

On the voyage, however, Darwin made observations of species that were hard to explain by special creation. He also became persuaded by geology books sent to him during the voyage that claimed the earth was much, much older than previously thought. By the end of the voyage, he allowed himself to entertain ideas that would undermine the stability of species. On his return, it did not take him long to adopt, without telling anyone, the outrageous idea of what he called the transmutation of species. And then he stumbled on the idea of natural selection and knew he was onto something.[38]

Natural selection was the key for Darwin because it allowed him to produce a scientifically *respectable* evolutionary theory. The theories of which he was aware—his grandfather's and Lamarck's—were unacceptable because they assumed evolution was progressive, directed by an agency toward greater perfection. Further, they could not satisfactorily spell out exactly how evolutionary change proceeded. Erasmus had been content simply to proclaim that living things had developed from simple to complex. Lamarck had included mechanisms of change, appealing to both the primary power of life—a tendency of living things to become internally more complex—and the secondary laws of the inheritance of acquired characteristics. But his theory had been thoroughly denounced by all the leading figures of British science. The geologist Charles Lyell had destroyed it in his review in the first volume of his detailed study. When the anonymous author of the *Vestiges of Creation* (1844) embraced an evolutionary theory very much like Lamarck's, thunder descended from every corner. Herschel, who had called for an explanation of new species by natural as opposed to supernatural causes, denounced what *Vestiges* cast as a law of progressive development. Such a speculative law of development could never, he believed, serve as a scientific explanation.[39]

Darwin's theory of natural selection, however, had no predictive power at all. It guaranteed change, but not development to perfection. All it said was that there would always be variations in the traits of offspring (what Darwin called individual differences) and that some of these traits would be preferred because they fit the environment better than others. As the environment changed, so would the traits selected. Given enough time, the traits could change sufficiently to make a new species. There could be no talk of guaranteed progress since there was no way to predict which of the individual differences would better fit the environment into which they came.

Darwin's theory worked equally well whether God was present or absent in nature; natural selection also guaranteed no purpose to the history of living things. In addition, it faced several scientific difficulties that would take well into the twentieth century to work out. Throughout the remainder of the century, natural selection thus remained controversial. But one service Darwin did render was to make the idea of evolution in nature more acceptable, even if natural selection won relatively few adherents. Metaphorically, if one purchased stock in evolution in 1860, by 1900 the investment would have produced very high returns. If, however, one had also purchased stock in natural selection at the same time, one would have lost money at the end of the century.

Along with the acceptance of the evolution of species over time grew an insistence on naturalistic explanations in science. By the century's end, the scientist had largely usurped the clergyman's role as authoritative interpreter of nature's meaning in the larger scheme of things. Darwin's work gave impetus to portraits of science in conflict with religion, first in Germany and later in England and America. Public depictions of such a conflict in Germany became front and center with the writings of the scientific materialists of the 1850s and particularly with the work of the Jena zoologist Ernst Haeckel. In a letter to

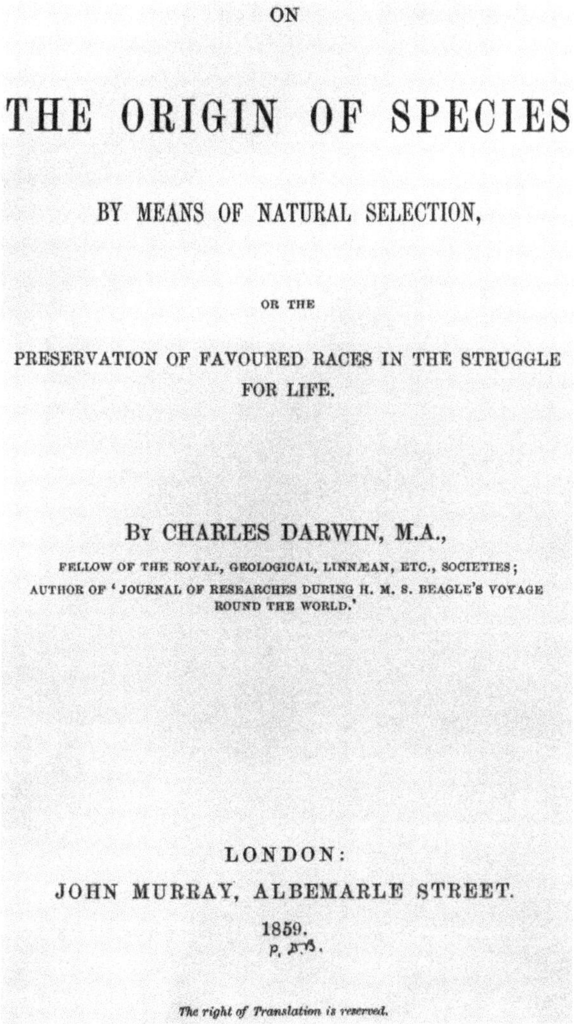

ON

THE ORIGIN OF SPECIES

BY MEANS OF NATURAL SELECTION,

OR THE

PRESERVATION OF FAVOURED RACES IN THE STRUGGLE FOR LIFE.

By CHARLES DARWIN, M.A.,

FELLOW OF THE ROYAL, GEOLOGICAL, LINNÆAN, ETC., SOCIETIES;
AUTHOR OF ' JOURNAL OF RESEARCHES DURING H. M. S. BEAGLE'S VOYAGE
ROUND THE WORLD.'

LONDON:

JOHN MURRAY, ALBEMARLE STREET.

1859.
P. 5.3.

The right of Translation is reserved.

FIGURE 5.3 Title page, *The Origin of Species*, 1859.
Few books have had the impact of Charles Darwin's study
of 1859 on the idea of nature and its larger meaning. ©
Bettman / Getty Images.

Darwin in 1864, Haeckel related that his wife endearingly referred to him as her German "Darwin-Mann."[40]

Beginning in the mid-1860s, Haeckel promoted an idealistic version of Darwinism that harked back to the pantheistic idealism of Schelling. Haeckel polemicized against dualistic and teleological interpretations of nature and bitterly opposed the established Christian churches. By the 1870s, he was aggressively taking on prominent established natural scientists, declaring at the annual meeting of the Society of German Natural Scientists and Physicians in 1877 that "evolutionary theory must lay claim to its legitimate influence in the schools as the most important means of education; it will

FIGURE 5.4 Ernst Haeckel. Ernst Haeckel's campaign for evolution and
against the Church helped establish long-lasting antagonism between
religion and science. © Corbis Historical / Hulton Deutsch / Getty Images.

not be merely be tolerated, but will become standard and leading."[41] The ensuing
denunciations of Haeckel's promotion of Darwinian evolution among natural scientists
and politicians in the German Reichstag made the idea of nature in progress hard to
miss by the German public.

The widespread visibility of Haeckel's polemicizing against traditional religion in
the name of evolution in the years between the mid-1860s and the end of the century
contributed more than any other single factor to the idea that evolutionary science was
materialistic and nontheistic, if not aggressively atheistic.[42] Yet, as Bernhard Kleeberg
has eloquently shown by following Haeckel's development from religious youth to
mature secular scientist, Haeckel, along with the devotees of the monistic movement he

founded, were able in the end to find a higher purpose in the experience of beauty in nature and the assurance of progress that scientific certainty provided.[43] Nor did Darwin himself permit his natural selection to imply, as in twenty-first-century neo-Darwinism, that the universe itself is so purposeless as to be the result of blind chance. Writing to the Irish philosopher William Graham in 1881 about the latter's book, *The Creed of Science*, Darwin expressed disagreement with the conclusion that the mere existence of natural laws implies purpose, but then conceded that the author had expressed his "inward conviction, though far more vividly and clearly than I could have done, that the Universe is not the result of chance."[44]

In England and America, evolution was not the focused critique of traditional religion that it was in Haeckel's diatribes. There the attacks were not against Christianity per se, but against dogmatic religion and rigid interpretation of scripture, symbolized particularly in Roman Catholicism. John Draper's *History of the Conflict Between Religion and Science* of 1874 and Andrew Dickson White's *Warfare of Science* of 1876, later expanded into his two-volume *History of the Warfare of Science with Theology in Christendom* (1896), made the case that whenever religion sought to constrain science, it ended up doing harm to both enterprises. In their eyes evolution did not contradict religion but added to a fuller understanding of its truths. It is safe to conclude, then, that the idea of evolutionary nature at the end of the nineteenth century could be used to support the optimistic belief that civilization was continuing to progress.

THE FLOWERING OF THE MECHANICAL VIEW OF NATURE

The program of explaining natural phenomena through the quantified forces of matter governing them has been called the "Newtonian dream."[45] It was hardly the eighteenth century's sole line of approach, as Stephen Gaukroger has so persuasively shown. But the dream of doing for other sciences what Newton had accomplished for mechanics persisted below the surface. If one could identify the material particles of whatever natural wonders were to be explained and quantify the force laws governing their movement, as Laplace had promised, one would have understood the phenomenon. When Albert Einstein and Leopold Infeld looked for a spokesman from the middle of the nineteenth century for what they called "the mechanical view," they chose the German physicist Hermann von Helmholtz, who characterized the problem of physical science "to be to refer natural phenomena back to unchangeable attractive and repulsive forces, whose intensity depends solely on distance. The solubility of this problem is the condition of the complete comprehensibility of nature."[46]

As the nineteenth century dawned, however, attempts to realize the Newtonian dream in sciences other than mechanics did not fare as well as they had in Newton's work. For example, attempts to quantify the force laws of chemical interactions went nowhere and were replaced in the work of John Dalton by quantifying the units of chemistry.[47] Nor did a Newtonian approach to the marvels of heat, light, electricity, and magnetism prove to be the most successful first line of inquiry in the first decades of the nineteenth century.

However, theoretical considerations of the relationships among forces of mechanics, heat, light, electricity, and magnetism led to intriguing results, from the recognition that electricity and magnetism were aspects of a single force to the conclusion that such forces could neither be created nor destroyed but could be transformed from one form into another. Discoveries like the wave theory of light, electromagnetism, the conservation of force (later clarified to the conservation of energy), and the second law of thermodynamics reinforced the impression that natural science was making great strides. And much of this occurred as the mid-century mark neared, just when natural science was being enthusiastically touted by some as the replacement for religion.

With the growing insistence on natural causation and on the material basis of reality, a secularized version of Newton's original program came back before the public after mid-century. Physicists successfully employed the mechanical view to create the kinetic view of matter, in which they accurately depicted the behavior of gases from the motions of their molecules. They could not describe the motion of an individual molecule, but their statistical description of the molecules as a group enabled them to explain experimentally measured properties of the gases. And in the early 1860s, the Scottish physicist James Maxwell created a model of the machinery of an all-pervading medium called the ether in which the motions of the machinery's parts not only corresponded to the effects of electricity and magnetism but also revealed *why* the effects occurred together. In 1867, Maxwell told another physicist that the purpose of the model was "to show that the phenomena are such as can be explained by mechanism."[48] His mathematical description of the mechanical interaction, known as Maxwell's equations, astonishingly revealed that light was an electromagnetic wave.

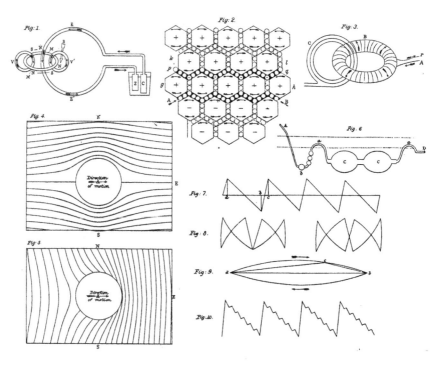

FIGURE 5.5 Illustration from James Maxwell's "On Physical Lines of Force." By mathematically describing the forces involved in the deformation and motion of the parts of this mechanical model, James Maxwell clarified the relationship between electricity and magnetism and discovered that light was an electromagnetic wave. © Wikimedia Commons (public domain).

But it was less technical results like these than popular explanations of the mechanical view that shaped the image of science in the public eye. Especially important were the popularized proclamations of the mechanical materialistic worldview from the likes of Vogt, Büchner, Molesschott, and others in Germany and elsewhere that banned suprasensual entities from science and insisted that matter in motion was the basis for all realistic scientific explanations. The mechanical interaction of matter in motion became once again the paradigm for scientific explanation. In his famous *Force and Matter* of 1855, Büchner referred to "the identity of the laws of thought to the mechanical laws of nature," and much later, quoting the psychologist Wilhelm Wundt, proclaimed that "Mechanics and logic are identical."[49]

In spite of past limitations of the mechanical approach, Büchner did not hesitate to assume that everything unknown would one day yield to the penetrating gaze of mechanical materialism. The scientific materialists resented any claim that there were things beyond the pale of science, characterizing them as "theological." To the German physician Emil du Bois-Reymond's famous declaration that "we shall never know" how to give a material explanation of consciousness, Büchner retorted that it was only because of our ignorance of the fineness (*Feinheit*) of matter. If we can but get to this level of matter, such metaphysical problems would be solved.[50] To some it seemed as if physical science were closing in on a complete explanation of nature. As one physicist put it, the future truths of physical science are to be found in the sixth place of decimals.[51]

Of course, most people did not think of nature in such bold and radical terms as did the reductionist and anti-religious scientific materialists. But in the emerging worldview, it became more and more common to assume that modern science had confirmed nature to be, in fact, an impersonal machinery. Nature would grind on deterministically in accordance with the natural laws governing it, unmindful of the concerns and wishes of humans. One could always hold in reserve the belief that the Great Mechanic could interrupt these laws should He wish to do so, an option retained by many to this day. But it was, by the end of the nineteenth century, becoming the task of the *scientist* (itself a neologism) to discover the mechanism causing whatever needed explanation. That mechanism might not yet be described in terms of the motion of particles of matter, but it someday surely would. Such views of nature came to dominate opinion in the second half of the nineteenth century, an era that has been called the Age of Realism.

BEGINNINGS OF THE BREAKDOWN
OF THE MECHANICAL VIEW

In spite of many successes, there were ominous signs within the physics community that not all was well with the mechanical view of nature. To be sure, no one regarded these difficulties as fundamental challenges that could not be met. Physicists regarded such challenges as the kind of puzzles that defined the ongoing agenda of research. They were occasions to learn more about nature and did little to shake the confidence that mechanical explanations would be found.

One such difficulty emerged from the successes in thermodynamics leading to the conservation of energy; in particular, it became clear that irreversible physical processes were present. But since the Newtonian dream assumed that mechanical explanations could run backwards as well as forwards, the mechanical interactions of whatever matter was involved would be reversible. If there were natural processes that ran in one direction only, then it appeared that they could not be described with mechanical explanations. Further, an implication of this irreversibility was that nature was running down and would suffer a "heat death" in the remote future. Some used this development to argue against materialists for a divine creation of the world, since, if the world were infinitely old, the heat death would already have occurred.[52]

And there was trouble with Maxwell's ether. While his model had been amazingly successful in explaining electromagnetism and in showing that light traveled through space as waves in the ether, the ether itself possessed qualities that were inconsistent with common sense. For example, to produce the results it did, the ether had to be a solid that was more elastic than steel and at the same time so extremely rarefied that it offered no resistance to things moving through it! But the most puzzling result came out of attempts to measure the speed of the earth with respect to the ether. One could not expect the earth to be the only body in the universe to be at rest with respect to the ether, yet attempts to detect differences in the speed of light as the earth moved directly away from and perpendicular to a distant light source showed no change. It was as if the speed of light remained the same whether the earth traveled with the light or at right angles to it. Physicists had no explanation for this result and went to rather strange extremes to account for it.

It was not until after the turn of the century that Albert Einstein's theory of special relativity made the luminiferous ether superfluous. His extension of his own finding a decade later to general relativity and Max Planck's unconventional assertion that energy was not radiated and absorbed continuously but existed in packets called quanta seemed to erode the very bedrock on which the classical mechanical view rested. Eventually in the 1920s, quantum mechanics replaced classical physics and thereby eroded the old confidence that nature *had* to give way to rational explanations. In the life sciences, natural selection withstood challenges of the early decades of the twentieth century, emerging in the 1940s as part of a wholly secularized evolutionary synthesis.

The breakdown of the Age of Realism was not restricted to the field of science. The old progressive order of civilization in the West collapsed with the outbreak of the Great War, a development reflected in art, literature, and philosophy too. Along with the loss of certainty, once the goal of Western thought, came an existential anxiety about the future. It is no wonder that it has been said of the nineteenth century that it was the last time in which one *knew* what one was doing.

CHAPTER SIX

Religion and the Divine

THOMAS KSELMAN

At the turn of the nineteenth century, defenders of Christianity had every reason to feel embattled as they looked back over the last fifty years. The campaign of dechristianization at the height of the French Revolution in 1793–1794 led to shuttered churches and assaults on the clergy, a political manifestation of the rationalist critique of Christianity that became an important stream of the Enlightenment in the second half of the eighteenth century. Although most of the *philosophes* remained deists, convinced still of the existence of God, critics such as Voltaire ridiculed the dogmas and practices of traditional Christianity, and others, such as Holbach and Diderot, openly defended atheism. The intellectual and political attacks on Christianity from the late eighteenth century stand in the background of all the efforts by nineteenth-century thinkers to reimagine the divine and to consider anew the nature of God, the significance of religion and religious institutions for society, and the appropriate relationship between man and God.

Two works established a new basis for the understanding of religion that resonated throughout the nineteenth century, and, for that matter, to the present day: Friedrich Schleiermacher's *On Religion: Speeches to its Cultured Despisers* (1799) and François-René de Chateaubriand's *Genius of Christianity* (1802). These were crucial first of all for setting the agenda for those who sought to defend religion, and especially Christianity, against the rationalism associated with the Enlightenment. In a paradoxical turn, they contributed as well to a modern critique of religion that affirmed its value and its experiential reality, but also undermined its supernatural claims and the ecclesiastical structures that supported them. After considering the arguments of Schleiermacher and Chateaubriand, this essay will take up this critical perspective as represented in the work of Ludwig Feuerbach, David Strauss, and Ernest Renan. Looking especially at Feuerbach's *Essence of Christianity* and Strauss's and Renan's studies of the life of Jesus will allow us to see how ideas about religion and the divine were transformed by philosophical critique and historical methods, by hermeneutics and historicization. This school of thought is generally responsible for the judgment that the nineteenth century was an age of the "secularization of the European mind," a position that scholars now regard with some skepticism, without being able fully to discount it.

Revisionists and critics were challenged in turn by powerful voices defending orthodox beliefs, whose persuasive force was based not only on their deep faith but also on their sensitivity to the problems posed by modern reformers and doubters. The life and work of John Henry Newman, an Anglican priest who converted to Catholicism in 1845, reveals the sustained power of Catholic orthodoxy, but also of evangelical Christianity and of the new paths followed by both of these traditions. The Danish thinker Søren Kierkegaard offers a final example of the resilience of Christian orthodoxy in his challenge to readers to abandon their tawdry absorption in material affairs, tepid religiosity, and shallow rationalism in favor of a faith that seems absurd.

The rethinking of religion in the nineteenth century involved amending, criticizing, and defending ideas inherited from the past, in particular those associated with the Christian tradition. It is important to note that Jewish thought followed a broadly similar pattern. Religious leaders such as the German rabbi Abraham Geiger established a reform movement that sought to preserve a connection with Jewish tradition interpreted with the tools offered by modern philosophy and philology. Orthodox rabbis vigorously opposed him, producing a division in Jewish religious life that endures to the present.[1] Beyond the struggles within traditional faiths, however, by the end of the century a number of alternative religions emerged in response to the shifting conditions in European culture. These innovations marked a break with the past, for they either marginalized or rejected the Christian tradition within which reformers and critics chose to work. The range of alternative religions was broad, and grouping them in a single category is a matter of convenience that should not hide the spiritual diversity they represent. Nationalism and spiritualism were especially important examples of the religious experimentation that was a principal characteristic of nineteenth-century European culture. Friedrich Nietzsche's late-century assertion that "God is dead" and his critique of the Judeo-Christian moral code resonated throughout the twentieth century. The emergence of these alternatives illuminates a shift in the conceptualization of religion, an expanding category that extended far beyond the traditional religions of Europe. Through the disciplines of comparative religion and the sociology of religion, European culture acquired a novel perspective that allowed the sacred to be regarded with sympathy and respect, even while it was examined critically in its complex relationship with political and social forces.

SCHLEIERMACHER AND CHATEAUBRIAND: RELIGION DEFENDED, RENEWED, AND REDEFINED

Friedrich Schleiermacher, as the son of a chaplain in the Prussian army, had direct experience of the challenges facing Christianity at the turn of the nineteenth century. After a period of doubt in the 1780s that left him estranged for a time from his father, Schleiermacher recovered his faith and became an ordained minister and a professor of theology at the Universities of Halle and Berlin. Chateaubriand also looked back on experiences as a young man that shaped his ideas on religion and its relationship with society. A French aristocrat, he briefly sided with the Revolution before joining the counter-revolution in defense of the Bourbon monarchy. He was wounded fighting against the revolutionary armies, lived for years as an impoverished exile in London, and then returned to France to have a distinguished though controversial career as a politician, diplomat, and writer. Although Schleiermacher and Chateaubriand lived very different lives, both were deeply troubled by the spiritual and social disorder of the revolutionary era, and both saw the need to re-establish faith in Christianity in terms that would respond to the challenges of the Enlightenment.

Schleiermacher's essays of 1799, entitled *On Religion: Speeches to its Cultured Despisers*, emerged from the circle of writers in Berlin led by Friedrich Schlegel, a key figure in

German Romanticism. The two, who lived together for a time, shared a belief in emotion as the central element in human experience, expressed in art, literature, philosophy, and religion. They were convinced of the necessity of reinfusing life and thought with feeling as the only way to make whole again the broken world produced by the revolutionary decade of the 1790s. Schleiermacher's essays provoked a major response when they were first published and form the basis for his reputation as the "most influential and revered Protestant theologian since the Reformation" and "father of modern theology."[2] Addressing the cultivated elite, Schleiermacher castigated them for despising religion, for "making your earthly lives so rich and many-sided that you no longer need the eternal."[3] Schleiermacher had a broader target in mind as well, for he also shared with his presumed audience of religious sceptics a rejection of the "crude superstitions of our people" and the "poorly stitched together fragments of metaphysics and morals that are called rational Christianity."[4] Both of these groups were profoundly mistaken in their understanding of religion, he insisted, which they confused with simple appeals for supernatural help or with metaphysical truths and moral codes. In his second essay, "On the Essence of Religion," Schleiermacher goes so far as to deny that immortality and even the concept of God are necessarily related to religion. "For me divinity can be nothing other than a particular type of religious intuition ... In religion, therefore, the idea of God does not rank as high as you think."[5] In the place of folk religion, metaphysics, and morals, Schleiermacher offered a definition of religion rooted in the human experience of an infinite which escaped any easy characterization. "Religion's essence is neither thinking nor acting, but intuition and feeling. It wishes to intuit the universe, wishes devoutly to overhear the universe's own manifestations and actions, longs to be grasped and filled by the universe's immediate influences in childlike passivity."[6]

From such a passage it is easy to see why Schleiermacher was accused by critics of a mystical pantheism that could not be reconciled with Christian belief and practice. Karl Barth, the most prominent theologian in the neo-orthodox movement of the twentieth century, described Schleiermacher as concerned with "pious self-awareness" for whom "proclaiming God means proclaiming one's own piety."[7] Schleiermacher nonetheless worked as a Christian theologian and preacher and spent his mature years in Berlin insisting on a special place for Christianity in the hierarchy of religions, seeing Christ as the fullest expression of God-consciousness and a model for how the finite and the infinite should stand in relationship to one another.

As with so many other thinkers of the Romantic era, echoes of Rousseau's Savoyard Vicar can be heard in Schleiermacher, who also acknowledged the influence of the "theology of the heart" developed within the Moravian Brethren, the tradition in which he was raised. For Jaroslav Pelikan, Schleiermacher's "affectional transposition of doctrine" stands as the culmination of this older tradition, but also as a transitional moment, looking ahead to a century in which religion could be understood first of all and, for many thinkers, exclusively as a psychological and social experience without any necessary reference to the supernatural.[8] Schleiermacher's turn to the feeling self as the starting point for religion ultimately allowed for a more sympathetic appreciation of other religious traditions. In *On Religion*, he called on his readers to "seek out an infinite number of finite and specific forms in which religion reveals itself" and to "abandon [their] vain and futile wish that there might be only one religion."[9] The emergence of the comparative and scientific study of religions in the nineteenth century has many origins, but it owes a great deal nonetheless to the assertion of the value of non-Christian traditions by the leading Protestant theologian of the early nineteenth century.

Identifying religion as an emotional state also contributed to a broader sense of what might constitute religion in the first place. The strong feelings evoked by art and literature, acknowledged by Schleiermacher as in some ways analogous to religion, could be used to identify aesthetic experience as sacred. Throughout the nineteenth century, many artists and writers came to see themselves as priests and prophets of a new religion centered on a divinized self. More ominously, feelings of dependence and self-transcendence, when associated with political movements and the emerging nation-states of the nineteenth century, sacralized these institutions, creating new forms of religiosity that could both link with and compete against established religions. We will explore these alternatives briefly at the conclusion of this chapter, but here it is worth emphasizing that Schleiermacher, even as he probed the meaning of religion, remained a Christian theologian and condemned alliances between churches and states as destined necessarily to produce corrupt religious experiences, oriented toward the finite, rather than connecting the finite and the infinite.

As a theologian and a preacher, Schleiermacher spent his life pondering, speaking, and writing about the nature of religion and religious experience. Chateaubriand used the success of *The Genius of Christianity* to launch himself on a career in politics and diplomacy. The work itself explicitly evokes the political context of France and Europe, which remains only a shadowy background in *On Religion*. For Chateaubriand, religion is beautiful, but it is also a social necessity, ideas that are inextricably linked in *The Genius of Christianity*. As in other nineteenth-century works, the relationship between religion and society is central to the book. Chateaubriand concludes his work with thirteen chapters devoted to the "services rendered to society by the clergy and the Christian religion." These include hospitals, schools, commercial fairs, agricultural innovations, science, the rule of law, and representative assemblies, a list corresponding to institutions that he believed define European civilization. From Chateaubriand's perspective, these services deserved gratitude and the continued support of governments. From the perspective of social theorists and anticlerical critics in the century that followed *The Genius of Christianity*, such connections between religion and social institutions warranted critical investigation and, for many, the limitation or elimination of clerical and Christian influence. Chateaubriand's appreciative catalog of Christian services thus raised the issue of the role of religion in public life and of the relations between church and state more generally, problems that would remain central to intellectual and political life through the nineteenth century and down to today.

Popular devotions were singled out by Chateaubriand for particular attention as socially beneficial beliefs, even if they appeared ridiculous from a rational perspective. The visits of pilgrims to healing shrines, the belief in omens of death and requests of prayers from the souls in Purgatory: these and other manifestations of popular belief formed a basis not only for religion but also for morality. Chateaubriand warned rationalist critics of popular practices to avoid "declaiming against superstition, for in doing so you open the door to all the crimes."[10] The passage suggests a pragmatic interpretation of religion as a mechanism of social control, but this was not all Chateaubriand had to say about popular devotions, which he praised as well for their poetic beauty and ability to establish harmony between nature and humanity. Chateaubriand imagined, for example, a fictive shrine to "Our Lady of the Woods," at which mothers would pray to lessen the pains of childbirth and young women would look for the faces and voices of lost lovers. In his treatment of popular devotions, Chateaubriand struck an ambivalent pose toward beliefs that he presented as beautiful and useful, while stopping far short of denying their supernatural efficacy. We will see this tension between the aesthetic/moral values of religion and the truth claims that underlie them build in subsequent religious thought toward sharper and in some cases hostile distinctions that Chateaubriand covered over but did not resolve.

In addition to the sublimity of nature and the charm of popular devotion, Chateaubriand embraced the Christian art and architecture of the Middle Ages, becoming a key figure in the Gothic revival that began in the late eighteenth century and continued through most of the nineteenth. For Chateaubriand, as with the German Romantics who gathered around the brothers Augustus and Friedrich von Schlegel in Jena and the followers of the architect Augustus Pugin in England, Gothic art embodied an era of universal faith and offered models for capturing and recreating a sense of spiritual depth that had been lost in the enthusiasm for the classical standards identified with the Renaissance and the Enlightenment. In his paean to Gothic cathedrals, Chateaubriand brought together the different elements of his religious sensibility, comparing them to forests, "the first temples of Divinity," and similarly evoking "a feeling of awe, of mystery." This linkage of sublime nature and medieval Christianity achieved a visual representation in the art of Caspar David Friedrich, as in *Abbey in an Oak Grove* (1810).

Friedrich, along with artists such as Karl Friedrich Schinkel and François Granet, often represented Gothic ruins, suggesting the erosion of Christianity as well as a longing for a period of lost faith.[11] Chateaubriand expressed this sense of loss as well, when he praised "those venerable cathedrals, overgrown with moss, full of generations of the dead and the ashes of their forefathers." This experience of Christian ruins set in nature as providing access to the divine was a common theme for Romantic writers across Europe as well. In *Lines Composed a Few Miles Above Tintern Abbey*, William Wordsworth looks down on the ruins of the medieval monastery, set against the River Wye. Wordsworth experienced "a sense sublime / ... A motion and a spirit, that impels / All thinking things, all objects

FIGURE 6.1 Caspar David Friedrich, *Abbey in an Oak Grove*, 1809–1810. © DEA Picture Library / Getty Images.

of all thought, / And rolls through all things."[12] Eugène Viollet-le-Duc, the architect who restored the cathedral of Notre Dame between 1844 and 1864, described cathedrals as "great coffins in the midst of our populous cities," but he similarly acknowledged as well that on days of great public celebration "they regain their voice."[13] In the Romantic recovery of religion, Christian beliefs, rituals, and monuments were regarded with awe for their beauty and with respect for their power to create social cohesion; but they also evoked a melancholy sense of the divine as buried in a past that could be idealized and remembered, yet not fully recovered.

FEUERBACH, STRAUSS, AND RENAN: THE CRITIQUE OF CHRISTIANITY

Defenders of religion in the first part of the nineteenth century began their analysis with the human experience of the divine, and, from this starting point, worked back to a belief in God and an affirmation of Christianity. In the generation that followed, a number of intellectuals centered in Germany rejected this move and claimed instead that human experience of the divine circled back on itself, never gaining access to a transcendent realm. Ludwig Feuerbach was a central figure of this group. His *Essence of Christianity* (1841) offered a critical response to his teachers at the University of Berlin, Schleiermacher and G. W. F. Hegel. Feuerbach's critique of religion was then taken up and amended by Karl Marx and from him passed into the socialist and communist movements that emerged later in the century.

The great creative act for Feuerbach was not God making man, as presented in Genesis and affirmed in Christian dogma, but man creating God, projecting onto him the attributes that define humanity's deepest values. Feuerbach developed his ideas within the intensely serious philosophical and religious climate of German universities in the first third of the nineteenth century. At the University of Berlin, Hegel challenged the claims of his colleague Schleiermacher in a series of lectures in the 1820s on the philosophy of religion. Like Schleiermacher, who held a chair in Theology, Hegel sought a new basis for understanding religion, but instead of the feeling self, he turned to speculative reason in order to provide "a conceptual understanding of the religious faith that the members of his audience already possessed."[14] For Hegel and some of his followers, this meant not replacing religion but demonstrating its truth in the complementary but higher domain of philosophy; from this perspective, Hegelian philosophy and orthodox religion shared the same content but took different forms. For Feuerbach and other young Hegelians, the application of reason led to a more complicated result that affirmed religious values, but only after they had been properly interpreted as human projections with no relation to a transcendent reality. This philosophical approach to religious truths led ultimately to a rejection of orthodox Christianity on the part of Feuerbach.

Feuerbach developed his ideas in a series of works in the 1830s, culminating in *The Essence of Christianity*, where he presented with great rhetorical force a paradoxical argument that affirmed religious values while rejecting Christian orthodoxy. Feuerbach saw his task as constructive as well as destructive. In the first section of his *Essence*, he dealt with "religion in its *essence*, its *truth*," establishing the positive values in Christianity and other religious expressions; in the second, he studied "its *contradictions*," exploring how religion, when it denies its origins in human nature, produces an alienated subject unable to recognize himself in the divine predicates that are attributed only to God.

Openly acknowledging his atheism, which cost him the chance for a university position, Feuerbach insisted nonetheless that atheism "is the secret of religion itself; that religion itself ... in its heart, in its essence, believes in nothing else than the truth and divinity of human nature." Feuerbach was engaged in translating theology into anthropology, but he also insisted that his argument worked in the opposite direction, exalting anthropology into theology. "Christianity, while lowering God into man, made man into God."[15]

In his positive appropriation of religious truths in his first section of *Essence*, Feuerbach pursued subjects familiar to theologians: the Trinity, the Incarnation, the Virgin Mary, Providence, redemption. In each case, he interpreted orthodox doctrine to expose the this-worldly and human meaning of supernatural claims. The passion of Christ, for example, does not represent the sacrifice of God's son for the redemption of humankind, but affirms the value of loving self-sacrifice. "God suffers—suffering is the predicate—but for men, for others, not for himself. What does this mean in plain speech? Nothing else than this: to suffer for others is divine; he who suffers for others ... is a God to men."[16] Orthodox believers might follow Feuerbach part of the way in his analysis, in which Christ's sacrifice is a model for Christians to follow, but many objected to his claims that reduce divinity to its human dimension, and to his hostility toward institutionalized religion that accompanies his praise for religious values.

Feuerbach's writing reveals that religious beliefs, and Christian doctrine in particular, were liable to positive interpretations when subjected to a particular hermeneutic approach that combined Hegel's philosophical critique with an ontological materialism. But the approach also led to a set of negative judgments, for the projection of positive values onto God left man debased and devalued. "God is not what man is—man is not what God is. God is the infinite, man the finite being; God is perfect, man imperfect; God eternal, man temporal; God almighty, man weak; God holy, man sinful," Feuerbach wrote.[17]

Feuerbach's position, condemned by the religious establishment, was famously taken up by Karl Marx, most conspicuously in his 1844 critique of Hegel's earlier *Philosophy of Right*. Here Marx restated with perfect clarity Feuerbach's essential argument that "religion is the self-consciousness and self-feeling of man who has either not yet found himself or has already lost himself again ... Religion is the sigh of the oppressed creature, the heart of a heartless world, just as it is the spirit of a spiritless situation. It is the *opium* of the people."[18] Marx, however, went beyond Feuerbach, criticizing him for failing to abandon fully a Hegelian framework in which the self-conscious realization of the true character of religion was in and of itself the goal. For Marx, on the contrary, the critique of religion was a first step, crucial but insufficient, in overcoming human alienation. That goal also required the destruction of the material conditions and social structure that supported political and religious institutions. Through Marx, Feuerbach's critique of religion and a policy of open hostility toward religious institutions exerted a powerful influence on the socialist and communist movements of the late nineteenth and twentieth centuries.

THE QUEST FOR THE HISTORICAL JESUS

Karl Barth's remark that, for Schleiermacher, "the historical element in religion ... the Lord Jesus, is a problem child" could be extended to religious thought in general during the nineteenth century, when the quest for the historical Jesus was taken up with the tools of philology that had formerly been applied to classical texts.[19] This quest had roots dating back to the Enlightenment and before, but it gained new energy and influence in the work of David Strauss, another participant in the circle of German philosophers and theologians that included Feuerbach. Feuerbach, however, was concerned with Christian dogma and theology and showed little interest in the historical Jesus. Strauss, by contrast, recognized that theologians and especially pastors needed to resolve questions about Jesus as a historical figure that were left open in Hegel's system. Does the life of Jesus, his preaching, his miracles, his death, and resurrection, belong to the essential content of Christianity, or are they representations, forms through which philosophical truths are expressed but upon which they do not necessarily rely? Without explaining how they viewed the person of Jesus, Strauss believed, theologians and philosophers were avoiding a central issue in their reconstruction of religious thought and failing to provide the guidance ministers needed in their preaching and teaching.

Strauss's publication of *The Life of Jesus* (1835–1836) came to a clear conclusion, though one that was challenged by orthodox opponents. His work rejected unequivocally the two most important models of Jesus inherited from previous scholarship: orthodox views that accepted the supernatural claims of the Gospel narratives *and* rationalist interpretations that labored to identify natural causes for their miraculous elements. For Strauss, any miracle was dismissed immediately, for in the modern world as he viewed it, "the belief in a supernatural manifestation, an immediate divine agency, is at once attributed to ignorance or imposture."[20] Strauss accompanied this rejection of the miraculous with a historical interpretation that saw the Gospel narrative as infused with mythic elements derived from the Jewish culture of the first century. Working within the Hegelian tradition, Strauss sought to preserve the essential truth of Christianity and insisted that "the essence of the Christian faith is perfectly independent of this criticism."[21] But Strauss struggled to specify the content of this new form of Christianity, "to re-establish dogmatically that which has been destroyed critically."[22] In general terms, Christianity affirms that "heaven and earth are reconciled ... The servile relation of man to God, as it existed under the law, has ceased; love has taken the place of the fear of the punishment threatened by the law."[23] Reconciliation and love thus become the central message of the Gospels, derived through historical criticism that distinguishes these universal values from the mythic shell of first-century Judaism. Strauss's approach to sacred scripture represents the larger movement to create what Jonathan Sheehan has referred to as "the Cultural Bible," a book that could be said to embody the values of Western civilization, but was not a historically accurate record of the life, miracles, and redemptive suffering of Jesus.

German philosophy and biblical criticism by the likes of Feuerbach and Strauss exerted enormous influence on European intellectual life in the first half of the nineteenth century. In England, readers could consult Strauss's *Life of Jesus* and Feuerbach's *Essence of Christianity* in translations by Mary Ann Evans, who wrote her novels as George Eliot. In France, Ernest Renan took up the quest for the historical Jesus, borrowing from but also amending the work of his German colleagues, in particular Strauss. Renan's *Life of Jesus* (1863) became one of the best-selling works in nineteenth-century Europe, making available to a broad audience a critique that denied the supernaturalist claims of orthodox Christianity. Renan's success was based on both style and substance. Strauss had approached the life of Jesus as a series of problems to be solved through a detailed and technical analysis of the sources; from his perspective the historical Jesus was hardly discernible at all, hidden as he was within the mythic constructions of messianic Judaism. For Renan, the Gospel accounts could be used in conjunction with other sources to construct an appealing narrative in which the historical Jesus appeared as a living being and not as a symbolic representation of Hegelian philosophy.[24]

Edouard Manet's painting of *Jesus Mocked by the Soldiers*, presented at the Paris Salon in 1865 and now at the Chicago Art Institute, offers a visual representation of the humanized Christ made fashionable by Renan. Portrayed in the fashionable realist style of the middle years of the nineteenth century, Christ is a tortured and vulnerable human, modeled on a local artisan. Contemporary critics saw the work as a denial of the divine status of Jesus, echoing the message of Renan's work. Manet's painting can be placed

FIGURE 6.2 Édouard Manet, *Jesus Mocked by the Soldiers*, 1865. © Corbis Historical / Fine Art / Getty Images.

within a larger story of "the progressive naturalization of religious art," an attempt to depict the life of Jesus and the Bible in general based on historical research and eschewing any overt references to the supernatural, a style that managed eventually to win even the support of believing Catholics as appropriate for the nineteenth century.[25]

Renan accepted without reservation the need to "banish miracle from history," one of the fundamental intentions of Strauss, but he refused to banish Jesus from the historical past. For Renan, Jesus was not a figure shrouded in myth, but a man of the first century who achieved "the highest summit of human greatness" and became "an inexhaustible principle of moral regeneration for humanity."[26] Renan dealt with the miracles and other evidence of supernatural power attributed to Jesus as legendary additions to texts that nonetheless tell the story of a historic figure whose life and teachings marked a revolutionary moment in world history. Renan was forthright in acknowledging Jesus as preaching an ascetic ideal in the expectation of the imminent coming of the Kingdom of God. Unlike the "Christ of the Barricades" described by socialists interested in recruiting him to their political cause, Renan's Jesus was apolitical, even as he saw himself as a messiah who would usher in a Kingdom based on a morality that was, in Robert Priest's words, "anti-dogmatic, anti-hierarchical, individualistic, idealistic and libertarian."[27] Renan's interpretation of Jesus' teachings in this vein reflects this French scholar's commitment to a version of universal values that were nonetheless deeply entangled with the culture of nineteenth-century Europe. Jesus taught "a pure religion, without forms, without temple and without priest," a historical judgment on Renan's part, but also a criticism of the institutional churches and clergy of his own era.[28] Renan's Jesus also reflects nineteenth-century assumptions about gender: he is a sweet and gentle preacher who appealed first of all to women and children.

What is more, Renan's sense of the revolutionary nature of Christianity borrowed from ideas about racial difference and historical progress that his work both affirmed and expanded. Christianity marked a sharp break from the dominant form of Judaism as it had long existed in ancient Jerusalem, "a city of pedantry, acrimony, disputes, hatreds and littleness of mind," as Renan put it.[29] Jesus was a native of Galilee, a province known for its verdant landscape, ethnic diversity and a peaceful and joyous population, a context that helps explain Jesus's estrangement from the religion of Jerusalem, dominated by the Pharisees. Renan's thoughts on race were complex and do not fit into the strict biological framework that emerged later in the nineteenth century. The Galilean Jesus Renan described has an ambiguous racial status. Despite his origins, Renan asserted, "Jesus was no longer a Jew ... He proclaimed the rights of man, not the rights of the Jew, the religion of man, not the religion of the Jew, the deliverance of man, not the deliverance of the Jew."[30] This language evokes a theme common in the anti-Semitism of the nineteenth century: that Jews are narrowly tribal and concerned exclusively with themselves. Renan balanced this assessment with a clear affirmation of the Jewish contribution to world history, describing them as the originators of monotheism. Renan's confused efforts to criticize but also embrace Jewish tradition and to infuse a racial dimension into his religious reflections reflect a general pattern for Christian religious thinkers. Renan ultimately shared the view of orthodox Christians in his assessment that Christ preached a universal message of love that transcended the legalistic ethic of Judaism and thereby changed the world.

Renan and Strauss, along with other writers who applied a critical approach to scripture, saw their work as an effort to rescue the historical Jesus from an orthodox interpretation whose supernatural claims threatened the moral message of the

Gospel. Their judgments incorporated the pervasive sense of progress over time that characterized historical thinking in the nineteenth century, epitomized in the work of the French philosopher Auguste Comte. For Comte, humankind had moved from a religious to a philosophical and, finally, scientific or positive understanding of the natural and social world. From such a perspective, a belief in supernatural explanations would necessarily and correctly be replaced over time by metaphysical abstractions and by truths established through scientific empiricism. The evolutionary theory of Charles Darwin, presented in *Origin of Species* (1859) and defended by Thomas Huxley in a famous debate held at Oxford in 1860, is certainly the best-known example of how scientific explanations were understood to supersede religious myth; the creation story of Genesis was gradually replaced by the slow working of natural selection. In a broad sense, Hegel, Feuerbach, Strauss, and Renan all accepted a progressive view of history in which traditional Christianity would give way to a new form of religion based on philosophical and historical critique.

THE DEFENCE OF ORTHODOXY

In October 1845, the same month Ernest Renan walked out of the seminary of Saint-Sulpice, leaving behind Catholicism and its claims about the divinity of Jesus, the Anglican priest John Henry Newman was received into the Catholic Church. Newman was the most prominent of many English converts from within the Oxford movement, which in the 1830s and 1840s sought to reform the Anglican Church by affirming its ties to Catholicism and rejecting doctrines associated with the Protestant Reformation. Newman's journey was movingly recalled in his autobiographical masterpiece, the *Apologia Pro Vita Sua* (1864), a work that illuminates both the powerful appeal of orthodox doctrine and the ways in which it was reformulated in response to the challenges posed by critics and unbelievers.

As a young man, Newman was drawn to an evangelical form of Protestant Christianity, a set of beliefs that, "through God's mercy, have never been effaced or obscured."[31] Evangelicals, like Catholics, affirmed the Trinity, with God the Father, Son, and Holy Spirit as co-equal participants in a single godhead; the redemptive value of Christ's suffering for a mankind corrupted by sin; the eternal reward in heaven of those saved by their Christian faith; and the eternal punishment in hell of those who rejected Christ. Newman's autobiography looks back to his youth for common ground between Protestantism and Catholicism and describes a growing conviction that Roman Catholicism alone is faithful to the doctrines of the early Church. Newman embraced the Catholic view of the sacraments and thus affirmed the Real Presence of Christ in the Eucharist. He accepted the authority of the Church in defining and teaching doctrine and opposed the Protestant reliance on individual judgment in reading biblical texts. But Newman did more than reaffirm such confessional differences. Through his theory of the development of doctrine, worked out over the two years preceding his final conversion, Newman proposed to explain how changes in Church teaching could occur without violating the principle of continuity with the early Church. With the help of divine guidance, Newman argued, doctrines that were implicit or veiled in early Christianity gradually emerge and at a certain moment in history achieve a clear and definitive formulation.

This was true, for example, of the doctrine of the Immaculate Conception of Mary, proclaimed by Pius IX in 1854. For Newman, "the idea of the Blessed Virgin was as it were *magnified* in the Church of Rome, as time went on,—but so were all the Christian ideas, as that of the Blessed Eucharist. The whole scene of pale, faint, distant Apostolic Christianity is seen in Rome, as through a telescope or magnifier."[32] Newman accepted as well, though he thought it inopportune, the other major doctrinal innovation of the Catholic Church in the nineteenth century: the declaration of papal infallibility at the First Vatican Council in 1870. This doctrine, along with that of the Immaculate Conception, were centerpieces of the ultramontane movement, which advocated religious authority within the Catholic Church being increasingly concentrated in Rome. These doctrines were also supported by popular devotions to Mary and the Pope, which mobilized Catholics throughout Europe, especially after the occupation of Rome by the Italian state in 1870. The long reign of Pope Pius IX (1846–1878), and his vigorous critique of liberal doctrines, including freedom of the press and the separation of church and state, made him a powerful symbol for the distinctive quality of Catholicism and a lightning rod for attacks by both Protestants and secularists. Although papal infallibility was limited to matters of faith and morals, it was viewed by republicans in France and Protestants in Germany and Britain as compromising the attachments of Catholics to established states. The result was a *Kulturkampf*, a culture war, that produced discriminatory, anti-Catholic legislation in France and Germany and everywhere hardened the borders between Protestant and Catholic.

FIGURE 6.3 *Punch* cartoon—John Tenniel, "The Pope's Mad Bull", January 7, 1865. © Hulton Archive / Getty Images.

In his early attachment to evangelical Christianity, Newman was part of a powerful movement of religious revival with roots in the Reformation of the sixteenth century, but also in the more recent awakening of Christian "enthusiasm." In Britain and the United States, the Methodist movement founded by John Wesley continued to inspire conversions in outdoor services that featured emotional preaching and communal singing. Its influence reached the ruling elite in Britain, as evident in the career of William Wilberforce. Following his conversion in the 1780s, Wilberforce played a leading role as a member of Parliament in the successful campaigns to abolish the slave trade (1807) and slavery in the British Empire (1833). Wilberforce, like Schleiermacher and Chateaubriand, lamented the current state of Christianity, expressed in his *Practical View of the Prevailing Religious System* (1797), and he shared their sense that emotion rather than reason must play a central role in any authentic religion. But Wilberforce insisted as well on the importance of orthodox doctrine, on the historical accuracy and doctrinal authority of scripture, the fallen nature of man, and the redemptive power of Christ's death.

Evangelical Christians in both Britain and on the Continent expressed their activist commitment in creating missionary societies that spread Christianity both inside and outside of Europe and in organizing educational and charitable works designed to counter the impact of industrialization. The Salvation Army, for example, founded by the Methodists William and Catherine Booth in a working-class district of London in 1865, reached out to the poor with material assistance with the intent of converting them to evangelical Christianity. Roman Catholics were also active in reform movements, creating a "social Catholicism" that culminated in the encyclical of Pope Leo XIII, *Rerum Novarum* (1891), which defended the rights of labor and criticized the unrestricted operation of capitalism. Through these initiatives, orthodox Christians, both Catholic

FIGURE 6.4 Salvation Army Christmas Feast for Boys in Berlin, 1913. © Paul Thompson / FPG / Stringer / Getty Images.

and Protestant, sought to establish the continuing vitality and relevance of their beliefs in the midst of the dramatic social changes that, along with the intellectual objections of reformers and doubters, posed formidable challenges in the nineteenth century to inherited religious traditions.

Søren Kierkegaard fits uneasily into the category of orthodox religious thinkers, given the idiosyncratic nature of his work. Kierkegaard frequently employed pseudonyms and parables in his writings and held as a principle the impossibility of expressing Christianity in any systematic fashion. Raised in an austere and pious atmosphere by a guilt-ridden father, he spent his adult life exploring religious and philosophical ideas in works that had limited impact in his own time but would exert enormous influence in the twentieth century. Kierkegaard shared with other Protestant defenders of orthodoxy both a rejection of the attempt by Hegelians to produce a rationalist explanation of Christianity and an insistence on the primacy of a deep and personal faith relationship to God. He criticized the current state of Christianity as tepid and inauthentic with a strikingly original religious vocabulary that included concepts of the absurd and of despair, both employed in a powerful analysis of the modern spiritual condition.

Kierkegaard's understanding of faith as a tortured and profoundly difficult personal choice was best made clear in *Fear and Trembling* (1843), an extended reflection on the story of Abraham and Isaac. When God commands him to sacrifice his son, Abraham, faced with an absurd choice between conventional ethics and religious obligation, experiences dread: "he believed that God would not require Isaac of him, whereas he was willing nevertheless to sacrifice him if it was required. He believed by virtue of the absurd; for there could be no question of human calculation, and it was indeed the absurd that God who required it of him should the next instant recall the requirement."[33] In the twentieth century, the theologian Karl Barth and the existentialists Martin Heidegger and Jean-Paul Sartre found inspiration in Kierkegaard's analysis of the human condition, which seemed appropriate for a Europe shocked by the moral, religious, and political catastrophe of the First World War.

ALTERNATIVE RELIGIONS

In the nineteenth century, "the sphere of the religious," as Maurice Mandelbaum has written, "was enlarged beyond any confines of orthodoxy and in fact merged not only with philosophy but with all awareness of whatever was taken to be true or beautiful or good."[34] Conceived in such an expansive manner, the divine might appear to be everywhere, a possibility that led orthodox thinkers to identify pantheism as one of the major threats to Christianity in the nineteenth century.[35] But the divine was also embodied in more particular heterodoxies, marking the nineteenth century as a period of religious diversity and experimentation.

At the height of the Terror in France, the revolutionary leaders of the First Republic, even as they assaulted the Catholic Church, introduced a new religion in which the Supreme Being and the State were glorified together. This linkage of political and religious identity resonated in numerous ways throughout a century in which Europe was increasingly organized into a system of nation-states. In many cases, imagining the state in religious terms involved associating it with a folk culture based on popular practices and national languages—with a *Volk*, to use a term associated with Johann Gottfried Herder. Herder was primarily concerned with affirming the value of national cultures without advocating that they take a particular political form. This was not the case of Giuseppe Mazzini, the Italian writer and political activist who became the leading proponent of nationalism in the nineteenth century. In laying out *The Duties of Man* (1844), his most extensive statement of his beliefs, Mazzini began with God as the first object of human loyalty and the source of the moral conscience that compels us to act for the good of humanity. But in a crucial move Mazzini insisted that the nation was the providentially chosen means to fulfil God's commands: "Be your country your Temple. God at the summit; a people of equals at the base."[36]

Mazzini's democratic impulse was not always present in the different manifestations of the religion of nationalism as it developed; but the sense of the nation as imposing a sacred obligation on its people was an increasingly assumed dimension of European culture in the nineteenth century. Furthermore, the nation was sacralized in language, as with Mazzini, but also in state-sponsored liturgies, in art, and in music. The monumental "Altar to the Fatherland" raised in the center of Rome to honor Victor Emmanuel II (1820–1878), the first king of a united Italy, made no reference to Christianity and used only classical motifs to celebrate the Italian nation. Richard Wagner's operas constitute a significant example of how art might generate a new mythology sanctifying the nation based on folk traditions. In Wagner's case, moreover, the nation became an exclusive racial group, threatened by the quest for selfish material gratification that he identified in particular with Jews. And Christian churches, both Catholic and Protestant, collaborated in the sacralization of the nation, evident in the support that they offered for the nations of Europe as they entered into the murderous catastrophe of the First World War.

FIGURE 6.5 Altare della Patria, designed by Giuseppe Sacconi in honor of Victor Emmanuel II in 1885, inaugurated in 1911. © De Agostine / Getty Images.

Europeans might find the sacred in the grand, imagined space of the nation, but they discovered it as well in more intimate settings. In the 1850s, European newspapers were filled with descriptions of "talking tables," as small circles of men and women felt themselves in communication with the dead, channeled through mediums. Spiritualism was a diverse and amorphous movement, though it achieved some level of systematization in the best-selling works of the French writer Hippolyte Rivail, who took the name of Alan Kardec. According to Kardec, spirits communicated to their earthly contacts a vision of individual progress through reincarnation, an indication of how Spiritism responded to the increasing knowledge of Eastern religions in Europe. Kardec insisted as well, as did other Spiritists, that their doctrines could be verified using scientific techniques such as photography, a claim that was able to gain some support within the scientific community and in particular in the developing field of psychology. The Theosophical movement, founded in New York in 1875 by the Russian émigré Helen Blavatsky, offers another example of a religious innovation that moved away from traditional Christianity and claimed to accommodate both Eastern religions and modern science. Theosophists accepted evolution, but attributed the origin of the universe to a deity "who infused each particle of matter with a spark of the divine," a principle they claimed to take from the religions of India.[37] The works of Kardec and Blavatsky do not show up in any of the standard contemporary anthologies of religious thought, and their ideas about the divine might now be dismissed as shallow and syncretistic oddities, occultist fantasies created by leaders whose lives carry an odor of charlatanism. But they nonetheless reflect the range of religious options that had emerged by the turn of the twentieth century, and the search for contact with the divine outside the framework of established traditions foreshadows the New Age religious movements of the twentieth century.

RELIGION AND SOCIETY REIMAGINED: NIETZSCHE AND DURKHEIM

Friedrich Nietzsche and Émile Durkheim offer a final pairing of thinkers from Germany and France whose ideas about religion allow us to see some continuities with themes established by their predecessors, but also the dramatic ways in which they broke with the past. Both men grew up in devout families and early in life were pointed towards ministerial careers. Nietzsche was the son of a Lutheran minister in Saxony, and Durkheim the son of a rabbi in Lorraine. Both achieved early success, followed by sharply divergent paths. Nietzsche abandoned a promising academic career in 1879 to become a peripatetic and struggling writer, living in boarding houses in Switzerland, France, and Italy before mental illness led him to his sister's home, where he died in 1900. Durkheim became one of the most distinguished professors in the French Third Republic, renowned for work that made him, along with Max Weber, a founding father of the discipline of sociology. Both Nietzsche and Durkheim probed the ways in which religion shaped the moral foundations of society, but they did so from sharply different perspectives that illuminate the depth and range of ideas about the sacred in the late nineteenth and early twentieth centuries.

Nietzsche's declaration that "God is dead" in 1882 stands as a landmark moment in the history of religious ideas, as does his corollary rejection of the Judeo-Christian ethical standard of charity, humility, and self-sacrifice, which he condemned as "slave morality."[38] Nietzsche's critique of what he observed to be the flaccid religious and moral atmosphere of contemporary Europe resonates with many of the religious thinkers who preceded him. But his diagnosis and prescription went far beyond what had previously been imagined. Feuerbach, for example, was an atheist and a materialist who nonetheless affirmed the principles he saw in Christianity. God did not exist, but his attributes represented human ideals to be embraced. Christ was not divine, but it was a human obligation to act in accordance with his teachings of charity and self-sacrifice. Nietzsche held in contempt the divine attributes and ethical standards that emerged from the Judeo-Christian tradition. Any reader of his most famous work, *Thus Spoke Zarathustra* (published 1883–1885), will sense immediately that Nietzsche saw himself as a religious teacher, speaking through a prophet who descended from the mountains to find disciples and teach them a new religious dispensation. He called on his readers to acknowledge their role in murdering God and to create a new religion of human self-affirmation, the religion of a "superman" that, like the paganism of ancient Greece and Rome, would embrace physical strength, courage, sensuality, and cruelty. In Nietzsche's view, this older and noble understanding of the good had been overthrown by the weak and resentful Jewish people, who had invented the concept of evil, attributed it to their oppressors and generated a new and degraded understanding of good as altruism that was then adopted by Christianity. Scholars have rightly pointed out that Nietzsche condemned unequivocally the vulgar anti-Semitism on display in Europe at the end of the nineteenth century. But Nietzsche's assault on the Judeo-Christian tradition, most clearly in *The Genealogy of Morals* (1887), warrants him a unique and significant position in the history of nineteenth-century religious ideas.

Durkheim shared with Nietzsche the assumption that religion was a human creation, but in his classic work *The Elementary Forms of Religious Life* (1912), he established a new basis for understanding the nature of religion and appreciating its moral and social significance. Drawing on ethnographic studies of the totemic cults of Australian and North American native people, Durkheim sought to identify the fundamental essence of religion, which he saw as "first and foremost a system of ideas by means of which individuals imagine the society of which they are members and the obscure yet intimate relations they have with it."[39] Critics have pointed out the deficiencies of the evidence he used and questioned a method in which he claimed that studying the supposedly "primitive religions" can yield universal truths about religion in general. But Durkheim's approach can be read as elevating our regard for the religions of native or non-Western peoples, whose beliefs and rituals deserve the same respect as those of modern European religions.[40]

And if Durkheim has been criticized for reducing religion to society, his *Elementary Forms* is more appropriately read as weaving back and forth between the two, showing their intimate connections and the creative force that religion plays not only in morality but also in the construction of the basic categories that humans use in thinking and acting in the world. Durkheim was a key figure in supporting the secularization carried out by the French Third Republic in the 1880s, a program that included creating a public school system that would teach a "secular morality" which "is not derived from revealed religion."[41] But in addressing the Union of Free Thinkers and Free Believers in 1914, Durkheim called on his audience to "confront religion in the same mental state as the believer." "There cannot be a rational interpretation of religion," he continued, "which is fundamentally irreligious; an irreligious interpretation of religion would be an interpretation which denied the phenomenon it was trying to explain."[42] There was, in other words, an obvious tension in Durkheim's approach to religion, which combined skepticism about particular truth claims with respect for the "religious nature of man" as a "fundamental and permanent aspect of humanity."[43] Moreover, Durkheim's appreciation of religion as an essential part of our humanity links him to his predecessors Schleiermacher and Chateaubriand, even as he abandoned their effort to see Christianity as the highest expression of this universal impulse. When placed alongside Nietzsche, however, he seems to move back into the inclusive religious framework constructed within European culture throughout the nineteenth century.

CHAPTER SEVEN

Language, Poetry, Rhetoric

PATRICK MCGUINNESS

> The decadents did not like reality, but they did know reality, and that is what distinguishes them from the romantics.
>
> —Osip Mandelstam

In the manuscript of T. S. Eliot's *The Waste Land*, one of fellow poet Ezra Pound's comments, written in the margin at the bottom of the first page of what became "A Game of Chess," reads: "Il cherchait des sentiments pour les accommoder a [*sic*] son vocabulaire":[1] *he was looking for feelings to fit them to his vocabulary.* It is not clear which lines Pound is highlighting, or who the *il* (he) refers to. Is it Eliot the poet, with some of the dud, congested lines that Pound edited with such stringency? Or does Pound mean the Prufrockian persona, rich in diction but poor in experience, already in danger of becoming Eliot's trademark voice? A third option is that it is both: that the poet and his creation have become one, and that irony, the device for setting you at one remove from what you mean, is also the perfect way of owning, without owning *up to*, what you meant.

The final possibility is a fusion of all of these: that Pound is alluding to the supposedly modern malady of sophistication, part of the late nineteenth-century inheritance of the symbolist and decadent writers he and Eliot had absorbed in their quest to *make it new*. The Eliot lines alongside Pound's comment are "My nerves are bad tonight. Yes, bad. Stay with me"—lines that survived, though in slightly altered form, from the original manuscript of "He Do the Police in Different Voices" into the final version of *The Waste Land*. For the 1922 reader, knowing their Laforgue and their Verlaine, their Mallarmé and their Corbière, the nerves had displaced the heart, the mind, and even the body as the motor of literary sensation. Having more language than one had feelings had become a feeling in itself, and it, too, needed the right language to express it.

PROGRESS AND ITS ILLUSIONS

Arthur Symons, so influential in bringing French symbolist and decadent writing to an English-speaking audience, described Jules Laforgue in *The Symbolist Movement in Literature* (1899) as "the sickly modern being with his clothes, his nerves: the mere fact that he flowers from the soil of his epoch."[2] Laforgue's art, argues Symons, is "what all art would tend towards if we followed our nerves to the end of their journeys." It is an arresting remark: we traditionally think of the heart's "journey," or the mind's "journey," as the narrative of an emotion or a thought. Hence we have novels or poems about the growth or decline of love, or about the processes of either disillusionment or education (sometimes the two are the same) seen in the *Bildungsroman* and its offshoots. This is because feelings and thoughts have narrative arcs, even if, as in Marcel Proust or Virginia Woolf, or Henri Bergson and William James, they do not have conventional beginnings, middles, and ends. We suppose emotions and thoughts to be linear, even if they are not straightforward.

But we rarely think of the nerves in narrative terms—on the contrary, we think of them as disruptors of our mental and emotional arcs. Compulsion, repetition, interruption, recapitulation—the frazzled circuitry of the modern self, located in the gray area between our brains and our bodies. To use the language of early radio, if thoughts and emotions are frequencies, nerves are the interference. But as the philosophers knew from the start, the gray area is us; it is where what we call ourselves takes place.

To feel out of step with one's epoch, one's milieu, and one's own self, Symons suggests, is a sign that one is, paradoxically, in step with all three. The genuine *Zeitgeist* is a club that only admits those who feel excluded by it. The language of nerves, neurosis, and hyper sensitivity was also part of the *Zeitgeist*. We could say that the nerves were to the late nineteenth century what the humors had been to the Renaissance: not just part of the language of medicine in general currency, as in the work of the French neurologist Jean-Martin Charcot and others, but a fund of metaphorical language for writers of all kinds—poets, novelists, historians, journalists, philosophers, and political theorists. This language crossed over into poetry (as in an 1883 collection entitled *Les Névroses*, or *Neuroses*, by Maurice Rollinat) and fiction, most famously in the work of Émile Zola, and also determined the way history and literary history, not to mention racial and national discourses, were envisaged: hence the idea of the "decline" of the West, the "degeneration" of races, or the "decadence" of culture.

In an article on the Goncourt brothers, published in book form in *Mes Haines* (*My Hates*) in 1866, the great French writer Zola diagnosed his period in the following manner:

> The body, as in the great days of mysticism, is singularly in decline among us. It is no longer the soul that we exalt, but the nerves, cerebral matter. The flesh is battered by the deep and repeated shocks that the brain imprints on the whole organism. We are ill, that is certain: ill from progress. The brain is hypertrophic, the nerves develop at the expense of the muscles, and these, sickly and enfeebled, no longer uphold the human machine. The balance between mind and matter is ruptured.

> We would do well to think about the poor body while we still have the time. The victory of nerves over blood has determined our customs [*moeurs*], our literature, our entire epoch.[3]

Zola reveals his characteristic mix of genuine scientific understanding and colorful analogy as he tries to define a new paradigm for modernity: progress is our sickness. The same Progress promised by Enlightenment values and by Romantic idealism had turned sour. And yet Zola writes this in the 1860s—hardly what we would think of as the "*fin de siècle*" or the "decadent" era. Besides, it is mostly writers and artists who believed in ideas such as decadence, decline, and degeneration, or at any rate attributed any moral or religious value to such terms, let alone any form of regulative agency.

Reading the literature of the period, it is important to remember that big, sprawling terms like *decadence* represent not so much worldviews, but *a* view of *a* world. In the "real world," nineteenth-century scientists are busy establishing the laws of thermodynamics or plotting the periodic table; physicians are inventing medicines; engineers are building trains, railway stations, and canals; and town planners are creating hygienic sewage systems and safer roads. Diseases are being eradicated, populations are being educated, and people (albeit only white men) are being given the vote. Infant mortality is decreasing, illnesses that were once a certain death sentence are being cured or managed, and literacy rates are rising. That hardly resembles decline or decadence, and, on the contrary, looks a lot like beneficial advance—even if the idea of "progress" is put into question by the way advances in medicine are used for biological warfare, advances in engineering feed the manufacture of weapons, and advances in transport and infrastructure benefit the deployment of colonial troops in one direction, and the extraction of natural resources from the colonies on the other. But the dissonance here—that "progress" can also come in the shape of negative and destructive advance—arises from the fact that we tend, wrongly, to attribute a form of *moral* value to technical and scientific developments.

The poet Charles Baudelaire, who was also a penetrating cultural critic, understood that while human beings stayed the same, the things human beings could do were constantly evolving and increasing in scope and sophistication. To assume that scientific or technological progress was in and of itself moral and able to change morality, and that human nature followed a similar upward curve of advancement and improvement, was, as Baudelaire put it, a "heresy." It ignored "original sin," though Baudelaire's notion of it was more philosophical than religious. This powerful idea was not original to Baudelaire, but it was hugely influential, not least upon T. S. Eliot and the strand of critical and creative thought we might label "modernist classicism": while scientific and technological progress are a one-way ratchet, in which previous gains and advances are "banked" and successively built upon, human nature is no different now from how it was when people lived in caves, or burned witches at the stake, or ate their defeated enemies.

The heresy, Baudelaire holds, is to imagine that what we can do changes what we are—it is to apply the rules of one sphere (science, say) to another sphere (human nature). Religion was useful because it reminded us of our bounded nature, our fallen state, our imperfectability. But in a post-religious age it is all too easy to forget the things religion once reminded us of, and which kept humanity's hubris in check. In terms of poetry, we might put it this way: we have all those new words and sophisticated rhetoric, all those surprising images and nuanced metaphors, but it is still the same old feelings that we are stuck with. Many of these debates in the nineteenth and twentieth centuries coalesced around terms such as "Romanticism" and "Classicism," two of the long nineteenth century's defining artistic keywords. It is best put, even now, by the influential English poet and thinker T. E. Hulme, who in his essay "Romanticism and Classicism" (1911) wrote this:

> Put shortly, these are the two views, then. One, that man is intrinsically good, spoilt by circumstance; and the other that he is intrinsically limited, but disciplined by order and tradition to something fairly decent. To the one party man's nature is like a well, to the other like a bucket. The view which regards man as a well, a reservoir full of possibilities, I call the romantic; the one which regards him as a very finite and fixed creature, I call the classical.[4]

The point he was making is not a religious one: Hulme did not believe in God, calling questions about the existence of God "secondary chatter." It is a cultural one, and it enjoins us to take what he calls a "religious attitude," in other words to retain, from religion, the sense of humanity as fallen and bounded. We might add that Hulme also warns us against the dangers of Enlightenment thinking, which he sees as essentially a Romantic faith in rationality: the belief that all can be understood, explained, and ordered; and that, once understood, explained, and ordered, it can be controlled. Like Baudelaire before him, Hulme argued that Progress was a dangerous illusion, the ultimate nineteenth-century fantasy. And yet its allure remains—so much so that we use it to organize our own more modest narratives of artistic development.

Victor Hugo, in his pseudo-revolutionary poem "Reply to an Act of Accusation," celebrates "divine Progress," thus linking the religious with the technical and the moral. In the poem, Hugo forges analogies between political freedom (the storming of the Bastille) and poetic freedom (the way he claims to storm the dictionary and free the ordinary words derided by poetry). The poem explicitly yokes revolutionary freedom to literary and artistic freedom. This yoking represents a belief both in Enlightenment values and in Romantic values as guarantors of Progress as a new secular deity capable of changing social and political reality. That revolutions are followed by counter-revolutions, that action is followed by reaction, is as true in politics and history as it is in art and literature.

CONTENT IN SEARCH OF FORM

"Looking for emotions to fit them to his vocabulary": can there be any more devastating comments on a poem-in-progress? Withering as they might be, those comments nonetheless contain an element of real cultural diagnosis: where once we felt more than we could say, we can now say more than we feel. The line Pound quotes is from Henry-D. Davray, the English literature correspondent of the venerable French review *Mercure de France*. Davray had written the "English Letters" column for periodical since 1896, the high-point of French Symbolism and decadence, and was also the translator of—among others—H. G. Wells, Joseph Conrad, and Oscar Wilde. It comes in his review of Edward Marsh's *Georgian Poetry, 1916–1917*:

> These young people are masters in the art of writing before they have lived. Thus they are looking for feelings to accommodate them to their vocabulary, and not words to express their passions and their ideas.[5]

Davray sees English poetry as comfortable, insulated, and middlebrow, and goes so far as to imagine a line of German trenches through Kent, with the cathedrals of "Cantorbéry [*sic*] and Winchester beneath the shells of Kultur." Then, suggests Davray, perhaps "these young people's serenity might be somewhat ruffled."[6] The implication is a standard one, however dramatically expressed: authentic experience creates authentic literature. That the anthology contains war poems by Siegfried Sassoon and Robert Graves (both in the trenches at the time) is overlooked because Davray's purpose is to deprecate a poetry where words come before, and thus instead of, feelings. Pound's line is all the more barbed for the fact that he also writes the German word *Echt*—meaning real or true or genuine, the antonym if not exactly the opposite of *Ersatz*—three times in his *Waste Land* marginalia. Between them, the German word and the French phrase raise questions about the authentic and the inauthentic in literature, and about the relationship of words and language to feeling and experience. What is at stake in Pound's comments? An attitude to feeling or an attitude to writing? Or, to put it more grandly, what comes, or should come, first: the feelings or the words?

Posed like that, the question, so local and specific in its asking, becomes something we can ask about any literature, any poetry, and any language that is designed to persuade. If we were to sketch the traditional narrative of the move from Romanticism to Modernism via Decadence, we might start with the claim that feelings come first, and that language strives to keep up with them. As old as rhetoric itself is the rhetorical manipulation of the trope of the unsayable, of the place in emotion and experience where words cannot go and do not reach. Part of being eloquent is to advertise the inadequacy of our eloquence in the direction of our subject, of projecting a sense of language as shortfall, whose failure to match its subject becomes the proof of that subject's worth. All the arts confront this limit-situation and work with it to express the grandeur, the beauty, the horror, or the elusiveness of their subject: some artists might see it in the sublime, others in the hyper-ordinary, but all artists in command of their means understand what it is to reach the edge of what can be expressed and to invoke what lies on the other side.

That is Romanticism's "official story." According to this theory, there was a time when feelings were constantly in excess of words (for words we can substitute musical notes on and off the sheet, paint on brushes, the sculptor's tools or the dancer's limbs). But, taking Pound/Davray's line, by the end of the nineteenth century and into the early twentieth (so this theory goes), language had finally exceeded emotion: our linguistic palette had become more variegated and richer than ever before, yet we had nothing left to say. As our techniques advanced, what we had to express had not. As Paul Verlaine begins his 1888 poem "Saint Graal" with the declaration that we are "dying of the period in which we live"—another version of Zola's claim that we are "ill from progress."

As we see just from Zola and Verlaine, who come from opposing points in the literary field—Naturalism and Symbolism—"progress" is at best an ambiguous force, and understood ambiguously even at a time when we might have expected people to be more positive about it. When critics talked about progress, they really meant a followable, mostly linear, narrative of artistic change made up of incremental and usually causal development, conventionally assumed to be gain, as distinct from random, aleatory, or even violent transformation. We are all in our different ways beholden to narratives of progress because they give us the comfort of continuity and help us organize material: literary, political, artistic, philosophical, scientific. This is partly why self-styled avant-garde movements such as Futurism, Dada, or Surrealism claim to be convulsive and discontinuous in their novelty, defining themselves as standing outside both cyclical and linear artistic time. It is not enough to be new; we must rupture the linear paradigms on which old and new depend. When André Breton claimed in the 1920s that Surrealism would discover new emotions, he was indicating that a renewal of artistic language (spoken, written, acted, painted, composed) could not happen until there were new feelings to express. To do this, human beings had to change or be changed—an ambition shared by movements as different (or, in this respect at least, as differently similar) as Futurism and the Socialist Realism. For better or for worse, that ambition has remained unfulfilled, though there have been historical moments when political regimes and artistic movements coincided in their attempts to change human nature, either through freedom or through its abolition. It is perhaps the most romantic ambition of all, and one Baudelaire would have ridiculed.

It is tempting, therefore, to see the passage, over less than a century, from Romanticism to Decadence less as an idea of "progress" than as an idea of reverse continuity. This process happens in a sort of dual-time: as the arts expand and advance in terms of technique, the human subject remains static. As Hulme might have put it: technique and expressive range are deepening wells, but human beings will always be buckets—who imagine themselves as wells. The age of artificiality and empty virtuosity succeeds the age of natural and unfettered authenticity—or so the story goes. We get versions of that story, a sort of de-creation myth of creativity, in J. K. Huysmans's *Against Nature* (1884), when the protagonist Des Esseintes compares the literature of his own period with the flowering of decadent literature at the end of the Roman Empire. Already in 1834, one of Huysmans's sources, the classicist Désiré Nisard, had defined the "decadent style" as technical virtuosity over content. The Latin decadent writers were, he claimed, "poets without inventiveness, without genius, but not without a certain talent for style."[7] Views like these were not confined to literary and artistic circles; in 1889, the French philosopher Jean-Marie Guyau neatly defined things as follows: "Periods of decadence know more but can do less."[8]

If we cast backwards from the *fin de siècle* to the beginning of the nineteenth century, where our canonical Romantic writers are found, we are encouraged to think that there was a time when feeling overran language. Poets were constantly fresh-minting language in order for poetry to keep up with emotions and intellects. The same can be said of painting or music or sculpture: that the form strains to hold the content, and that the truth of the artwork lies *in* the straining. This is a central element of the Romantic inheritance: that language's job was to keep up with the discoveries of the inner life, an inner life lived at the extremes, both of what could be inwardly endured and what could be outwardly expressed.

Along with this view came, unsurprisingly, a wealth of images and examples taken from the natural world. These examples emphasized the excess, the overrunning-*ness* and untameability of Nature: waterfalls, volcanoes, abyssal gorges, tumultuous seas, and bank-bursting rivers, and a whole spectrum of different weather phenomena, from the deep and calm and still to the thunderous, lightning-strafed tumult of the electrical storm. As Madame de Staël wrote: "Natural phenomena ... have a philosophical meaning and a religious goal which even the most attentive contemplation will never understand the scope of."[9] And in her novel *Corinne* (1807), she describes Vesuvius in ways that are typically "romantic":

> This lava advances without hurry and without losing a moment; if it encounters a high wall or any kind of structure that stands in its way, it stops, it builds up in front of the obstacle its black and bituminous torrents, and finally swallows it up in its burning waves.[10]

The correlatives to these images can be found in the way many nineteenth-century writers described the writing process, as well as the way they expressed the "subject" of their writing: self as still pool or self as raging storm, and all those other *Sturm und Drang* (German Proto-Romantic) clichés of the self. As well as the obvious matter of the "pathetic fallacy," where writers seek either meteorological assent for their feelings and states or, conversely, meteorological indifference and contrast, metaphors of natural processes were used to explain Romantic artistic creation too. In other words, metaphors of composition (the "how" of writing, composing, painting) were often extensions of the "what" (extreme feelings, excessive emotions, or conversely calm, profound stillness, unplumbable depths).

Perhaps the best-known of descriptions, and a staple of the schoolroom, the university seminar and the national poetry-day soundbite comes from the English poet William Wordsworth. As Wordsworth defined it in a well-known but insufficiently scrutinised line from the preface to *Lyrical Ballads* (1798): poetry was the "spontaneous overflow of powerful feelings." *Spontaneous, overflow, powerful.* All the elements for a critical as well as a creative ideology are there: something uncontrollable, the sense of overrun, liquid exceeding the vessel. For something to overflow, it needs to be contained, even if the container is not sufficient. In fact, the container *must* be insufficient, because lyric poetry is more than mere flow: it is the pressure of constraint invested back into the momentum of escape. In other words, it is *form*: a mutually supportive antagonism between container and contained. Yet, by the time we reach the poetry of decadence and modernism, we seem to have arrived at its opposite: language, not emotion, is the excess or the overflow, and spontaneity has given way to something Pavlovian: a verbal stimulus, a twitching in the dictionary, thesaurus reverb. That is, barring a few differences, how we tend to think of the changes between Romanticism and Decadence, between the beginning of the nineteenth century (which started earlier) and the end (which ended later).

But Wordsworth did not quite say this; more specifically, the line itself is qualified in ways that rather alter the meaning it is often used to illustrate:

> For all good poetry is the spontaneous overflow of powerful feelings: and though this be true, Poems to which any value can be attached were never produced on any variety of subjects but by a man who, being possessed of more than usual organic sensibility, had also thought long and deeply.[11]

Wordsworth makes this grand and much-quoted statement about emotions precisely in order to add nuance to it, and them, with a statement about thought. Further along in the preface to *Lyrical Ballads*, he reprises:

> I have said that poetry is the spontaneous overflow of powerful feelings: it takes its origin from emotion recollected in tranquillity: the emotion is contemplated till, by a species of reaction, the tranquillity gradually disappears, and an emotion, kindred to that which was before the subject of contemplation, is gradually produced, and does itself actually exist in the mind.[12]

What is significant here is the way Wordsworth describes a *process* by which the poet generates a secondary emotion, "kindred" to the original, through contemplation. The word "reaction" has clear scientific undertones too, reminding us that many nineteenth-century poets—Wordsworth and Coleridge no less than Goethe, Hugo, and Novalis—were fascinated by scientific developments and kept attentively abreast of them. The idea that science and poetry were opposed or mutually antagonistic is a modern fallacy and damaging to our understanding of the period. For Wordsworth, thought, here at least, is the engine-room of poetic creation itself—not the opposite of feeling but a gateway to it.

We remarked earlier that poetic language was designed to persuade. So far so clear. But to persuade whom? When we think about rhetoric, we ask, logically enough, what it exists to persuade us, as readers or listeners, of. The next question should be: what is the rhetorician trying to persuade *him- or herself* of? In Wordsworth's recipe, the poet must inhabit and believe in the feelings, even if he or she has generated them in order to make the poem. The art of persuasion is, here at least, an art of sincere self-persuasion.

In Benjamin Constant's *Adolphe*, a hugely influential novel published in 1816, we find an attitude to language and emotion, and to the relationship between the two, that is altogether less positive. Adolphe, the narrator. An introspective, melancholy son of a wealthy establishment family who goes in search of experience, seeking to make his life match up to the poems and stories he has read. The experience he seeks is love. Adolphe presents the contortions of aimless (male) feeling, a sort of *otium* of the privileged, which both mistakes and projects itself as a kind of cosmic hunger with universal resonance. It called itself the "*mal du siècle*," the century's pain, though "*mal*" in French can range from pain and suffering to the more banal "mal" of "malaise." It can also mean evil, as in Baudelaire's *Les Fleurs du mal*, though it is the spectrum of affect—pain or suffering modulating, by way of sickness, to mere inconvenience—that concerns us here.

The "*mal du siècle*" was much in vogue, and like many terms that present themselves as "universal," then as now, they are really only "universal" to a subsection of white men of a certain class, from a dominant culture in a specific historical period. The peasant or the mill-worker, the farmer or the innkeeper, the merchant or the builder, were not suffering from "*mal du siècle*" (too busy), and needless to say few women (of any rank or social standing) were allowed to apply. The "*mal du siècle*" typically affected rich, French, titled, or educated young men caught in a post-revolutionary limbo, haunted by the era of heroes, and caught between the disappointment of arriving too late and the restless anticipation of arriving too early. It was not just the sense of being out of time, but the sense that the time itself was both post- and pre-. "The time is out of joint," we might say, following Hamlet, the ultimate nineteenth-century romantic (in)action-hero: there is something dislocated about history itself.

But surely everyone feels this, not just artists and writers and composers, but also scientists, economists, businessmen, and politicians? People like us today feel it, too: the mix of vague anticipation and vicarious nostalgia, the sense of living in a period that is no longer anchored by the past but where the future has not yet taken shape. And in any case, surely it all depends on what one does with this feeling. An economist and political theorist like Karl Marx had as accentuated a sense of the in-betweenness of his era as did nineteenth-century writers such as Giacomo Leopardi, François-René de Chateaubriand, Goethe, or Hugo. But just as we risk being Eurocentric in our point of view, so, even within Europe, we privilege the literatures of, notably, France, England, and Germany. If we look at the literature of smaller nations and the not-yet-nations, or of languages without nation-states, we could consider Adam Mickiewicz writing the Polish national epic, the *Pan Tadeusz* (published in Paris in 1834) in a Lithuania under Russian rule, or Sandor Petofi, a Hungarian born in a Slovak town, writing the Magyar "National Song" and leading the Pest chapter of the Hungarian uprising in 1848.

These people were not wandering around in a haze of *otium* (let alone opium). They were harnessing their historical moments to actions. Our canon-distorted sense of the "*mal du siècle*" is of little help when we try to understand their situations. We might also consider France Preseren choosing to write in his native Slovenian rather than the imperial German in which, under the shadow of Goethe, he wrote his earliest poetry. Europe has never been synchronized, and the regions and languages of Europe always had their own artistic temporalities upon which we must be wary of imposing our own. For Catalan writers, for example, and for the literature of the Catalan language, the early nineteenth century is called the Renaixença or Renaissance (though it was, in terms of literary identity, a "romantic"-led phenomenon), and the early modern period and the eighteenth century were the Decadència. Our French or British or German categories are not their categories, and though the winds of Romanticism and Enlightenment blew across them also, they did so with very different results. The world looks different from the emerging nation, or the minority culture, the stateless nation, and the nationless state.

THE *MAL DU SIÈCLE*: A FORM IN SEARCH OF CONTENT

Baudelaire called his epoch, which, despite being only a few years later, was not the same as Constant's, an interregnum. That sense of betweenness reigned, we might say, right across the nineteenth century, and not just at strategic points along it. The *"mal du siècle"* was not so different from the *fin-de-siècle* mood, since both shared that sense of nervous fatigue, thwarted energy, and temporal dislocation: they were endings wrapped around beginnings wrapped around endings … *ad infinitum*. Anatole Baju, editor of the *Décadent* magazine in the 1880s, called his *fin de siècle* a "foetal," "preparatory" period, while the composer Erik Satie wrote with his trademark blend of mischief and melancholy: "I have arrived very young into an era already very old."

The Romantic *"mal du siècle"* was, in other words, just one, rather limited and introspective, way of responding to that sense of prolonged crisis, and of mapping personal dislocation with an imagined cultural one. The *"mal du siècle"* was also a social, not to say socialized phenomenon; it was mundane, even, in the French sense of the word *mondain*: of and in society. And the history of the term *"mal du siècle,"* like that of the altogether more elemental German *"Weltschmerz,"* is of writers fitting, as Pound implies, their personal experiences and feelings to pre-existing verbal categories. Maybe they were the early equivalent of memes, looking for feelings to attach themselves to?

If Chateaubriand did not invent the *"mal du siècle,"* he is the author who gave it its most powerful image in his novel *René* (1801). Like *Adolphe*, this is a first-person narrative, albeit framed by other voices both inside and outside the book. We might reflect here that the first-person narrative, a mode in which we (or the 1801 and 1816 reader) might expect direct access to the felt truth of emotional life, actually shows us just how fickle the first-person narrator is, how prone to self-deceit, self-justification, unreliability, and neediness he can be. As in Jean-Jacques Rousseau's *Confessions*, we are faced with the possibility that the self, the bedrock of who we are, our orientation-point in a tumultuous world, is in fact just as dark, complicated, contradictory, and paradoxically deep and shallow, as what lies outside it. The correlative of this is that the first-person narrator *begins* as an unreliable narrator. Far from the unreliable, ironic, duplicitous narrator being a modern invention, it exists right from the beginning of the form; it is an intrinsic part of the form's habitation of itself as it stretches into its possibilities.

Unreliability, we could also say, is coeval with reliability. The untrustworthy narrator is not some endpoint of a literature of decreasing sincerity or truth and increasing sophistication, as Progress-narratives would encourage us to think. It is inherent in the form and is tapped as a resource right at the beginning of that form—not inherent in the form's decline or gradual self-imbrication over time. Just as trick photography and hoax images of fairies or ghosts were produced at more or less the same time as the earliest "genuine" photographs, so the lie is coeval with the truth, bad faith is coeval with faith, self-delusion is coeval with self-scrutiny, mock-heroic is coeval with the heroic, and so on. It is worth reiterating this as a guard against one-size-fits-all Progress-narratives where we imagine a fresh, energetic, sincere, and overflowing Romanticism declining into a jaded, weary, ironic, and dried-out Decadence.

ROMANTIC SELF-FASHIONING
AND THE MANUFACTURE OF EMOTION

We should be prepared to see, at the beginning of the nineteenth century, in writers such as Goethe, Constant, Chateaubriand, and even the long-deceased Rousseau, a great deal of the sophisticated questioning of form and feeling that we recognize, because we are told to look for them, eighty or ninety years later and into the twentieth century. Chateaubriand's René is another Romantic connoisseur of volcanoes; indeed, they are an important prop to his self-image:

> One day, I climbed to Etna's summit, a volcano burning in an island's midst. I saw the sun rise in the immensity of horizon below me, Sicily narrowing to a point at my feet, and the sea stretching into distant space ... [B]ut while my gaze perceived these things on one side, on the other it plunged into Etna's crater, whose burning innards I could see amongst black clouds of vapour.

> A young man full of passion, seated on the rim of a volcano, and weeping over the mortals whose dwellings he can barely see at his feet, is he not, venerable fathers, truly an object worthy of your pity; ... it is thus that throughout my life I have had before my eyes a creation, at once immense and subtle, an abyss yawning at my side.[13]

This is romantic self-fashioning at its most sophisticatedly naive, which may be the same as disingenuous: the young, ardent man seeking out the symbols that will sponsor his self-image, grandiosely third-personizing himself in order to leave the reader with a framed symbol of his deep and complicated self. On the one hand, he sees great vistas (the poet as seer, the poet as visionary, the poet as prophet); but on the other, there is also, inside him, the raging volcanic turmoil. This is an image of dualism that has been with us since the Greeks, via Descartes and others, and we may also recognize something of Nietzsche's or Freud's great dualities: the Apollonian and the Dionysiac, or the Ego and the Id. This is the cult of the sublime, but already it is staged and stage-managed; already it is being used as part of a narrator's exculpatory strategy. In 1801, one year into the new century, the symbol is being manufactured: the cliché arrives at the same time as the original picture, the stylized trope at the same time as the freshly minted image. The two men listening to him, a native Indian and a French priest, are not fooled: they both tell him, in today's parlance, to *get a life*. What hope is there, we might say, for the Romantic hero when even his fellow-fictional characters do not buy into his self-image?

Many years later, Chateaubriand wished that he could destroy René. "If René did not exist, I would no longer write him," he wrote. "If it were possible for me to destroy him, I would: he has infested the mind of a large part of our youth, an effect I could not have foreseen, since I had wanted, on the contrary, to correct it."[14] Just as Goethe's *Sorrows of Young Werther* had spawned a genre not just of literature but of behaviors and temperaments, so the "*mal du siècle*" spawned a "pullulation," in Chateaubriand's words, of copycats. Europeans worried about the young men who read Goethe's *The Sorrows of Young Werther* (1774) and killed themselves, in much the same way as today's parents worry about their children copying behaviors from social media or advertising or computer games. At the other end of the century, Huysmans's Des Esseintes, a rich, impotent, cynical, uncreative, and malicious snob, whom Huysmans invented as a cautionary tale or counter-example, became, instead, a *fin-de-siècle* hero. And, *Against Nature* turned into, as Arthur Symons said, "the breviary of decadence," even though

Huysmans was clear that it was meant to be an absurd satire on the decadent mentality and its dead-end, self-consuming omphalocentrism. The key word is breviary: a book of liturgies to be learned and repeated. Like René eighty-three years before him and Werther 110, the literary character launched "real-life" imitators. Literature—the imaginative life—is contagious; it *is* contagion.

It is no coincidence that in Mary Shelley's *Frankenstein* (originally 1818), the monster reads and is affected by *Werther*, which he/it finds among his/its maker's belongings. Just as it is a creature made of other human body parts, so its emotional and intellectual life is made of literary parts. But perhaps all writers, and all readers, are made up of similar parts, monsters of intertextuality? Like René, like Werther, or like us, the monster is a product of the literature it has read. Once a term like *"mal du siècle"* or *"Weltschmerz"* exists, it attracts, like a lightning conductor, all sorts of loose human material—feelings, thoughts, instincts, sensations, anxieties, moods, and spasms in the cultural nervous system—which, in attracting, it also shapes. To name is to create, in literature at least, and Pound's question remains: are feelings in literature the cause or the effect of literature?

To read Constant's *Adolphe* with these questions in mind shows us just how the language of feeling and authenticity, meaning and intention, was compromised from the beginning of the nineteenth century. The decadence, etymologically, the "fall," from language of feeling was already evident. *Adolphe* appeared in 1816, the year Coleridge published *Kubla Khan* (written almost twenty years before), with its attendant myth of the poem arriving as in a dream, ready formed, only to be cut short by a banal visit from "a person on business from Porlock." A staged encounter between the life of the transported mind (helped, let us say, by what we could euphemize as "opioid enhancement") and the intrusion of reality, the story of *Kubla Khan* is the narrative *par excellence* of inspiration and verbal creation. Constant's novel shows us a different side to the "spontaneity" and "overflow" of words. Adolphe is hungry for experience, on a quest for the feelings that might give all his words, written and read, some anchor, some mooring, in lived life. Adolphe determines to take an older woman as a lover. Initially, the woman resists—she has children and a partner, though she is unmarried. But when she gives in, seduced by Adolphe's words of passion, she gives in completely. Adolphe himself—one part of himself doing, the other watching and noting—does not.

What was and remains most disturbing about the book is the way it depicts a relationship between words and feelings that is already riven with self-consciousness and self-deceit. Moreover, *Adolphe* shows a man not simply persuading someone to love him through deft use of the vocabulary of passion—that, after all, is standard procedure—but persuading *himself* of that love. In one passage, he describes how writing the letter generated in him some of the emotions to which his rhetoric laid claim:

> The struggles I had fought for so long against my own character, the impatience I felt at not having been able to overcome it, and my doubt about the success of my plan, cast into my letter an agitation which bore a strong resemblance to love. Besides, aroused as I was by my own style, I felt, as I finished writing, a little of the passion I had sought to express with all possible force.[15]

Perhaps the most troubling element of this statement resides in the words "a little": while words urge us on to experience emotions we do not spontaneously have, they also produce a reduced version, a sort of scaled-down simulacrum of them. This should remind us of Wordsworth's idea of the "kindred" emotion created by contemplation: related to, but not exactly the same as, the first or the original emotion. But it is differently deployed here, since it is deployed to create a falsehood, to fool oneself just enough to proceed to fool the other completely, rather than, as in Wordsworth, to gain access to a related but distinct feeling that might terminate in a new truth, not to mention a new verbal object: a poem.

The really poignant element here is that "a little" is enough: in the currency-inflation of the language of love, a little emotion is all you need, since words, or rhetoric, will multiply it by the necessary factor. What makes Adolphe's language so devastatingly false is, in fact, that it is *a little* true. French readers in 1816 might well have been struck by the difference between the weakness, indecision, and rhetorical clumsiness of Adolphe and the priapically eloquent, libertine amorality of Valmont, the libertine hero of Pierre Choderlos de de Lachlos's *Les Liaisons dangereuses* three decades earlier (1782). What Adolphe the man and Adolphe the rhetorician shows us is that by far the largest category of humanity is neither morality nor immorality but, merely, weakness.

This attitude to language as an instrument for fooling oneself as well as another—that is to say, language as alibi—enables Adolphe to pretend that he is as much a victim of language as Ellénore, the woman whose life he ruins. As she writes to him in her final letter, when his words of feelingful excess have turned into words of unfeeling shortfall: "You are good; your actions are noble and devoted: but what actions could efface your words?"[16] By telling Adolphe that it is not him but his words that have caused her harm, and by separating words from actions and feelings, she also absolves him from his responsibility. Ellénore is ruined, her children are removed from her care, she is excluded from society, and she dies of an illness brought on by heartbreak. Adolphe meanwhile returns, as he was always destined to, to the safety of his father's world where a job and a respectable life await. Reality has won its war of attrition. He blames "society" for forcing him to return to the safe male place that was, in truth, never really in danger: his *"mal du siècle"* was the calculated overflow, we might say, of powerful failings.

There is a Romantic hero in the book, one for whom language is not enough to express feeling, and whose love is measured not just in the way it exceeds and eludes language, but in the way it stakes everything, even life itself, on emotions. But that hero is a heroine, and it is Ellénore. She exceeds and eludes language not just because of the intensity and authenticity of her emotions, but because she dies of them, and because her words become the unanswerable silence from which all language comes and to which it all returns. Here silence, not words, becomes the marker of truth and feeling. In *Adolphe*, silence is authentic, and words are the falsehood. As Cordelia says in *King Lear*, replying, in an aside, to her father's order to describe in excessive language the excess of her love: "Love, and be silent." The compression of her line gives it double the power: it expresses causality, in the sense of *"because* I love I am silent" (feeling beyond words), and it expresses the imperative: "I love, so will be silent" (feeling debased by words). After so many words in *Adolphe*, silence is not only a refuge but a place of authenticity, and the prestige of silence in literature—as a sign not only of what exceeds verbal expression but of what is *diminished by* verbal expression—is a story of its own.

Adolphe was ferociously successful, not just in France but across Europe. It is a book about failure, but not the grand shattering failure of the age of heroes such as Napoleon (defeated at Waterloo the year before the book appeared), but the failure of the unremarkable, the average. The failure comes with no real loss because there was never really anything hazarded, and that is perhaps the worst loss of all. While Adolphe was held to epitomize an entire generation's shortcomings, he was, in fact, simply one branch of a family tree that had begun long before him and continued to ramify long after. He may have felt unique, but he was, in fact, a type: struggling with his burdensome singularity and discovering that everyone else has pretty much the same singularity as he does. Adolphe has ancestors and he has descendants, but here, even in the midst of the Romantic revolution, and long before the self-entangling ironies of Laforgue, early Eliot, Fernando Pessoa, and others, words are not just a debased currency but a counterfeit one.

Samuel Taylor Coleridge's *Kubla Khan*, published in the same the year as *Adolphe*, is perhaps more important for the fable of its drug-infused genesis than for the poetry it contains. This is because it still calls on us to consider where poetic language (and by extension any artistic language) "comes from" and also who "owns" them. Though Coleridge was glad of the transports that had helped him write the poem, he was also afraid of the power of words to control, rather than to serve, the poet. One of his nightmares was that he might become a verbal automaton, that the words might rule him rather than he them. The idea of the "automaton poet," in thrall to language and not its orchestrator, haunts him, as the exultations of being inspired merge with the terrors of being possessed—a classic Romantic seam which is itself part of the paradox of creativity. In this respect, Coleridge was reckoning with one of Romanticism's most compelling clichés, a paradox that comes to its clearest and most critical point much later in Surrealism and the dream of automatic language. But Coleridge's automaton poet is a negative—because mechanistic—version of the lyre of Orpheus, a particularly tenacious myth of creativity that has remained potent up to the Beat poets and beyond. At the other end of the century, for instance, the French poet Arthur Rimbaud talks in the famous "lettres du voyant" of how the poet is analogous to the copper that finds itself a clarion, and that the true poet does not say "I think," but rather "I am thought." "Je est un autre," he writes, with a deliberate grammatical dislocation: "I *is* another": "bad luck to the wood that finds itself a violin."[17] What Rimbaud is referring to here is the poet's agency in relation to language: on the one hand, he masters language; on the other, he is mastered, he is its instrument. Rimbaud's contemporary, Stéphane Mallarmé, a poet who more than any other explored the fine line between craft and chance, writes of "ceding the initiative to words."[18] Control of language and abnegation of control are closely tied, and have a far more complicated relationship than simple opposition.

How much opium Coleridge had consumed before starting *Kubla Khan* is thus less of an issue than the role played by the image of drugs and alcohol in the myth of artistic creation: they become symbols of the verticality, the ways of reaching heights or depths of the self, through which the creative paradox of self-escape and self-realization can lead to art. But the other, and some might say the true, function of drugs and alcohol is to wear off; they help us exit Time briefly only to remind us that Time wins. Drink and drugs are attractive to creation's self-mythologizing because they play out and are correlatives of the nature of creation: the fight against Time. The amateur drug- or drink-taker consumes them for the high; the real professional knows that it is the lows that give you the best lines. We should also note that when Baudelaire writes *"enivrez vous sans cesse"*—"inebriate yourselves without ceasing,"—he does not necessarily mean drink or drugs, but anything (he suggests poetry and virtue as well as wine) that takes us out of the *now*, saves us from becoming the "martyred slaves of Time."[19] In Baudelairian terms, our drug of choice might just as well be religion, or model trains, or Norwegian box sets.

For Coleridge, all this is more complex than a mere theory of inspiration: language is creative in that it has an affective power that can shape reality through its power to create feelings not just in the reader or listener but in the one who uses it. As he wrote to his friend William Godwin, "I would endeavor to destroy the old antithesis of *Words & Things*, elevating, as it were, words into Things, & living Things too."[20] But a suspicion of one's own eloquence is attendant both upon the "spontaneous overflow" of which Wordsworth speaks, and the calculated pseudo-overflow with which Constant's character manipulates both Ellénore's emotions and his own. Coleridge writes of the "prodigality of beautiful words, which are as it were the half embodyings of Thought, that make them more than Thought, give them an outness."[21] That word "outness," a characteristically Coleridgean noun, suggests something not quite three-dimensional but almost: like bas-relief or an embossing, where the joint between inner and the outer is delineated but the two are neither fully separate nor fully one. Words, we might say, are inter-dimensional things, or things that play, like holograms, with the illusion of interdimensionality. I use the word *things* deliberately here, because in his notebook of January 1, 1806, Coleridge embarks on a piece of what he calls "metaphysical Etymology" in which he connects the Latin verb *reor* ("I think") to the word thing, *res*. He stays true to this idea, writing in 1818, "To think (*Ding, denken*; *res, reor*) is to *thing*ify."[22]

THE LANGUAGE OF SILENCE

Beside Coleridge's "metaphysical Etymology" for *thingification*, we might set one of Mallarmé's later wordplays: the etymological connection between one of his favorite words, *rien*, nothing, and *res*, thing. From *res* to *rien* and *rien* to *res* lies the whole Mallarméan drama, which is the drama of language and silence itself: something to nothing, nothing into something.[23] As Coleridge might have put it, to use language is to thingify and to de- or un-thingify. "Thing" and "Nothing," words as everyday as they are metaphysical, share a single etymological root, and each implies the other. What links all the disciplines, artistic or scientific, is that they ask the same question: what came first? Something or nothing?

There is a rich anthology of nineteenth-century silence that goes hand-in-hand with nineteenth-century excess and overflow. This may at first seem counter-intuitive; after all, why would writers who take language to its apogee of feelingful surfeit need to resort to silence? The answer is that, for many of them, silence becomes another form of expression, a language that comes both before and after words, and functions as a point of origin for words as well as their point of disappearance. Words can be answered; silence cannot. Thus the insufficiency of language becomes more and more of a trope, precisely *because* language is doing and saying more and more.

Consequently, invoking silence and unsayability has always been a rhetorical tool: a way of signaling that language is coming up against feelings, experiences, facts, spiritual or scientific discoveries, for which words fail. Language is insufficient in the direction of Life, or Nature, or God, or the Sublime. Or how much we love another person. Silence comes to the rescue, not just as language's opposite, but as its underwriting force, its guarantee. Thus, silence has the paradoxical effect of both negating language and coming to its aid by validating its subject, and thus language's deep roots in feeling or visionary height. Perhaps the greatest example to the English Romantics was John Milton, the great limit-pusher of the seventeenth century, whose apophatic rhetoric was built on asserting language's inadequacy in describing and knowing God. It was also a version of Protestant iconoclasm, the idols to be shattered here being human language and human words. And just as Milton used angels and prophets to mediate between human reality and heavenly truth in *Paradise Lost* (1667), so the Romantic paradigm of the poet-as-prophet depends on the image of the poet as intercessor, through an imperfect language, of something unknowable and beyond comprehension.

Silence is also a way for the poet to turn away from words, and to inject a sense of the world having its own, non-human language. In Victor Hugo's poem "Le Silence du soir," silence is not inexpression or lack of communication but the opposite. "This silence of the night, / Is not silence. Listen!," the poem begins, then runs through the permutations of silence's expressiveness. The poem ends with a flourish: "And when all goes quiet all begins to speak."

> Ce silence du soir
> Ce n'est pas le silence. Écoute!
> Et dès que tout se tait, tout commence à parler.[24]

Hugo, like many Romantic writers, was intent on showing how much we do not hear, how much we do not understand: silence becomes the place in the culture where we keep the unknowable. Some might say it is the place in the culture where we keep religion or the religious attitude, a place where our words do not go. But it also pays to be suspicious of what Hugo was doing: by imposing the language-paradigm upon Silence, in other words arguing that silence is also communication, he was also colonizing silence, and colonizing the unknown. Thus, the poem, whose surface "argument" alleges that silence is unknowable, makes a deeper claim that the unknown bears strong structural resemblance to the known and functions in the same manner. This is typical of Hugo, incidentally: there is in his work a strange conservatism of imagination, where the unknown can only remain unknown on the condition that it is unknown in known ways.

This is very different from, say, Novalis or Hölderlin, Rimbaud or Nerval, or Leopardi, as in his poem "The Infinite" (1835). Here silence functions differently as a marker of the infinite, of what is timeless against what is made of time, that is, us in the noisy, fleeing, here and now:

> And when I hear the wind rustling through the trees
> I compare its voice to the infinite silence.
> And eternity occurs to me, and all the ages past
> And the present time, and its sound
> Amidst this immensity my thought drowns
> And to founder in this sea is sweet to me.[25]

Here the idea of being wrecked (*naufragar*) is soothing, not frightening. Oblivion is attractive. This is not simply because of the grandeur of the silence, but because Leopardi's speaker is comforted by the fact that the infinite still exists, that the depths have not been plumbed, and that the mysteries of life and death are still there—however much we may, with our language, science, and philosophy, try to explain the world. Silence here is the guarantee of the infinite, the unknown, the non-human, the trans-temporal, and the absolute. This poem is a religious poem without a religion. If we have not killed silence, then we have not (yet) killed God.

In Mallarmé's "A Throw of the Dice," a poem whose radical spatial experimentalism takes as its central image the idea of shipwreck, silence and blank space are cognates of each other. The precarious words on the page signify the precarious hold the actions of our minds—words, thoughts, theories, poems, mental edifices—have upon the infinite. They teeter, follow their narrow paths, and are scattered, submerged, or wrecked against it. In the poem's Preface, he writes: "The 'blanks' indeed take on importance, at first glance; the versification demands them, as a surrounding silence, to the extent that a fragment, lyrical or of a few beats, occupies, in its midst, a third of the space of paper: I do not transgress the measure, only disperse it." In other words, Mallarmé aims to use blankness, or silence, as a way of pacing the reading, of showing how the ideas, the mental constructions, shine and then fragment or disappear against it. We note, too, that he reminds us how he has not altered the ratio of words to silence, poem to page space, only "dispersed it."

Mallarmé seems to be telling us that any poem, even a poem confidently settled in the traditional middle of the page, splendidly occupying center-stage, is surrounded and perhaps threatened by the blankness. It is only an optical illusion, a metaphysical sleight, a romantic/enlightenment trick of distribution, that makes us forget this. For everything we think we know, Romantic-Enlightenment-Progress followers that we are, there exists a larger portion of unknown. Is that unknown something, or is it nothing, asks Mallarmé, for whom all of these poetic-aesthetic questions have an existential timbre.

To compose poetry, or make language, is also to shape non-language, to craft the void and make it perceptible. Everything we say displaces its own weight in what is unsayable. The idea of "composing" silence may not be new, but for Mallarmé it is central to poetic creation. In his poetry, the act of composition extends into the silence, the emptiness, the void, as if to measure itself against them.

In the symbolist theatre of the Belgian playwright Maurice Maeterlinck, a precursor to the playwrights Samuel Beckett and Eugene Ionesco, silence replaced language and waiting replaced action. This was part of Maeterlinck's theory of the "everyday tragic," conveyed in a series of powerful one-act plays which he called the "theatre of waiting." In these dramas of the 1890s, Maeterlinck created long pauses between dialogue, depicted characters devoid of actions, and made use of darkness and low lighting to give spectators the sense that the play's underlying forces lay just on the other side of language, away from "dramatic" events, beyond the stage and deep inside the shadows. Maeterlinck deliberately toyed with the anti-theatrical and the non-dramatic to create what he called a *"théâtre statique"* or static theater, in which silence had semantic variety and depth while language remained a thin, brittle surface.

Some fifty years later, in 1937, soon after finishing his novel *Murphy*, Beckett wrote a famous letter to a German acquaintance, Axel Kaun:

> And more and more my language appears to me like a veil which one has to tear apart in order to get to those things (or the nothingness) lying behind it ... It is to be hoped the time will come, thank God, in some circles it already has, when language is best used when most efficiently abused ... To drill one hole after another into it until that which lurks behind, be it something or nothing, starts seeping through—I cannot imagine a higher goal for today's writer ...

> Is there any reason why that terrifyingly arbitrary materiality of the word surface should not be dissolved, as, for example, the sound surface of Beethoven's Seventh Symphony is devoured by huge black pauses, so that for pages on end we cannot perceive it as other than a dizzying path of sounds connecting unfathomable chasms of silence? An answer is requested.

One wonders what sort of answer Beckett might have expected from his poor correspondent. But what is clear from this letter is Beckett's grasp, which he was later to turn to powerful dramatic effect, of the mutually enriching, mutually deepening relationship between language and silence. Beckett's frustrations here—dissatisfaction with language, suspicion of eloquence, fear that words stand between us and the world rather than enabling us to gain access to the world—are all recognizably Romantic, part of the long nineteenth century's legacy to modern literature and art.

CHAPTER EIGHT

The Arts

JULIAN JOHNSON

INTRODUCTION: ART AS HISTORY

What is the historian to do with art? What, for example, can Manet's 1880 painting of a lemon tell us about history? We might have things to learn from the genre of history painting, from representations of kings and generals, revolutions and war, but surely not from a still life centered on a lemon. Yet the telling of art history implies, and often develops, a sense of connection with the telling of history as a whole.[1] Of course, art is historical like anything else; it has its key events, agents, movements, and leaves behind a trail of empirical evidence. But the elision of art and history implies a relation that is more than merely external, more than just a chronology of individual artists, institutions, patrons, and publics. It includes the idea that, in its material substance, in matters of aesthetic form, style, and technique, art connects in profound but essentially unprovable ways with the unfolding history of other things—of society, politics, technology, culture, religion, philosophy, and the changing sensibility of everyday life.

FIGURE 8.1 Édouard Manet, *The Lemon*, 1880. © Christophel Fine Art / Getty Images.

On the one hand, artworks are historical texts and objects like any other—clocks, clothes, steam engines, newspapers. On the other, they make a claim to be more than objects or historical records. To denote something as art is to propose it as the focus of aesthetic experience whose criteria are quite different to those of historical method— which makes the task of the art historian unusually complex. It involves a concern with the social practice of the arts, their reception and changing ideas of style, function, and value, but it also involves exploring the ways in which artworks, in their own techniques and forms, are historical texts. A string quartet may seem to say nothing of history, but it is shaped by traditions, techniques, and technologies that are thoroughly historical in ways that exceed the realm of music. For that reason, a musical work is not only the result of historical agency, but has the capacity to acquire historical agency itself. Such a claim derives from the fact that the idea of an autonomous subjectivity appears in parallel with the idea of autonomous art. More than being simply a representation of the bourgeois subject, in the nineteenth century art became one of the most powerful means for enacting its emancipation.

Any attempt to give a synoptic overview of the arts between 1800 and 1920 in a single chapter would soon be defeated by the sheer volume of material. So, instead of the familiar narrative of stylistic change, I offer below a set of interrelated categories through which to explore the tension between the historical and the aesthetic, ideas that connect rather than divide the early twentieth century and the late eighteenth century. There is, however, a less pragmatic and more important reason for proceeding in this way: an account of the arts as an accelerating process of development reproduces the very myth of the nineteenth century that a critical study should question. So, the first of my six categories is history itself—the way in which art is bound up with ideas of historical progress, with the rush forwards of a *modernist* sense of future-orientation, while at the same time thoroughly *historicist*, compelled to reflect on the past through the traditions it perpetuated even as it sought to overturn them.

NARRATIVES OF PROGRESS

No period forces us to think about the relation between art and history quite as much as the long nineteenth century because no other period was quite so obsessed with its own historical self-consciousness. Reinhart Koselleck has shown how, in the aftermath of the French Revolution, time was experienced as accelerating at an alarming rate: "No time has ever been so strongly, so closely, so exclusively, and so generally bound up with the future than that of our present," wrote Friedrich Schlegel in 1828.[2] The experience of time as rushing forward like a torrent or avalanche was a product both of the rapidity of turbulent political change and, increasingly, of new technologies of production and transport. But it was also powerfully embodied in art, and nowhere more so than in music, the art of time.

In an essay on Beethoven's *Eroica* Symphony (1803), Reinhold Brinkmann draws fascinating parallels between the work's enactment of a future-oriented teleology and the sense of accelerating historical time set out by Koselleck.[3] The *Eroica* was, at one point, to be dedicated to Napoleon, but it is the temporal urgency of the work that really defines its revolutionary nature, an unstoppable current that was both thrilling and terrifying for its early audiences. Amid the tumultuous and violent years of the Napoleonic Wars, here was a work that set out to make sense of the conflicting emotions of rapid change, of revolutionary hope as much as the terrifying forces it had unleashed. Two years after its premiere in 1805, Beethoven's contemporary, G. W. F. Hegel, published *The Phenomenology of Spirit* (1807) in which he sketched out an entire philosophical system based on a similar idea—the development of self-identity through the progressive unfolding of historical time.[4]

Koselleck further suggests that the bewildering experience of nineteenth-century life derived not simply from the rate of change, but also from the unprecedented *simultaneity* of its time frames.[5] The poet Charles Baudelaire pointed to something similar in 1859 with his remark that "Modernity is the transitory, the fugitive, the contingent, which make up one half of art, the other being the eternal and the immutable."[6] The imperative to be new defined the modern spirit; in the wake of failed attempts at revolutionary social change, the claims of art to remake the world carried a weight that was variously political, moral, and even spiritual. By this logic, the important artists were ground-breaking and cutting edge—pioneers and explorers, at times even prophets and visionaries. So when, in 1873, Arthur Rimbaud insisted that "Il faut être absolument moderne" (we must be entirely modern), he was, paradoxically, articulating an idea nearly a century old.[7] And if the definitive sense of the *Neuzeit* was an accelerating rush toward the future, it was equally the case that a sense of being fractured from the past, while not yet having arrived at a promised future, produced a peculiar sense of homelessness at the heart of modern life.

A preoccupation with the gap between the present and the past was thus also a central component of modern art. A. W. Schlegel, writing in Jena in 1801, expressed the essential sense of present loss: "The poetry of the ancients was … the poetry of possession, while ours is the poetry of longing; the former is firmly rooted in its present, while the latter hovers between remembrance and anticipation."[8] So, while familiar narratives of modernism tell a singular story of progressive change, artworks themselves suggest something more conflicted and contradictory. Wilhelm Wackenroder's *The Heartfelt Effusions of an Art-Loving Monk* (1797), for example, articulated a profound nostalgia for a more ancient, simpler, and spiritual life centered in art, specifically the life and work of Albrecht Dürer (1471–1528). Partly inspired by Wackenroder, a group of artists in Vienna, self-consciously identifying themselves as the "Brotherhood of St. Luke," set out to cultivate the same values in their own work. Led by Franz Pforr and Friedrich Overbeck, they moved to Rome in 1809 (where they became known as the Nazarenes) and made their home in a deserted convent.

Their deliberately archaic style might seem extreme and a world away from a radical Romanticism, but this contradictory tug of old and new is everywhere evident in nineteenth-century art. Contemporary with the elemental violence of Eugène Delacroix, the studied historicism of J.-A.-D. Ingres looks back to the Renaissance world of Raphael. After composing *Tristan and Isolde* (1859), a work which would become a touchstone for musical modernism for the next fifty years or more, Richard Wagner composed *The Mastersingers of Nuremberg* (1868), a work set in a medieval city in the sixteenth century and which brings the most modern of musical styles to bear on an opera about the social role of art and the renewal of tradition.[9]

Nowhere was this conflicted sense of history more immediately visible than in architecture; for all the Romantics' emphasis on the individual, when it came to the expression of public values, the model was definitively archaic. The so-called Gothic Revival was a feature of architecture across Europe, Great Britain, and even North America. In London, the Houses of Parliament and Palace of Westminster, constructed between 1835 and 1868 to a design by Sir Charles Barry, with internal styling by Augustus Pugin,

FIGURE 8.2 London St. Pancras station and hotel, 1868–1876.
© Hulton Archive / Heritage Images / Getty Images.

provide a good example of a new building that was intended, from the start, to appear old. As Parliament was completed, work began on the Midland Grand Hotel adjacent to St. Pancras Railway Station (built 1868–1876). Designed by George Gilbert Scott in High Victorian Gothic with medieval towers and arches, it was nevertheless constructed on an iron frame and as part of a modern railway complex. The French writer Théophile Gautier's observation that railway stations had become the cathedrals of the modern age is apposite here, not just in terms of the grand designs that they produced, but in the sense of replacing the sacred communal space of one with the functional communal space of the other.

Reading against the familiar narratives of progress and evolutionary development reveals some striking parallels between the early 1800s and the early 1900s. The call to order after 1918 was perhaps not so different from the repressive political atmosphere of post-1815 Europe. In both cases, the broken promise of social change and the disasters of war were experienced in apocalyptic terms—as the catastrophic ending of historical time rather than its fulfillment. The vast and sensational biblical landscapes of the English painter John Martin, such as the *The Fall of Nineveh* (1829), share common ground with the apocalyptic landscape paintings of Ludwig Meidner produced in Berlin between 1911 and 1916. William Blake's eschatological works around 1800 seem similarly to anticipate themes in the expressionist poetry of Georg Trakl or Kurth Pinthus, summed up in the title of Pinthus's 1920 collection of poems, *Menschheitsdämmerung* (*The Twilight of Mankind*).[10]

THE CLAIMS OF ART

Art is fiction, artifice, invention, make-believe. It is also frequently entertainment, diversion, pastime, ornament. And yet, the art of the long nineteenth century is shaped by a remarkable claim to truth without which it is quite impossible to understand much of what is most celebrated and still valued from this time. This claim, that art somehow discloses aspects of experience and understanding not available to other kinds of discourse or communication, may be summed up in a single word, though it is one singly misunderstood: metaphysics.

There are two versions of the metaphysics of art. The first and popular form, which still has social force today, is that art gives access to a metaphysical realm "not of this world"—that it offers a glimpse of something beyond the usual limits of human understanding, that it speaks what everyday words cannot, and is thus a kind of revelation. Such a view clearly relates to the idea of the artist as a special kind of person (the notion of "genius" comes into its own at this time), an individual of extraordinary insight who nevertheless finds forms through which to communicate this vision to others.

The second form of art as metaphysics is a negative version of the first, connecting the Romantic irony of literature and music of the late eighteenth century with the breakdown of common languages of art around 1900. In place of delivering, in concrete form, the vision of something beyond everyday reality, this kind of art accentuates the limits of its own language. Music, because of its lack of any tangible content or subject matter, came to be understood as the highest form of this idea of art as ineffable.

It is impossible to understand the history of the arts, from Goya and Turner through to Cézanne and Mondrian, from Beethoven and Berlioz to Schoenberg and Debussy, without acknowledging this defining idea. If art in the eighteenth century was essentially a secondary activity—the imitation or representation of aspects of the real world and human experience—in the nineteenth century the shocking claim of art was that it was more true than the apparently real world. While the latter, as the German philosopher Arthur Schopenhauer set out in *The World as Will and Representation* (1819), was merely the fleeting appearance of phenomena, the moving force behind such ephemeral forms could only be expressed through art—above all, music.

It is no coincidence that Friedrich Schiller's *Letters on the Aesthetic Education of Man* (1795) was published just a few years after Immanuel Kant's *Critique of Aesthetic Judgement* (1790). The so-called Third Critique proposes art as one of the key ways in which the essentially divided mind of modern consciousness could be brought into some kind of harmony. Schiller was one of many German Romantics who drew the conclusion that art (in the words of Jürgen Habermas) had the "historical task of reconciling a modernity at variance with itself," and thus of taking on "a virtually social-revolutionary role."[11] In his lectures on aesthetics in 1802–1803, Friedrich Wilhelm Joseph Schelling proposed art as the highest form of human knowledge, equal to philosophy. By 1880, Wagner was able to claim that "it is reserved for art to save the spirit of religion."[12]

After 1918, in a more chastened twentieth century, these claims of Romanticism often seemed dangerously exaggerated. But to understand the nature and the role of the arts across the long nineteenth century requires taking seriously its claims to be an alternative way of knowing the world. The enduring validity of such claims is a question for the philosopher, not the historian, but it remains a historical fact that art exerted the social force that it did and was central to a reimagining of the world. Around 1800, art thus moved from a secondary function (decorative, mimetic, illustrative) to be understood as one of the most powerful ways of mediating key aspects of human experience. Far from being mere illustrations to the book of "real" history, art came more and more to be understood as a powerful form of social practice and agency.

This claim was made particularly about the art that might seem most distant from social reality, that of music. Students of aesthetic modernism have made commonplace the observation of the English critic Walter Pater, in 1877, that "all art constantly aspires to the condition of music," but the idea goes far beyond the intermingling of the arts at the *fin de siècle*; its full resonance draws on the astonishing rise in the status of music in German Romanticism around 1800.[13] The claim that instrumental music could be a kind of thought exemplified a wider sense that art was an expression of what, to language, remained unknowable and unsayable. Art was thus fundamentally allied to metaphysics and the claim that its counterfactual nature gave it a critical distance from everyday life. This post-Kantian idea of art, as bridging the gap between the world and its knowability, joins the Romantic generation of Schlegel, Novalis, and Hoffmann with twentieth-century modernists such as Klee, Schoenberg, Mallarmé, and Rilke. For these figures, art was not a mystery in the sense of something completely irrational, but precisely a search for order by means of a different kind of logic.

THE DIVIDED SUBJECT

These grand claims for art were also claims for the artist. Art could only be special because the artist was a special kind of person. But, in this, the artist represented a collective ideal, standing for the heightened sense of subjectivity that was the single most important invention of the nineteenth century.[14] More powerfully than almost any other social practice, art enacted and articulated this ideal. Being an artist thus meant embodying the profound divisions and contradictions at the heart of the idea of subjectivity, trying to balance out the notion of a unique individual who was also a citizen and social being, to cultivate inwardness and interiority while nevertheless acting in the public sphere. If the crisis of modernism by 1900 was a bifurcation between the insistence on a highly personal mode of expression and the demand for public meaning, this was a crisis already in the making by 1800.

In *The Metropolis and Mental Life* (1903), the German sociologist Georg Simmel analyzed how, in modern life, individuality has to be exaggerated in order to survive at all. When particularity is suppressed by a faceless money economy and the dominance of the intellect, intensely subjective forms of expression are cultivated as a kind of compensation. "This results in the individual's summoning the utmost in uniqueness and particularization in order to preserve his most personal core. He has to exaggerate this personal element in order to remain audible even to himself."[15] Simmel's analysis offers one way in which we might understand the proliferation of "-isms" around 1900: the uniqueness of the artist's vision is marked by a similar uniqueness of style, voice, technique.

Central to that idea was that the artist should speak in the first person—as in lyric poetry, the autobiographical novel, or the self-portrait. These genres are not specific to this period, but from Jean-Jacques Rousseau's *Confessions* (1782) to the self-portraits of Delacroix, Van Gogh, or Schiele, the searing sense of uncompromising self-analysis is highly distinctive. Far more important than the subject of the self-portrait, however, was

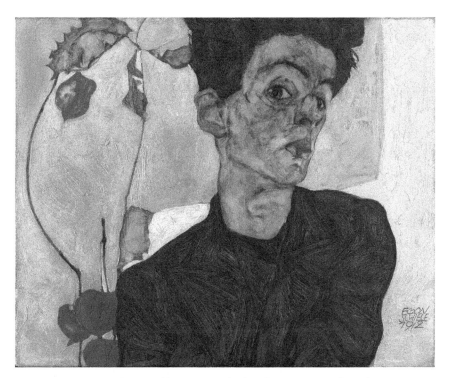

FIGURE 8.3 Egon Schiele, *Self-Portrait with Physalis*, 1912. © Wikimedia Commons (public domain).

singularity of style, the uniqueness of the artist's vision, as evident in a still-life as much as a self-portrait. Similarly, when Frédéric Chopin played the piano, it was understood to be an emanation of his soul, a wordless disclosure of unspoken and unsayable feeling. But more than that, Chopin's music was taken to speak on behalf of its listeners, finding expression, in a way that they could not themselves, for their most intimate and private feelings.

One consequence of this wordless communication meant that music, piano-playing and song in particular, defined a peculiarly intimate mingling of private and social space. It was one in which women, under cover of music's apparent lack of content, could find a rare space in the nineteenth century for a relative degree of performative freedom. This was true not just for amateur pianists and singers, but also for professional pianists and, occasionally, composers—witness Fanny Mendelssohn, Clara Schumann, Cécile Chaminade, Amy Beach, and Lili Boulanger. In painting there were also a few signs that the notion of equality promised by the French Revolution might yet begin to permeate the otherwise strict gender divisions of the nineteenth century. Painters like Adélaïde Labille-Guiard and Élisabeth Vigée Le Brun were certainly the exceptions, but their self-portraits of women *as artists*, in the act of painting, formed part of a slow process of asserting a new kind of active role in the art world, realized later in the century by painters such as Rosa Bonheur, Mary Cassatt, and Berthe Morisot.

The difficulties in carving out a public persona as a female artist can hardly be underestimated, however, a fact amply demonstrated by the number of female writers who felt obliged to publish under a pseudonym—George Eliot, George Sand, the

Brontë sisters. Some women writers had access to this world by dint of marriage or family (Mary Shelley, Christina Rossetti, Elizabeth Barrett Browning, Virginia Woolf), while others did not (Jane Austen, Louisa May Alcott, Harriet Beecher Stowe, Emily Dickinson), but the considerable struggle to be published and thus to be heard, in each one of these cases, stands as an odd indictment of Romanticism's rhetoric of progressive emancipation.

For all artists, being "a special kind of person" often brought with it a precarious sense of being a social outsider. Beethoven, increasingly reclusive on account of his deafness and ill health, became emblematic of artistic genius in this respect. But the heightened subjectivity of the artist—an affirmation of subjectivity in general—was derived from turning away from the world to cultivate one's inwardness. There is a clear parallel between Caspar David Friedrich's advice that "the artist should not only paint what he sees before him, but also what he sees within him" and Paul Klee's insistence, a century later, that "the purpose of art is not to reproduce the visible, but to make visible." It is not that the art of this period rejected the outward appearance of things, but that the artist's task was to discover there a corollary of inward experience. This is what connects E. T. A. Hoffmann with Sigmund Freud, J. M. W. Turner with Henri Matisse. Such an inward focus opens up what a later age would call the Unconscious, precisely the irrational realm that the Age of Enlightenment had attempted to contain. At the dawn of the new century, one of the most telling of the Spanish artist Francisco Goya's *Los Caprichos* (1799), a series of eighty satirical prints, was "The sleep of Reason produces monsters."

Familiar accounts tell us that it was around 1900 that the rational order of art broke down through violent eruptions of repressed Unconscious drives, not least in the embrace of so-called Primitivism, as an attempt to return to an undivided subject. But the deformations of Expressionism have their parallels in Romanticism around 1800—witness the fascination with the supernatural and the uncanny in the stories of Hoffmann and Jean Paul, or in operas like Carl Maria von Weber's *Der Freischütz* (1821) and Heinrich Marschner's *Der Vampyr* (1828). The exploration of dreams connects Henry Fuseli's *The Nightmare* (1781/1791) with the dreamscapes of Giorgio de Chirico painted around 1914. An extreme version is found in depictions of madness, from Goya's *Courtyard with Lunatics* (1793–1794) and Théodore Géricault's late portraits of the insane (1822/1823), to Alban Berg's opera *Wozzeck* (1914–1922).

This interest in madness can be understood as part of a wider turn to the grotesque. Béla Bartók's *Two Portraits* Op. 5, for violin and orchestra (1911), are titled "Ideal" and "Grotesque."[16] One could base a study of the entire history of nineteenth-century art on this definitive tension: from William Blake's pairing of *Songs of Innocence* (1789) with *Songs of Experience* (1794) to Hector Berlioz's *Symphonie Fantastique* (1830), from Charles Baudelaire's "Spleen and Ideal" (1857) to Arnold Schoenberg's *Pierrot Lunaire* (1912), the grotesque haunts the ideal as its accusing, negative inversion. It frequently found expression in the figures of the *commedia dell'arte*, and most particularly in the sad clown Pierrot—witness the troupe of such figures in the work of Hoffmann, Schumann, Verlaine, Baudelaire, Picasso, Seurat, Satie, and Stravinsky.

Such negative extremes might be considered atypical of nineteenth-century art more generally, not least because one of the dominant themes of the early 1800s was the heroic subject. After Napoleon emerged into the public sphere as First Consul of France in November 1799, he quickly became the heroic subject of art. The French painter Jacques-Louis David's larger-than-life *Napoleon Crossing the Alps* (1801) represents an elision of art and politics that was perhaps not matched again until the art of totalitarian states in the twentieth century. Ingres similarly drew on the technique and formats of classical painting to invest the new leader with timeless authority in works like *Napoleon on the Imperial Throne* (1806). Antoine-Jean Gros similarly used history painting as a kind of "contemporary reportage" in *The Battle of Nazareth* (1801) and *Napoleon in the Plague House at Jaffa* (1804).[17]

But, almost at once, the heroic topic was subject to a kind of critical interrogation. In Théodore Géricault's pairing of *The Charging Light Cavalryman* (1812) and *The Wounded Heavy Cavalryman* (1814), the precariousness of Napoleonic power is finely balanced. And in Turner's anti-heroic *Snow Storm: Hannibal and His Army Crossing the Alps* (1812), widely understood to refer to Napoleon, the painter reduces "the heroic protagonist Hannibal to a speck atop a microscopic elephant barely visible on the far reaches of the valley floor."[18] By 1848, the heroic ideal of David's depiction of Napoleon astride a rearing stallion had contracted to the (factually more correct) version of Paul Delaroche's *Bonaparte Crossing the Alps*, in which the weary and defeated emperor is shown seated on a donkey.

THE AUDIENCE

On May 29, 1913, a riot erupted in Paris, not on the streets, as so often at pivotal moments of French history, but in the normally reserved interior of the Théâtre des Champs-Élysées. The occasion was the premiere of *The Rite of Spring*, presented by Sergei Diaghilev's Ballets Russes. The angular style of Vaslav Nijinsky's choreography was certainly part of the problem, but it was the primitive violence of Igor Stravinsky's score that really unsettled the audience. It was not the only musical riot that year. On March 31, a performance of music by Schoenberg and some of his pupils, in the hallowed space of the Musikverein in Vienna, had ended in a brawl and a subsequent court hearing. Such events mark an extreme opposition of art and audience at the heart of aesthetic modernism, a world away from the situation of Joseph Haydn, a servant to Prince Nicolas of Esterhazy from 1761 to 1790, writing music to order and to please his aristocratic patron. But, in Haydn's lifetime, the decline of aristocratic patronage and the rise of a commercial audience was already evident. When Prince Nicholas died in 1790, Haydn suddenly found himself a free agent, and was promptly engaged by the impresario Joseph Salomon to come to London. His two periods of residence there were hugely successful, both artistically and financially, bolstering a new-found economic independence. The twelve London Symphonies (1791–1795) may be remarkably silent on the topic of Revolution, but their very existence is rooted in a new democratization of music. How different was the case of Mozart who died a pauper in 1791, having fatally misjudged the market conditions in Vienna.

At Beethoven's death in 1827, for all his huge reputation, the most famous and popular composer in Europe was the Italian Giacomo Rossini, a figure who much better exemplifies the new economics of the arts. His hugely successful career ran for less than two decades, from *Tancredi* (1813) to *Guillaume Tell* (1829), after which he fell almost silent as a composer until his death in 1868. But in the nine years from 1810 to 1819, by which time he was just twenty-seven years old, he had composed twenty-nine operas. In both the opera house and the concert hall, the audience was changing: in its social make-up, its behavior, its tastes, and its expectations.[19] As Mark Evan Bonds underlines, the symphony after 1800 was heard "as the sonorous manifestation of an ideal state, a society in which every voice could maintain its own distinct identity while contributing to a harmonious whole. Such perceptions reinforced the growing idea that the performance of symphonies ... represented a kind of ritualized enactment of community, be it civic, regional, national or universal."[20]

The monumental style for big public works required big public spaces. The public exhibitions of painting in Paris via the official Salon was itself a kind of spectacle, complete with the politics of style and censorship that provoked radicals to establish alternative spaces—thus the Salon des Refusés (from 1863) and the Salon des Indépendants (from 1884). The Great Exhibitions of the nineteenth century, and the huge buildings that housed them, were physical embodiments of a new alliance of art, industry, and an increasingly mass public—witness the Crystal Palace (1851) in London with its spectacular use of iron and glass or the enduring symbolism of the Eiffel Tower (1889) in Paris. But the public was not simply invited to view monumental art works; they were increasingly the subject of them. From the new power and centrality of the chorus in Verdi operas to the presence of the crowd in the novels of Balzac, Dickens, Zola, and Dostoyevsky, nineteenth-century art aspired to represent a collective whole as much as the individual.

The changing audience, allied to changing urban spaces, innovative institutions, and new technological possibilities, did not leave art unchanged. The popular, far from remaining simply a subject for art, also necessarily generated its own forms. Serialized novels, published in weekly parts in newspapers, appeared in Paris as early as 1829 to create what Arnold Hauser calls "an unprecedented democratization of literature."[21] Honoré de Balzac's Le Pére Goriot (1835–1836) and Charles Dickens's The Pickwick Papers (1836) were early successes, though the real master of the new form was Alexandre Dumas, author of The Three Musketeers (1844). The development of the upright piano in the 1820s, led by the French firm Érard, created an explosion of domestic music-making; by 1845 there were an estimated 60,000 pianos in Paris alone and around 200 piano manufacturers in England, mostly in London. Was everyone playing Beethoven on the parlor piano? Apparently not, since, by 1860, the most popular form of musical entertainment in London was music hall and, in Paris, operetta.[22]

Such rapid social changes impacted not only the practice of the arts, but also what one might call the politics of representation. The Romantic claim for the critical and even emancipatory function of art had been linked to an idea of radical newness, of challenging and transcending conventional forms. The claim that revolutionary art enacts a revolutionary politics goes back to Beethoven, but it was alive and well with Wagner in the 1850s, and it would continue to echo in strategies to engage a wider public with modern art in the socialist republic of "Red Vienna" in the 1920s.[23] But by the mid-century it had produced an awkward paradox since, in practice, the opposite was often true: radical art seemed to show a contempt for ordinary people, a high-minded and hermetic self-sufficiency. As Christopher Butler puts it, the claim for the avant-garde rests on the faith that advanced art "provoked the emancipation of the subject out of bourgeois conformity." But did it? Given the social base and structure of artistic institutions, was "revolutionary art" not an oxymoron?

In the face of such a contradiction, a number of artists attempted to break down the gap and genuinely politicize art in a broadly socialist cause. In 1849, Gustave Courbet painted "three colossal pictures that changed the history of art"—The Stonebreakers, A Burial at Ornans, Peasants of Flagey returning from the Fair.[24] All three were shown

FIGURE 8.4 Jean-François Millet, *The Gleaners*, 1857. © Wikimedia Commons (public domain).

in Paris the following year. The powerful realism of Courbet's representation of rural workers, in a manner that seemed to derive from their own world rather than being idealized by an elite and urban aesthetic, was read as a political challenge, redefining the social purpose of art by its powerful representation of the conditions of the working class. Jean-François Millet's *The Sower* (1850) and *The Gleaners* (1857) made a similar impact through the directness with which the rawness of rural labor was brought into the salon.

While the turn to realism in painting and naturalism in literature redirected art towards material social conditions, a more long-standing tradition that was repurposed in the nineteenth century was that of art as satire, especially in the "low" forms of prints, etchings, engravings, and aquatints. Goya's *Los caprichos* was deemed to be sufficiently incendiary that it was "withdrawn" from sale two days after it appeared. A similar kind of censorship operated in Metternich's Vienna in the 1830s, evidence enough that art was judged to have powerful social influence. Conversely, where the art of the caricaturist flourished, as in the work of James Gillray, Honoré Daumier, and Jean-Jacques Grandville, political dissent was probably alive and well. Using art to indict society, at its more extreme, caricature became an indictment of the institution of art itself. When the German poet Hugo Ball opened a cabaret in Zurich in 1916, he initially called it the Cabaret Voltaire. Home to the notorious Dada movement, the name was surely intended to underline that the possibility of enlightened critique was exhausted and all that was left, he believed, was nonsense or the babbling of infants. Amid the carnage of the First World War, it must surely have been hard to avoid a sense of profound frustration and bitterness that art had failed in its promise to change the world.

NATURE AND TECHNOLOGY

Within a few decades after 1800 the genre of history painting moved from a position of pre-eminence to one of peripheral status. By contrast, the importance of landscape painting grew rapidly to become "the defining genre of artistic renewal."[25] This might be understood as part of an inward migration from politics and the public sphere to questions of a more personal relationship to the (natural) world, history, and ideas of community. The English critic John Ruskin was one of many to note, in his *Modern Painters* (1843–1860), the rise of landscape painting as emblematic of a wider task of art, as he saw it, to re-articulate the spiritual content of nature in the face of an industrialized society. Such a vision could certainly be found in the work of artists like Philipp Otto Runge, Samuel Palmer, and Caspar David Friedrich. For the latter, landscape may have entailed a mediation of nature and spirit, but it was one hard fought rather than easily won. His *Monk by the Sea* (1810) poses the relation between mankind and the natural world as a problem, a question, a mystery—something to be worked out in solitude rather than being underwritten by any system or faith.

Ruskin made his home in the English Lake District, thus making common cause with the Lake Poets (Wordsworth, Coleridge, Southey) of an earlier generation. But it was Turner who was the key figure for Ruskin, a painter whose work submits the abstract idea of representation to a powerful assault of sensory intensity. Grand historical themes, and the fate of men great and small, were situated precariously amid powerful natural forces, often on the brink of being overwhelmed—witness his fondness for storms at sea and in the mountains. It is a world away from the work of his contemporary, John Constable, a man who once said that his "limited and restricted art may be found under every hedge."[26] While Turner traveled across Europe and Britain, Constable's art hardly ventured beyond the cycle of rural life around his birthplace in Suffolk. In the 1820s he produced a series of monumental "six footers," not of heroic figures or great events, but of unknown localities in a rural backwater, most famously *The Hay Wain* (1821) and *Dedham Vale* (1828).

It is hard not to be struck by the obvious contradiction of an art that dwells on representations of rural tranquility in an age of rapid industrialization and urbanization. Turner is, again, interesting here because his work engaged the tension between these in fascinating ways, as in *Rain, Steam and Speed—The Great Western Railway* (1844). Just as the Renaissance pastoral was understood to be played out outside the city walls (rather than in a total wilderness), so nineteenth-century painting increasingly acknowledged the tension between nature and technology in landscapes located within sight of the city, as in Turner's *London from Greenwich Park* (1809) and Georges Seurat's *A Bathing Place, Asnières* (1884), or where the city is merely implied by the presence of the railway, as in Claude Monet's *Railway Bridge at Argenteuil* (1874).

A very particular version of that tension is played out in art in the United States, given the ambivalent attitude to wilderness as both a potential economic resource, to be tamed through technology, and (for transcendentalists like Ralph Waldo Emerson and Henry David Thoreau) a necessary counterweight to the advance of human society. In a landscape with a railway, such as George Inness's *The Lachawanna Valley* (1857), that tension is merely implied; in a painting like Asher B. Durand's *Landscape, Progress (The Advance of Civilization)* (1853), the message of the dangers of technological domination is clear. Similarly complex and political issues were at stake in the way in which art dealt with the notion of distant places. In orientalist operas, from Giacomo Meyerbeer's *L'Africaine* (1865) to Léo Délibes' *Lakme* (1883) and Giacomo Puccini's *Madam Butterfly* (1903), the format repeats itself over and again: the exotic is fantasized as feminine, erotic, available. It was, of course, technologies of transport and industrial production, on the back of colonialism, that had opened up Europe to the world, and the world cultures that the composer Claude Debussy and his contemporaries saw as "exhibits" at the Paris Exhibition of 1889 (and many others like it) were strangely divorced from this social reality. The echoes of the sonority of the Javanese gamelan in Debussy's piano music, of Japanese prints in Whistler, Degas, and Van Gogh, or African masks in Matisse and Picasso thus have to do with the struggle of European art within its own world, not with any real exploration of a different one.

It is another example of Koselleck's idea of the simultaneity of different times that modernism's fascination with the idea of the primitive coincided with a parallel interest in new technologies. It is nicely summed up by Debussy's rather disparaging remark about Stravinsky's *Rite of Spring*, that it was "primitive with every modern convenience." The impact of new technologies necessarily changed the sensory experience of everyday life. Stephen Kern, in his study of the period 1880–1918, lists innovations including the telephone, wireless telegraph, X-ray, cinema, bicycle, automobile, and airplane.[27] Sara Danius suggests, in turn, that the result of these was "a technologically mediated crisis of the senses" that shaped modern art from Marcel Proust to James Joyce.[28] In fact, the sensory impact of these changes was felt a good deal earlier and not always as a crisis. Many popular Viennese waltzes and polkas by the Strauss family, from the 1860s onwards, referenced recent developments ("Acceleration," "Without Brakes," "Non-Stop"), suggesting a pleasurable exchange between the thrill of bodily movement in the dance and that of the new transport technologies.

Nowhere was this embrace of new technology more immediately visible, however, than in the attempts of Italian Futurist painters to capture the sense of continuous motion in modern life. In some cases, such as Giacomo Balla's *Rhythms of the Bow* (1912), a study of the sequence of movements of a violinist's arm, this was derived from the example of chronophotography in which successive stages of movement appear in a single image. But the same idea is explored in *Simultaneous Visions* (1912) by Umberto Boccioni in which objects as such give way to a picture of motion itself. Similarly, nowhere was this new sensibility more audible than in the attempts of Futurist musicians to capture the chaotic counterpoint of noise in an urban landscape. In his *Technical Manifesto of Futurist Music* (1911), Francesco Balilla Pratella insisted that music should reflect "the musical soul of the crowds, of great industrial plants, of trains, of transatlantic liners, of armoured warships, of automobiles, of airplanes."[29] Luigi Russolo similarly argued, in *The Art of Noises* (1913), that today "we derive much greater pleasure from ideally combining the noises of street-cars, internal-combustion engines, automobiles and busy crowds, than from rehearing, for example, [Beethoven's] *Eroica* or the *Pastorale*."[30]

The invention of photography was undoubtedly one of the most important technological events of the nineteenth century.[31] The daguerreotype was publicly announced in 1839, but it was not until after 1850 that it saw widespread use, through the popularity of the photographic portrait. Baudelaire complained as early as 1859 that such a technology was inimical to art, an early sign of the modernist mistrust of the standardization produced by mechanical means based on the fear that the identity of the individual—that most prized construction of the Romantic age—would be dissipated by

FIGURE 8.5 Umberto Boccioni, *Simultaneous Visions*, 1912. © History and Art
Collection / Alamy Stock Photo.

mass culture. It is certainly true that photography at first became largely functional. André
Adolphe-Eugène Disdéri, "who almost singlehandedly established the portrait industry
in Paris," is credited with having standardized the portrait format in 1854, reducing the
image to the size of a visiting card reproducible in multiple prints.[32] The fixing of the
image in a stock repertoire of formats was later set out in Disdéri's *The Art of Photography*
(1862), confirming Baudelaire's worst fears (and anticipating those of a critical theorist
like Theodor Adorno) that the image was a simulacrum of individuality constructed by a
mechanical and repetitive model that denied the very thing it purported to affirm.

REPRESENTATION AND ABSTRACTION

A popular understanding of the difference between Romanticism and Modernism is
that one had to do with the depiction of real objects, people, and landscapes, while the
other had to do with more abstract forms, sounds, and colors. But this familiar account
misses the essential connection between the two—the extent to which artists across the
period were as much concerned with the *how* as the *what*, the materiality of art itself as
much as with ideas of representation. What is often called the "crisis" of modern art is

fundamentally a crisis of language, of the adequacy of language as a representation of the world. As language came under scrutiny, from Rousseau, Herder, and Novalis to Mauthner, Wittgenstein, and Saussure, so art explored its own capacity for a different kind of sense-making. This was clear even in the literary arts—witness the derangements and creative reorganizations of language in the work of Rimbaud, Mallarmé, Kafka, Joyce, or Woolf. But it was equally true in the case of the visual arts, music, dance, and even the new art of film; around 1900, conventions of representation in all these arts were called into question, reformulated and in many cases dismantled and discarded, from Picasso and Kandinsky to Schoenberg and Stravinsky. There are two principal ways by which this critical distance was made from art's older function of mimetic representation: firstly, by opening up an ironic space within art's own modes of signification; secondly, through a focus on the materiality of art itself.

In many ways, it took the foregrounding of irony in early twentieth-century art to reactivate an understanding of Romantic irony in the late eighteenth century. This is particularly the case in music where thinking about irony in Neoclassicism helped draw out the irony in the Classical style itself (witness the play of ironic wit in Haydn and Beethoven). This aspect of music was not so much forgotten as displaced by the hegemony of an idea of music as direct and authentic self-expression. The legacy of musical Romanticism has thus powerfully occluded a different view, exemplified by composers like Rossini, Offenbach, and Satie, of an art that foregrounds its own fictitiousness.

But closer scrutiny shows that the deconstructive force of irony ran through the arts of this period like a cold, fast-flowing river. Its function was always to disturb the stability of meaning wherever it had become too comfortable, too conventional, and taken-for-granted. One of its methods was to create a critical distance from tradition by citing familiar works or conventions while deforming them at the same time. The idea is

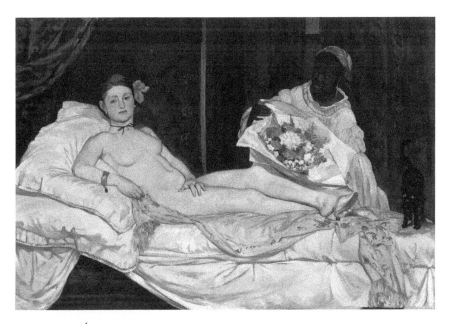

FIGURE 8.6 Édouard Manet, *Olympia*, 1863. © Wikimedia Commons (public domain).

exemplified in Manet's *Le Déjeuner sur l'herbe* (1863) and *Olympia* (painted in 1863 but not exhibited until 1865). Both are suffused with references to past paintings (by Titian, Giorgione, and others), classical works which they undermine in their ironic treatment of their subject matter as much as their rough and "unfinished" technique. And in subverting the historical genres on which they depend (the female nude and the pastoral), they also subvert the expectations of the institutions of art. It is hardly surprising that they were savaged by many critics.

Long before any theory of intertextuality, art had itself explored a complex web of textual connections as a mode of critical self-reflection. In *Le Bonheur de vivre* (1905–1906), Matisse references Watteau, Ingres, Giorgione; in the *Classical Symphony* (1917), Sergei Prokofiev takes a modern look back at the symphonies of Haydn and Mozart. By underlining the contingency and relativity of stylistic conventions, such works undermined the idea of an authorial voice or hand and thus of the idea of direct, unmediated, and authentic communication. As Stravinsky played with historical musical styles in *Pulcinella* (1920), James Joyce was writing the eighteen episodes of *Ulysses* (1918–1920) in as many different literary styles. Glenn Watkins has underlined how nineteenth-century ideas of organic form were displaced in the twentieth century by techniques of collage and "cut-and-paste assemblage."[33]

Ironic play with language, style, and quotation was one way in which art questioned received ideas of the world. But another, equally important way was the increasing focus on the sensuous material of art itself over any signifying or quasi-linguistic function. Poetry focused more on the tone and rhythm of the spoken word, painting on color, music on sonority. Dance provides one of the most striking examples of this new emphasis, since it foregrounds so directly the centrality of the human body over language. One of the great shocks of *The Rite of Spring* was the way in which Nijinsky's choreography seemed to ignore the long tradition of communicative conventions established in classical ballet. And just as Stravinsky's music seemed to distance itself from the refined language-like structures of musical phrase and motif to focus instead on the more elemental aspects of rhythm and sound, so too did Nijinsky's choreography work from a more immediate and physical sense of the body in motion. Nijinsky's lexicon of new movements came, in part, from the Eurythmics of the Swiss musician and teacher Émile Jacques-Dalcroze (via the dancer Marie Rambert). But this was part of a wider movement in modern dance in which a focus on the idea of "natural" human movement displaced the nineteenth-century focus on storytelling and highly refined conventional techniques. Key figures in this were two American dancers—Loie Fuller and Isadora Duncan—and two German dancers, Grete Wisenthal and Mary Wigman. What all four achieved was a new kind of dance derived from and centered in the natural body.

Key to the foregrounding of art's own materiality was also the interaction between different arts. Music was led by poetry and painting, while poetry and painting were led by music. The music of Debussy, for example, was partly shaped by a relation to literary Symbolism (particularly Mallarmé and Maeterlinck) as also to certain painters (Turner, Whistler, Monet, and the Japanese printmaker Hokusai). But, at the same time, literary Symbolism was indebted to music (to Wagner, above all) and painting would soon take music as its model (Wassily Kandinsky, most prominently, as in his series of works, after 1909, titled *Impressions*, *Improvisations*, and *Compositions*). For painting and literature, the case of music offered a way out of the constrictions of naturalism and realism that dominated the latter half of the nineteenth century. But in turn, in the form of a musicalized poetry, literature gave music a way forward of its own (hence the importance of the poetry of Richard Dehmel and Stefan George for Arnold Schoenberg's move toward atonality).

The focus of art became not the representation of an object but the act of aesthetic perception itself—of seeing, listening, moving. Mallarmé's famous quip to the painter Edgar Degas, that poems are made with words not ideas, chimes with Paul Klee's observation, in 1910, of the importance of "one's attitude to the contents of one's paint box."[34] In some cases, this led to extravagant claims for the power and significance of art's materials, such as Kandinsky's theories of color in *On the Spiritual in Art* (1911), and in the early twentieth century a number of key figures, Piet Mondrian being one of them, were attracted to the mystical ideas of theosophy. The move to abstraction itself bifurcated: on the one hand, painters like Mondrian and composers such as Anton Webern sought to create a world of pure forms behind the heterogeneity of phenomena. "We must ... see *through* nature," Mondrian insisted. "We must see deeper, see *abstractly* and above all *universally* ... Then we can see the external for what it really is: the mirror of truth."[35] On the other hand, artists like Klee and composers like Debussy questioned such a "rhetoric of purity" with explorations of the particularity of phenomenal forms.

For that reason, the term abstraction is a misnomer for much of the art of the early twentieth century. Far from being abstract, its focus was most often a kind of absolute materiality (of paint, color, sound, movement) rather than an "idea" of representation. The shift is underlined ironically by the idea of a cubist portrait. Picasso's *Portrait of Daniel-Henry Kahnweiler* (1910), as Christopher Butler points out, contains "no particularly Kahnweiler-like features, except perhaps the right eyebrow and the hair above it."[36] A painting from 1912 by Picasso is titled *Ma Jolie* (*Woman with a Zither or Guitar*). The lack of specificity in the subtitle, added later, helps disabuse the viewer of any expectation that representation of superficial reality is the purpose of the painting.

As we have seen in the case of each of my six categories, the "new" around 1900 is already present in the "new" around 1800. The exploration of color in Turner and Delacroix anticipates Matisse and Cézanne; the exploration of sound and gesture in Berlioz anticipates Debussy. This essentially Romantic move has often been understood as "a triumph of the irrational," but we might understand it better if we avoid this binary opposition to the supposedly rational eighteenth century.[37] What I have in mind comes closer to what Gilles Deleuze would later call a "logic of the senses," an emphasis on particularity and individuality that resists the tendency of abstract thought to displace the subject. Which brings us, full circle, back to Manet's *Lemon* of 1880, a painting that foregrounds particularity and affirms the irreducible individuality of the most humble of objects. In doing so, it affirms not only the subjective presence of the painter, through his act of remaking the world, but also that of the viewer through the act of looking. This affirmation of the irreducible particularity of ordinary things, including ourselves, was the extraordinary business of nineteenth-century art.

CHAPTER NINE

History

DONALD R. KELLEY AND BONNIE G. SMITH

In 1800, a London traveler to Burma noted that the ruler of the Kingdom of Ava had a larger library "than any potentate from the banks of the Danube to the border of China."[1] In 1829, appointed by the Ava king, a committee began compiling inscriptions, chronicles, and other sources to create the "Glass Palace Chronicle" of events back to the eleventh century. At about the same time, official annals-writers in the Ottoman Empire were similarly busy noting events and compiling records both past and present as part of their official duties. Occasionally these records took a critical stance toward past policies, but it was rare for one to bite the hand that provided the salary, even metaphorically. These "event writers," generally based in Istanbul, made their chronicles livelier by presenting a bit of biography alongside official views and analyses. Across the globe, history also appeared in poetic form during these years and in many other genres, including song, folklore, paintings, and needlework. A shift was, however, in the works.

History continued to take diverse forms in the course of the nineteenth century, much of it still emanating from courts and reflecting that point of view, even as the rise of the modern nation-state brought forth scientific standards, new ways of narrating earlier times, and exacting methods for approaching the past and thinking about it. Historical writing in an age of nineteenth-century imperial expansion tacked between a professionalizing history of the nation and comparatively much less expert or professionalized histories of the world. Given the intense globalization of the century, it may seem contradictory that newly professionalized history based on research and specialized erudition was most often nationally focused and inward-looking. Despite increased and growing knowledge of the world's peoples, the development of archivally sourced national histories in Europe (and soon thereafter, the United States) anchored the consolidating nation-state in a somewhat traditional march through political regimes. Because the acquiescence of the wider population was part of nation-building, moreover, this half-dynastically oriented history eventually came to depend on describing peoples and cultures, too.

More tightly administered nation-states with increasingly powerful, industrially produced weaponry were well positioned to increase their imperial holdings. These expanding holdings provided commodities for factories, including foodstuffs, but also a raft of global knowledge that fed into the work not just of the sciences but of history, ultimately inspiring history's broadening out. The West's professional expertise in charting the growth of the nation and its increasingly well-administered institutions covered over national theft of foreign resources, military savagery in empire-building, and most nations' use, to varying degrees, of slave labor, at home but especially abroad. In fact, the history of the Western nation-state showed the nation as a civilizing end in itself, tamed through the creation of scientific narratives about its past. Although often a narrative of wars, histories usually concluded with the national establishment of peace, legitimizing the nation-state as a political form.

Thus, the development of professional history was an important cultural arm of modern nation-building, especially as the rising nineteenth-century nation often encompassed imperial expansion. Aligned oppositionally to archival national narratives, writings on diverse peoples, topographies, and cultures characterized but a small fraction of the imperial side of historical work. Globalized philologists who professionalized the study of Sanskrit and other non-Latin-based languages in the West and those in other countries who studied indigenous and European languages did still other forms of historical investigation. In the eighteenth century, especially after the founding of the Academy of Oriental Languages in Vienna in 1752, travel, specialization, and diplomatic concerns led to an interest in the Orient as in the scholarship of Carsten Niebuhr, Edward Bunsen, and Edward Sachau. While these Germans and others lacked a specific national interest in the Orient, the study of non-Western regions would eventually contribute to the growth of cultural history. For almost a century, Western interest in the Orient was expressed in the academy chiefly in works of cultural history.

Beyond the horizons of professionalizers, the historical work of popular memory continued in the enactment of mythical stories, such as performances of the Ramayana, or the perpetuation of historical practices, such as the Japanese emperor's turning of soil and the empress's ceremonial commemoration of silk production. Native Americans, excluded often brutally from the new nations of North and Central America, maintained their origin stories. The world's peoples also lived history by supporting the building of public monuments, collecting family and other manuscripts, and keeping shrines, burial grounds, and other sacred spots alive in historical memory through regular pilgrimages and maintenance. Reciting the Qu'ran or the Bible or sutras on various occasions was not just a religious event but also a historical one.

Still, this was the heyday of "modernization" or professionalization in historical practice. New thoughts arose about the nature of history and the work of researching and writing it—that is, the modernization of historical heuristics—with German, French, and British states organizing these efforts and increasingly locating them in university scholarship. "An enlightenment without ground, a historical enlightenment without documents is no enlightenment at all," wrote Friedrich Nicolai in 1782, appearing to criticize former practices.[2] As Christoph Meiners noted in 1782, "There is almost no science, no fine or practical art, ... which has not found its historian in the past century."[3] The eighteenth-century Enlightenment has been associated with the fact-based profile of natural science and the "rationality" of philosophy, but the modern field of history was no less a product of the eighteenth century. After the eighteenth-century rhetorician Giambattista Vico had resurrected philology in his "new science," the German philosophers Johann Georg Hamann and Johann Gottfried Herder produced a "metacritique" of Kantian abstract reason that recalled thought away from pure reason to language as a form of sturdy, verifiable evidence.

Herder himself published his immense *Ideas for the Philosophy of History of Humanity* between 1784 and 1791, which emphasized individual languages and cultures of peoples, and others joined him in what involved, in J. C. Adelung's coinage, "cultural history" (*Kulturgeschichte*). This movement was reinforced by the academic study of history culminating in the founding of the University of Berlin in 1810 and the subsequent compilation of great archival collections and the establishment of the seminar system. Justus Moeser emphasized "local reason" (*Lokalvernunft*), and in the 1790s several scholars wrote of the "historicizing" of knowledge and philosophy, adding to the crucial term "historicism" (*Historismus*). For this brief moment, the potential for a German national history was infused with culture—language, folklore, and artifacts such as pots and implements—as its scientific, objective ground.

At the University of Berlin taught the great historian of ancient Rome, Barthold Georg Niebuhr, who rejected myth and other ephemera in favor of philology, archaeology, and recorded historical facts based on written records, and Karl Otfried Mueller, who also studied Greek antiquities and literature. Niebuhr, son of the Danish explorer Carsten Niebuhr, was not only a distinguished statesman but also, according to Heinrich von Treitschke, "the first among all men of learning."[4] With his emphasis on philology, Niebuhr became a founder of modern German historical science (*Geschichtswissenschaft*) to whom even the great later German historian Leopold von Ranke deferred. Histories of Rome and Greece based on an array of evidence as well as the study of language would become privileged foundations for the West's imperial nations, including the United States. The reliance on documents and other verifiable evidence became codified in the formula of Ranke, admonishing scholars to find out "what really happened" (*"wie es eigentlich gewesen"*), referring specifically to the Venetian archives containing written reports from resident ambassadors. "Only from a spiritually combined series of facts does the event result," suggesting that in the progressive but verifiable history of any institution there might reside a higher, spiritual, or philosophical form.[5]

Karl Friedrich von Savigny was, in the mid-nineteenth century, the leader of the historical school of Roman law, publishing a monumental history emphasizing its continuity over many centuries. In a similar spirit, Karl Friedrich Eichhorn studied the tradition of Germanic law and its national coherence, lending to Western professional historical methods their rule-abiding and impartial reputation, in contrast to the myth-making and more poetic effusions of earlier authors and supposedly less advanced societies. The "higher truth" of events in national histories emerged from professionalization, allowing these events to serve as enduring foundations for individual states.

The original historicism of the late eighteenth century distinguished facts of human experience from the abstract reason of philosophers. It had strong ties to philology and the humanist tradition, as illustrated by the classical scholar P. A. Boeckh, a leading Hellenist of the Restoration period, making use of inscriptions in his study of the material base of Greek history while also opposing the Romantic emphasis on myth. K. O. Mueller similarly turned to archaeology and, in a critical spirit, mythology. In a history of Greek literature, he pointed to language as the key to comparative prehistory—that world in which the less critical and less scientific peoples still lived—and eventually to the origins of a common past. Among the disciples of Boeckh and Mueller was Ernst Curtius, who taught at the University of Berlin, doing his best work in archaeology and geography. Even more famous was Heinrich Schliemann, who began the excavation of Troy in 1870. Another of Beockh's students was the German historian Johann Gustav Droysen, who

FIGURE 9.1 Leopold von Ranke, 1877. © ART Collection / Alamy
Stock Photo.

wrote especially on hermeneutics and historical method. Heuristics and the science of
interpretation continued to develop.

In his lectures at the University of Bonn in 1829–1830, Niebuhr celebrated modern
discoveries of the ancient world, beginning with Egypt. In his "'ballad theory'" Niebuhr
tried to go beyond, or find traces of historical fact in ancient myth, poetry, classical
historians, the work of Cicero, and ancient records and inscriptions. Always in a
Eurocentric mode, these historians grounded modern nations and cultures securely in the
deep past of state institutions or earlier empires, which could also serve as an imperial
claim. With the work of Theodor Mommsen came the turn away from philology and
"occult conjectures" to science in his study of the later period of Roman history. For
Mommsen, ancient history was a complete cycle of civilization, and modern history

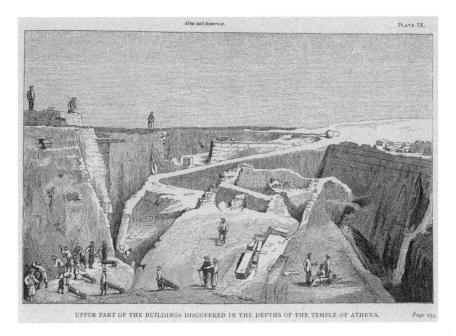

FIGURE 9.2 Excavation of Ancient Turkey. © Science and Society Picture Library / Getty Images.

a second wave; he looked into the real and more reliably sourced life of the people in ancient Italy. Mommsen believed "that there is a bridge connecting the past glory of Hellas and Rome with the prouder fabric of modern history," making explicit the relationship between ancient and present-day power.[6]

J. G. Eichhorn wrote in 1796, "The history of arts and sciences, their progress and various transformations can never be separated from the history of the social, for culture and literature are twin sisters."[7] His comments referred to the field of cultural history (*Kulturgeschichte*) that had originally included social behavior and patterns. Mommsen, however, professed to show in his studies that European cultures, scientifically and philologically studied, "have a very different sound from those of Asoka and Salmanassar; that Homer and Sophocles are not merely like the Vedas and Kalidisa," referring to Central and South Asian texts. Instead, scientific study proved that Europe grew "in our own garden—all of this is the work of Caesar."[8] World civilizations in an age of rising European empires, were, for Mommsen, irrelevant to the development of Europe's unique nation-state form and its enlightened culture. Greece and Rome alone mattered.

The stunning and complex political developments during the French Revolution turned still other historians in the West explicitly toward the study of the history of the state. The national resurgence after the French Revolution can be seen in the work of Heinrich Luden, who came to the University of Jena in 1806 and, with Johann Wolfgang von Goethe, discussed the nature of historical truth, which Goethe considered subjective. At Jena, Luden praised the unity of the national state, arguing that "in Germany all culture comes from the people," and yet he participated in the growing focus on and professionalization of political history.[9] In 1814, Luden began publishing his *General History of People and States*. Two of his contemporaries were Friedrich von Raumer, who published a *History of the Hohenzollern* (1823–1835), and Gustav Stenzel, who published a *History of the Frankish Emperors* (1827–1828) and a *History of Prussia* (1830–1837). Other national histories in this pre-Rankean age were those of Friedrich Wilken (1830), Friedrich Kohlraush (1816–1817), K. A. Menzel (1815–1821), J. K. Pfister (1829–1835), and Hans von Gagern (1825–1826). The Society for Germany's Oldest Historical Sources was founded in 1819, beginning with the Carolingian chronicles—again anchoring the state in a deep past verified in palpable documents. Erudition, despite avowals to the contrary, did not remain impartial in the period of national upheaval. Often it was devoted instead to the political unification of the "fatherland" and searching out the nation's higher truth.

The leading figure of this next stage of history in Europe was Ranke, who began with the study of antiquity but moved beyond the Roman Empire to the barbarian peoples whose history showed development toward the modern national states and their growing documentation. Ranke's first major work was his *History of the Latin and Teutonic Nations* of 1824, which was followed by his *History of the Popes* (1834–1836), elaborating on Rome as the center of European events, and *History of Germany in the Reformation*, concentrating on his major source of inspiration, Martin Luther. In his *Nine Books of Prussian History* (1846), Ranke narrowed his focus from the Holy Roman Empire to a principality aiming at a national state. Later Ranke turned his attention to the English and French monarchies. Ranke's last, multi-volume work, published in 1881, took up world history. The moment marked one highpoint in an age of modern empires. For Ranke, however, world history had a precise and relevant meaning: from the particularity of individual European nations could be culled world historical and universal insights. This history was less about the world's many regions in this age of empire than about the world as understood through the development of European institutions. It would remain so for many students of history long into the twentieth century.

Like Droysen and Mommsen, Ranke was the leader of an extended tradition of scholars over some five generations of disciples, producing an elite that monopolized the study of history in more than fifty German universities even into the Third Reich, not only though lectures but especially through the new seminar system. Into these generally all-male gatherings, avid professors carted compilations of documents for the instruction of historians-in-training. Many of these scholars were medievalists associated with the *Monumenta Germania Historica*, or the great records of German history. Increasingly after 1848, however, medievalists turned to modern history and were swept into the unification movement by which the many German-speaking states became unified as the German Empire. Among Ranke's students was Georg Waitz, who at Berlin had attended the lectures in the history of law of Savigny as well as Ranke's seminar. At the University of Kiel, Waitz began work on his history of Germany's constitutional development, the first volume of which he dedicated to Ranke. It made use of Jakob Grimm's fairy tales not as history but as evidence. Waitz, who with Friedrich Dahlmann had published a valuable bibliography of German history, became director of the *Monumenta Germania* in 1876. In 1878, while teaching at the University of Göttingen, he published the last of eight volumes of his major work, the *Constitutional History of Germany*, further solidifying the institutional foundation of the new German nation as it entered the imperial fray of the late nineteenth century.

Waitz's seminar at Göttingen was attended by Gabriel Monod, among others, who spread German historical methods to France. Another student of Ranke was Wilhelm

Giesebrecht, who first published a monograph on Otto II and, starting in 1855, his great *History of the German Imperial Era* (*Kaizerzeit*), which was never completed. The youngest of Ranke's major students was Heinrick von Sybel. He began with a *History of the First Crusade*, and in 1844 he published his *Origins of German Kingship*. In 1859, he founded the *Historisches Zeitschrift*, the first journal of scholarly history. He was also a champion of Protestantism, which brought him to the University of Marburg and explains his eventual attraction to modern political history. After 1848, German historical scholarship began shifting its focus from erudition to modern politics. Leaders of the Prussian school included Dahlmann, Ludwig Hausser, Max Duncker, Droysen, and Heinrich von Treitschke, the youngest and greatest figure, who lectured at Leipzig and in 1867 succeeded Hausser at Heidelberg. As these scholars intensified their studies of Germany, so the nation prepared itself not just for a national empire but for an overseas one as well.

The major representative of the nationalist Prussian school and son of an ennobled Saxon general, Treitschke thought an author should be "a microcosm of his people." Treitschke was a supporter of Otto von Bismarck, German Chancellor and founder of the unified German Empire, and no less a national historian-prophet than were Droysen and Sybel. He founded in 1858 the *Preussische Jahrbücher*, publishing in it essays on history, literature, and politics. Treitschke's major work is his *History of Germany in the Nineteenth Century* (1879–1894), a panoramic view of German politics and culture from the Thirty Years War to the eve of the 1848 Revolutions. In 1867, he succeeded Hausser at Heidelberg and in 1874 was called to Berlin. Treitschke wanted Germany to be not an empire but a racially unified state. He wrote that the disappearance of war "would turn the earth into a great temple of selfishness," and he disapproved of what he saw as the comparatively neutral stance of Ranke.[10] In this frame of mind, he moved history from "science" (*Wissenschaft*) to active politics, including the politics of imperial expansion. Treitschke cast scorn on other nationalities, especially the French and English. The militaristic Prussian school itself came to a culmination with his work.

Treitschke's nationalistic bravura arose from Prussia's victory in the Franco-Prussian War of 1870–1871. The rivalrous and yet parallel paths of historical scholarship in France and in the Prussian state had begun long before, with the French Revolution and the Napoleonic Wars. As the revolutionary era unfolded, amateurs outside the Prussian university system had adapted the romantic and cultural impulses of Herder and others, writing histories of people, their practices and beliefs but without the focus on language as a scientific ground of reality. Meanwhile, Germaine de Staël, writing in Switzerland, located cultural history in the artifacts of individual states and kingdoms of Germany. In a number of historical works, she surveyed the sentiments found in culture, outlining them in a variety of forms, including brief biographies of, and often paeans to, ancient women and short stories featuring global characters. In one of her novels, *Corinne* (1807), the heroine takes her lover on a historical tour of the various Italian states, inspiring romantic feelings not only of personal oneness in the couple but also of their oneness with the Italian and Roman past. Her heroine grasps that one may understand the past "through imagination rather than through ... critical judgment."[11] In this regard, as philosophers today also note, emotions were a form of cognition. De Staël included cultural influences as well in her own personal history of the French Revolution in her *Considerations on the Principal Events of the French Revolution* (1818).

De Staël had been preceded in her historical impulse by two very different pre-revolutionary women operating in a different arena. In 1792, Pauline de Lézardière published her *Theory of the Political Laws of the French Monarchy*, a collection of original documents and those found in ancient books. At the age of seventeen, Lézardière began the multi-volume work amidst the political crises of the 1770s and continued it through the 1780s and the beginnings of the Revolution, showing the rights of the French Parlements and national assemblies and situating France as a state in its history. Less legally minded, Louise Kéralio started publishing anthologies of women's poetry and fictional writing in the 1780s, thereby creating another form of historical documentation. (This impulse simultaneously existed among women in China: Wang Yun gathered up women's poetry from family archives across China to create a historical record of such accomplishments. Her granddaughters published several volumes testifying to this illustrious cultural past.)

Like de Staël, René de Chateaubriand also wrote on revolutions though earlier he, too, had written German-style Romantic novels such as *René* (1802). He then restored the emphasis on religion diverted by the Enlightenment: among the products of this shift of emphasis were his own *Genius of Christianity* (also published in 1802) and J. E. Michaud's *History of the Crusades*, the first volume of which appeared in 1812. Women historians—all of them amateurs like Chateaubriand and often, like him, in need of funds—were likewise moved by the revolutionary experience, producing history like him in a variety of styles, including historical fiction. They relied wherever possible on documentation, sometimes gaining access to the actual owners of family papers. However, again like Chateaubriand, they were sometimes first hand witnesses whose work in an age of rising national professionalization would, over the course of the century, become suspect. Mercy Otis Warren in the new United States of America wrote the first history of the American Revolution in large part because she and her family had participated in the struggle against Great Britain, which she saw as a paradoxical effort connected to independence from empire and freedom for the new United States to pursue further imperialist expansion, whose prohibition by Britain had in large part caused the war. Others created their own documentation opposing the new nation's drive for empire: early in the 1820s, Mary Jemison related her contentment with the Seneca Indians after being captured and integrated into their community in the 1750s. She had no desire, she reported, to return to the aggressive and brutal upstart US nation-state.

In France, the extremes of social and political change to which the generation of 1820 were exposed cast a unique light on the country's long pursuit of a trading empire. Having found "history among us," as Ernest Renan asserted, these writers were drawn to the past for explanations. The leaders of this new school in quest of national history included Augustin Thierry, François Mignet, Prosper Barante, Jules Michelet, and Chateaubriand, the last to hold the old regime title, Historiographe du Roi (Historian of the King). This generation owed many of its insights to what Thierry in 1840 came to call "the previously unheard-of events of the past fifty years which have taught us to understand the revolutions of the Middle Ages."[12] In the new historical studies of the early nineteenth century, several national areas of history were represented in the Collège de France, and in 1804 the historian Pierre François Daunou was appointed the second head of the National Archives—an institution destined to be as caught up in the nineteenth-century controversies over French history as the nation itself was. Along with these developments

FIGURE 9.3 Hôtel de Rohan, the original site of France's National Archives. © Julien
Elliott Photography / Getty Images.

came a concern for the social and cultural substance of the past and not just the political
and religious structure of European society.

The leader in the turn to the history of what was increasingly called "civilization"
was François Guizot, who came to Paris in 1807 and moved from the study of law to
engagement with literary and philosophical circles; he was also drawn to the study of
the medieval past, aided mightily in his work by his wife Pauline. Rejecting the "insane
pride" of eighteenth-century rationalism and abstraction, he turned to a broader view of
the European and even Arabic past that referred to both history and philosophy. Guizot
proposed to review the political history of Western civilization from a French perspective,
which meant the ideals of 1789 and the achievements of liberty and progress. Civilization
is "a fact like any other," he declared, "a fact susceptible, like any other, of being studied,
described, narrated." This was for him the fact *par excellence*: "the general and definitive
fact, in which all the others terminate [and] into which they all resolve themselves."[13]
Guizot saw history in three periods, that of the Roman Empire, the barbarians, and the
Roman Church; that of feudalism and religion; and that of the bourgeoisie, liberty, and
representative government. Such stages were emblematic of Western historiography as
they led from relative chaos to the triumph of the European form of state organization,
the nation-state. After 1848, Guizot went into exile in England and returned later to
France to write on the English Revolution.

Augustin Thierry, a collaborator with Henri de Saint-Simon, was the champion of the
"new history" of his generation, beginning with his *Letters on the History of France* (1820).
Thierry recognized three previous schools of history: the medieval chronicles, which were
now valuable as sources; Renaissance historiography beginning with Bernard du Haillan,
which he took to be full of prejudice and error; and the abstract and partisan history of the

previous century down to the Bonapartist period, which had its own misunderstanding of the substance of history. These three were followed finally by "the revolution in the way of writing history," which gave a better grounding to French patriotism.[14] From 1821, Thierry began working on his history of the Norman conquest, in which he also showed his concern for the social details of the changing past. In 1853, his history of the Third Estate appeared, which was an introduction to a collection of documents illustrating the progress of liberty down to the Revolution of 1830. In these efforts, Thierry was aided by his brother Amedée, who saw in races and peoples "collective persons." Indeed, both men sought out and grounded their "philosophical" history in material conditions, including those of race and class, thereby attracting and influencing the revolutionary thinker Karl Marx.

François Mignet wrote the first popular history of the French Revolution to appear in the Restoration. The work has been called the "Bible of liberal revolutions" for its focus on underlying causes and the conflict not just of ideas but of classes.[15] Historians of law and institutions admitted the destructiveness of the Revolution but acknowledged the continuity of customs, legal practices, and the legal mentality itself. Just before the revolutions of 1848, three histories of the Revolution appeared: those of Lamartine, Louis Blanc, and Michelet, all of whom were liberal idealizers of the Revolution. The Revolution was also the object of studies by the English historian Thomas Carlyle and the German historian Heinrich von Sybel, whose views were negative, conservative, and critical.

By contrast, Jules Michelet, echoing the fascination with popular politics of the French Revolution, announced, "My hero is the People."[16] Introduced to the work of Vico by the French philosopher Victor Cousin, Michelet grew fascinated by questions of origins as he began to teach, impelled in part by his own difficult childhood. In the 1820s, he developed a philosophy of history of his own, and the Revolution of 1830 inspired him to write his *Introduction to World History* (1831), which was a celebration of the contributions of France. He then began his history of France, breaking off in the fifteenth century to begin his seven volumes on the French Revolution, which were a poetic celebration of democracy, though he later returned to the narrative of the more distant past in which he indulged his enthusiasms and prejudices. In 1838, Michelet became professor at the Collège de France; he earlier had been appointed by Guizot as Head of the Historical Section of the National Archives, which Michelet had explored not just for political and social history, but also for biography, indeed the "biography" of France, as expressed in his passion for "the People." Michelet was critical of religion, yet his historical work elegantly recounted what he called "the Bible of humanity."

Along the way, the widower Michelet also married the studious Athénais Milaret, who was half his age. Unlike his first wife, Athénaïs did some of Michelet's research in accordance with their conversations about history, and, by his own admission, she wrote parts of his books. She also directed him toward writing joint histories of birds, insects, oceans, and mountains, while composing her own single-authored books.

Athénais Michelet was but one of the many women amateurs turning history in new directions. The study of French nature and geography meshed with what would become a focus of the French school curriculum on the topography, geography, and flora and fauna of France—most literally the "bedrock" of the nation. In the United States, women amateurs wrote of heroines of the American Revolution, of colonial furniture, or of manners and morals of the Republic. British-born Julia Pardoe wrote of moments in Italian, French, and British national history, but she also looked at the old empires on the eastern edges of Europe, exoticizing the Ottoman Empire in particular. Still other amateurs found in the history of women beyond Europe much to admire and even envy. Studying women's past in the Middle East, Olympe Audouard saw their rights as enviable.

Male historians, by contrast, built national narratives around biographies of heroes and, on occasion, villains. Across the globe, a variety of writers, dramatists, and amateur biographers imagined and reimagined historical figures as moral lessons for citizens. During the nation-building phase of the Meiji Restoration in Japan, historians fashioned Prince Shotoku (574–622) as the embodiment of civic "harmony" and especially credited him for introducing Buddhism to Japan. This historical fashioning in the aftermath of rebellions against the Meiji revolution not only served as a lesson to all Japanese to unite instead of fighting one another; the Prince's image in the coming decades of Japan's imperial expansion also metamorphosed in keeping with the state's announced motto of bringing harmony and enlightenment to those it conquered. However, as in Argentina, Brazil, and other Latin American countries emerging from decades of wars of liberation historians also produced smoothed-out biographical narratives of great figures from the period. These narratives, in the style of Manuel Belgrano of Argentina and José Bonifacio of Brazil, gave a sturdy and reassuringly stable cover to the horrifically bloody reality of nation-building.

Women historians contributed to this biographical, quasi-hagiographical effort in the cause of national history, too. The most prolific were the Strickland sisters, who produced series on the queens, princesses, and consorts from all parts of Great Britain in many centuries of its past. These showed a complex system of rule with its insistence on making explicit the heterosexuality of state institutions, especially the monarchy.

Queens regnant and consorts alike were often passed over except for their presence in royal genealogies; but in the age of Queen Victoria there was no ignoring them. The Stricklands' biographical series enjoyed multiple printings into the mid-twentieth century. Others, such as Julia Pardoe, romanticized and exoticized distant consorts, most notably in her portrayals of Ottoman concubines and wives. The Stricklands' work depended on archives, as did that of Arvède Barine, who researched notable women, including Queen Christina of Sweden. Moving far beyond the nation-state, US author and abolitionist Lydia Maria Child published her *History of the Condition of Women* in 1835, a work rich in evidence of women's lives, including both the privileged and the poor, across the globe. It was virtually unparalleled at the time.

Amidst this polymorphous, yet nationally focused historical work, intellectuals outside the European great powers began complaining about the very visible attachment of history in their own kingdoms to the regime in power, which implicitly and even explicitly shaped the content of historical narrative. As chroniclers typically included official opinions on people and events drawn from official repositories, such writing seemed backwards and hardly scientific to its critics. Chinese intellectual Liang Qichao, for example, a major champion of reform of the late Qing Empire, also championed a new history in his *Xin shixue* (*New Historiography*) (1902). In it, he wrote that the new approach should abandon the old recounting of imperial genealogy based on texts from centuries or even millennia past and in its place describe the development of citizenship, the spread of the rule of law, and the emergence of a national consciousness.

Others, such as Zhang Taiyan, held a different view, advocating that instead of jettisoning Confucian values and texts, historians should study them in terms of their

FIGURE 9.4 Agnes Strickland. © Wikimedia Commons (public domain).

broad historical context—that is, they should be historicized. Still others in turn-of-the-century China found such Western-inflected history entirely wrong-headed, critiquing, for example, its focus on ephemera as it also claimed to be universal. In fact, Zhang was converted to such a "Buddhist" approach: he advocated reaching beyond the veil or *maya* of a superficial reality that he felt modern historians were chronicling no matter how supposedly "scientific." Instead, he believed, they should strive to access a more cosmic, ultimately more traditional view of truth. Japanese historians, however, hewed even more forcefully in the nineteenth and early twentieth centuries than did Liang to the Western view of national history and standards adopted to anchor the power of the nation-state.

In England, scholars moved from "conjectural history" to cultural history to chart the nation's historical progress and to explain the stages of development celebrated in the

Enlightenment. The key idea was that "barbaric" and agricultural ages were followed by the commercial stage of history, which also brought about a concern for literary and cultural matters. After Gibbon, ancient Greco-Roman and Judeo-Christian history was carried on in England by William Mitford, Connop Thirwall, George Grote, who published a twelve-volume history of Greece, and Thomas Arnold, whose history of Rome was designed "to make Niebuhr known." Meanwhile, English historical scholarship was enriched by archaeological and anthropological discoveries and publications. The Anglo-Saxon past and its "Gothic bequest" attracted scholars, too, as did the accompanying legacy of British constitutionalism and liberty. Sharon Turner published a history of the Anglo-Saxon period (1799–1805) as marking the beginning of national pride and a unified state. Turner's work was succeeded and surpassed by John Lingard's *Antiquities of the Anglo-Saxon Church*, which began to appear in 1806; his later *History of England* (1819) was translated into French, German, and Italian. Turner's work was then continued by Francis Palgrave, whose *Rise and Progress of the English Commonwealth* (1832) continued the Whiggish tradition.

According to Palgrave, "The history of law is the most satisfactory clue to the political history of England"; and Henry Hallam, in his *Constitutional History of England* (1827), celebrated the limited monarchy of the Germanic tradition and the "essential checks upon royal authority on royal authority," including parliamentary consent, due process, and guarantees of individual liberties.[17] The great English historian Thomas Macaulay was largely in agreement with this view of English history. For several years after the Reform Act of 1832, Macaulay was a member of Parliament until he was "liberated" (in his own words) to return to his scholarship. Macaulay represented what Herbert Butterfield called the "Whig interpretation of history," emphasizing progress, representation, and democracy. Another contributor to the popularity of history in Britain was Carlyle, who in addition to his work on the French Revolution emphasized the role of singular individuals in a biography of Frederick the Great.

English historians continued the task of researching, writing, and revising national history after Macaulay. Among the British historians born in the second quarter of the nineteenth century were William Stubbs, J. A. Froude, J. R. Green, W. E. H. Lecky, Mandell Creighton, F. W. Maitland, and John Lord Acton, who wrote that "The great point is the history of history."[18] Prominent in their work, too, was what Stubbs called "the great hive of German workers."[19] Acton and Creighton were founders of the *English Historical Review*, following its counterparts, the *Historisches Zeitschrift* and the *Revue historique*. Many of these historians also had religious backgrounds, entering orders and, in some cases, moving into the Anglican hierarchy. J. H. Cardinal Newman represented an aberrant and somewhat negative influence because of his adherence to religious dogma. Nineteenth-century British historians disagreed about the relative value of religious, ideological, cultural, and comparative history, but almost all were in general agreement about the principle of historical continuity and the European state's progressive evolution.

The "Oxford school" began with the tenants of the Regius chairs, Stubbs, Froude, Green, and E. A. Freemen. The "Cambridge school" began with Acton, J. R. Seeley, and the ancient historian J. B. Bury, and included Creighton, first editor of the *English Historical Review*, and the legal historian Maitland, who had turned down the offer of Regius Professor. The history of law and institutions was turned in a comparative direction by Henry Sumner Maine, using the Roman Empire as the model but taking it in an "Indo-European" direction. Froude thought that history could be written to support any theory—whether of progress, corruption, or even the social contract—but theories too changed with history, and, like Ranke, Froude believed the historian's duty was "to the facts." G. M. Trevelyan saw historical practice as caught between science seeking cause and effect, on the one hand, and literary art aimed at giving pleasure and breeding enthusiasm, on the other.

Despite the "oriental renaissance" of the nineteenth century, British history was set largely in the context of the "Western," Greco-Roman-Christian-medieval tradition. For Seeley, for example, the Holy Roman Empire was the major link between the ancient and Victorian worlds, and he was followed in this opinion by many later imperial historians. In the nineteenth century, natural science increasingly exerted its influence on historical interpretation not only through empiricism but also through more explicit evolutionary patterns of progress. No less evident was the impact of the economics of industrial society. Examples are Auguste Comte's three-stage theory and Fustel de Coulanges's "positivism of the document," which led away from looking for general laws. In Germany, neo-Kantianism, especially as practiced by Wilhelm Dilthey, led back to the facticity of cultural history and a new understanding of "historicism." The "new historiography" of Italy, as Benedetto Croce called it, was created by liberal Catholics reacting against the superficial rationalism of the Enlightenment to establish a sense of national destiny. In Italy, Cesare Balbo's *Hope of Italy* (1845) celebrated Providence as the guarantee of Christian progress. Balbo also championed the work of German and French scholars and assembled modern collections of archival sources.

As British and other European legislation came to expand the national polity through the grant of suffrage to more and more men, historians reached outward from more or less elite histories to more numerous narratives of "the people" as a whole. When Green published his *Short History of the English People* (1874), he apologized for neglecting military and political history to focus on "the missionary, the printer, the poet, the merchant or the philosopher."[20] Married in 1878, Alice Stopford Green and J. R. Green worked together in writing social history, with the former turning, after her husband's death, to the study of Irish nationalism in *The Making of Ireland and Its Undoing, 1200–1600* (1908). Amateurs were often in the forefront of the democratization of the subjects of historical study and perhaps succeeded in bringing new awareness to questions of social justice. In Stopford Green's case, the issue was decolonization. The ambition was to turn public attention to the facts of conquest and the subsequent mistreatment of the Irish at the hands of the British. Others, such as Maud Gonne, emphasized in the same moment the revival of Irish culture, including the Gaelic language, as an antidote.

In Latin America, a similar impulse made itself felt to write the history of the new nations that had separated themselves from Spanish and Portuguese rule. Appearing as these new nations were being formed, "modern" histories of the nineteenth century often focused on a specific nation's relationship to the indigenous past. Many national historians—Mexican, Brazilian, Cuban, and others—integrated local people into their stories by depicting them as laying indigenous foundations for the modern nation-state in terms of the myths, poetry, songs, and other cultural elements of the pre-Columbian past. In so doing, these historians accepted the validity of non-written evidence, which some professionalizing historians in Europe found problematic. In nations on the western coast of South America, the histories of the Incas had become particularly important, especially by the later eighteenth century, when uprisings—precursors, many said, to the struggles for independence—were made in the name of restoring

FIGURE 9.5 Guarding Simon Bolivar's Tomb. © Eric Vandeville /
Getty Images.

an Incan heritage and values. As such, the return to the Incan Empire, in all its rich
rituals, beliefs, and practices, became historically important to the new nations of Latin
America. Instead of remaining an occluded set of esoteric events, Incan history was
made universally intelligible and politically useful to grounding the state's evolution.
Mexico and Brazil also served up past and even present indigenous beliefs that historians
typically translated, collected, and integrated into a common past in this heyday of
nation-building histories.

Latin American histories appeared with indigenous culture as the bedrock of
independence. "'That is what it is about: of being or not being savages', historian and
Argentinian president Domingo Faustino Sarmiento wrote."[21] The progressive motif of
history that had unfolded in European accounts beginning with the English Revolution

shaped Latin American histories, too. Historians here made strong claims to the trajectory from violence to the civilized, unified nation-state. Almost all the efforts on behalf of independent nation-states began drenched in blood only to emerge into order and freedom, or so the idea went.

Although new nations need new histories, the Haitian past and its stunning revolution got little attention, to the point of virtual erasure. For the United States, the story of this successful uprising and then nation-building by slaves and former slaves of African descent slaves was especially frightening, even after the enslaved gained freedom and former male slaves (briefly) enjoyed full constitutional rights. The past of Native Americans was similarly disturbing to professional US historians, albeit for both identical and different reasons. Just as professional US history was taking shape, the army and settlers were slaughtering Native Americans at an unprecedented pace, as well as driving survivors from their lands. Only much later, when most of the slaughter, though not other forms of victimization, had stopped, was their history published or demythologized and only then at a glacial pace. By that point, the end of the bloodshed indicated that the nation-state was ultimately a force for order and unity.

Still, outsiders to the US nation—that is, those within the nation whom white males kept from full citizenship and equality of rights—took up the cause of writing their own history. By the end of the nineteenth century, African Americans such as Jacob White of Philadelphia had been collecting documents and objects and writing histories for a substantial number of years. When the American Negro Historical Society was founded in Philadelphia in 1897 to serve as a site for holding some of these collections, it was one among many reading rooms and historical repositories for African Americans in urban centers in the late nineteenth century. Women acted in these societies not just as members but also as participants on boards of directors and other governing bodies. While men collected many of these documents and gained standing for founding these organizations' archive, their wives were generally the people responsible for cataloguing them, preparing them for use by historians and other scholars into the future. Outsider men and women from the elite across Western countries served largely invisibly as historical archivists. One exception was Daniel A. P. Murray, who promoted Black history from 1871 to 1922 as an archivist at the Library of Congress.

Native Americans also undertook historical work in the nineteenth century, aiming to show their past as members of coherent groups with foundational agreements, laws, and a rich culture. Zitkala-Sa, a Sioux given the name Gertrude in a missionary school, gathered up Native American lore and published collections of Sioux stories. White women also collected historical materials, Annie Abel and Emma Helen Blair foremost among them at the beginning of the twentieth century. Earlier, Helen Hunt Jackson, sometimes called a muckraker because her appraisals of the evidence were harshly truthful, produced *A Century of Dishonor* (1881) in which she highlighted documents showing that massacres by Indians "were *instigated* and *hired* by the English."[22] Seen as less fiery, Mary Austin's *Land of Little Rain* (1903), on Native Americans in the Southwest, and Blair's *Indian Tribes of the Upper Mississippi and the Region of the Great Lakes* (1911) were "scientifically" grounded in documentary evidence. The continuing significance of Austin's book, with its additional descriptions of the environment, topography, and other natural features of the land, is registered in its many editions since the original publication. As history became increasingly nationalized—which is to say, rife with claims about the nation-state that were idealized, exclusionary, and at times simply false—alternate narratives emerged, many of them based on committed sleuthing of facts that had seemed unimportant to professional historians. The unique features that distinguished such works as *Land of Little Rain* made them representative of a historical avant-garde.

Women were among the outsiders to "scientific" and professional histories. By the end of the nineteenth century, they had taken up the challenge to stretch the boundaries of historical writing just as many wanted to stretch the boundaries of citizenship. Women in the Middle East, for example, were transformed from being readers to being producers of history and other literature. They started numerous periodicals specifically for women, such as the Syrian-born journalist Hind Nawfal's *al-Fatah*, founded in 1892. In essays and biographies, they looked, for example, to the pharaonic past where women's power and cultural achievements laid the foundation of their claims to modern rights. Islamist women also focused on women's accomplishments, especially as relatives of the Prophet Muhammad and as interpreters of *hadith*. This trajectory of women's improvement provided an existential affirmation across time that was thought to indicate worth of national citizenship and civilization—an important acquisition given the designation of the colonized, and especially women, as not advanced enough for either personal or national autonomy.

Similar publishing efforts occurred in South Asia, where an array of journals by and for women arose, again including historical and political studies, perhaps in an effort to prove civilizational worth through "scientific" methods. Women in Europe and the United States had a somewhat easier time of it, though less so in terms of securing "professional" jobs and networking among scientific historians. Instead, once the heuristics for producing political histories of the nation had been established, leading scholars and activists alike set about collecting documents wherever women were admitted to work in archives. Susan B. Anthony and Elizabeth Cady Stanton produced a multivolume history of the US women's suffrage movement using copious documentation, including that contained in their scrapbooks of newspaper clippings, letters, and speeches. British amateur Charlotte Carmichael Stopes published *British Freewomen: Their Historical Privilege* in 1894, a work outlining the contradictory position of women in the issues of rights and showing that across time they had had many that in the nineteenth century men claimed they had never had.

Mary Sheldon Barnes and Lucy Maynard Salmon used the same methodology in their historical scholarship (and in the case of Salmon, the study of women) as did many Native Americans and African Americans. The two women had studied together at the University of Michigan with Charles Kendall Adams, who emphasized sources. As Barnes put it in her 1896 book on methods: "Indian relics, pictures of native Indians, photographs of historic sites and buildings, all the historic maps of the locality ... old costumes and uniforms, old dishes, utensils, tools, coins, stamps and portraits" could serve as the ground of history.[23] Salmon, from her position as Professor of History at Vassar, meanwhile, not only introduced her students to the seminar method but also used it to transform the notion of documentation. She had her students consider such ephemera as railroad schedules, cookbooks, and laundry lists and to scrutinize, as art historians have come to call it "the vernacular landscape," that is, urban boundaries, the placement of buildings on main thoroughfares, housing, and other physical aspects of towns and cities as source material. Salmon also urged the development of local historical societies and called on them to upgrade the science of history in terms of method by collecting evidence drawn from what we would now call material culture.

By 1900, the entire globe was re-urbanizing—that is, rebuilding civic centers that had been attacked by empire builders—or building vast cities on the sites of small towns and villages. Both old and new cities increasingly became adorned with museums, historic monuments that celebrated the heroes of nation-building and memorials to old and new empires. That is, new empires, such as the United States, charged public grounds with sphinxes and obelisks (e.g., the Washington Monument) and gave cities names such as Delhi, Memphis, Athens, Rome, and the like to ground their achievements in the past. World's fairs offered similar testimonials to the nation's goods as well as to traditions from around the world. In this iteration of history, the nation could look very old indeed. Even colonized regions were typically adorned with statues of imperial notables as well as the traditional architecture of the imperial metropole.

"One must be absolutely modern," wrote the French poet Arthur Rimbaud in 1871, and indeed "modernism" applies to the generation at the turn of the twentieth century. Modernism had early on been integral to the work of amateurs in the West. Among other Western scholars, Karl Lamprecht, Kurt Breisig, Henri Berr, Benedetto Croce, José Ortega y Gasset, and James Harvey Robinson began contributing to the wave of the "new history" that finally brought cultural, social, economic, and geographical questions and "historicism" into the professionalized realm of Western political history. Relativism also penetrated historical studies with the works of Max Weber, Ernst Troeltsch, Karl Mannheim, and Wilhelm Dilthey, who joined a "neo-Kantian" critique of historical reason to the Kantian critique of pure reason. Historians devoted to the national history of the major European powers were followed by the "mini-national" scholars of Finnish, Swedish, Danish, Polish, Romanian, Serbian, Czech, Lithuanian, Latvian, and Estonian history. However, in an age of growing empires, militant nationalism and new dictatorships across the globe, much history for the first half of the twentieth century still followed, or aspired to follow, the nineteenth-century paradigm designed by the professionals. Post-Second World War decolonizers and the efforts of those excluded from the academy and similar institutional perches both enriched and challenged historical science in all its nineteenth-century glory.

NOTES

Introduction

1 "France Under Louis Napoleon," *The Westminster Review* no. 70 (October, 1858): 194.

2 See 159 below.

3 See 44 below.

4 William Wordsworth, *The Prelude or Growth of a Poet's Mind* (London: Oxford University Press, 1933), 231, (ll. 73–7), 10, (ll. 351–55), 228 (ll. 376–77).

5 G. W. F. Hegel, *The Phenomenology of Spirit*, translated by A. V. Miller (Oxford: Oxford University Press, 1977), 11 (20).

6 Quoted in Wilfred Mellers, *Beethoven and the Voice of God* (New York: Oxford University Press, 1983), 25.

7 Friedrich Schlegel, *"Lucinde" and the Fragments*, translated by Peter Firchow (Minneapolis: University of Minnesota Press, 1971), 144, 145, 149, 247, 278, 256.

8 Andrea Wulf, *The Invention of Nature: Alexander von Humbold's New World* (New York: Alfred A. Knopf, 2015), 235–45.

9 Edmund Gosse, *Father and Son* (Oxford: Oxford University Press, 2004), 61–6.

10 Prudhomme and Michelet quoted in D. G. Charlton, *Secular Religions in France* (London: Oxford University Press, 1963), 26, 36.

11 Quoted in Linda Nochlin, *Realism* (New York: Penguin, 1991), 83.

12 Quoted in George Joseph Becker, ed., *Documents of Modern Literary Realism* (Princeton, NJ: Princeton University Press, 1963), 6.

13 Wulf, *The Invention of Nature*, 312.

14 Charles Baudelaire, "Le Peintre de la vie moderne," in *Oeuvres complètes*, 2 vols. (Paris: Bibliothèque de la Pléiade, 1976), vol. 2, 691.

15 Angus Maddison, *Phases of Capitalist Development* (Oxford: Oxford University Press, 1982), 48.

16 John Stuart Mill, *On Liberty* (Indianapolis, IN: Hackett Publishing, 1978), 70.

17 Stendhal, *Life of Henry Brulard*, translated by John Sturrock (New York: New York Review Books, 2002), 197.

18 Quoted by Richard Sheppard, "The Crisis of Language," in *Modernism: 1890–1930*, edited by Malcolm Bradbury and James McFarlane (New York: Penguin, 1976), 329; Hugo Von Hofmannsthal, "The Letter of Lord Chandos," in *The Whole Difference: Selected Writings of Hugo von Hofmannsthal*, edited by J. D. McClatchy (Princeton, NJ: Princeton University Press, 2008), 70.

19 Hugo Von Hofmannsthal, *The Lord Chandos Letter*, translated by Michael Hofmann (London: Syrens, 1995), 5.

20 Edmond de Goncourt, August 22, 1875, 9 vols., *Journal des Goncourt: Mémoires de la vie littéraire*, vol. 5 (Paris: Bibliothèque-Charpentier, 1891), 222–3.

21 Gustave Le Bon, *The Crowd: A Study of the Popular Mind* (New York: Macmillan, 1897), vii, 34, 35.

22 Auguste Javary, *De l'idée de progrès* (Paris: Librairie Philosophique de Ladrange, 1851), 1.

23 Jean-Antoine-Nicolas de Caritat, marquis de Condorcet, "The Sketch for a Historical Picture of the Progress of the Human Mind," in *Political Writings* (Cambridge: Cambridge University Press, 2012), 130.

24 Seung Jin Baek, *The Political Economy of Neo-modernisation: Rethinking the Dynamics of Technology, Development and Inequality* (London: Palgrave Macmillan, 2018), 331.

25 See Hannu Salmi, *Nineteenth-Century Europe: A Cultural History* (Cambridge: Polity Press, 2008), 35, 41.

26 Alfred de Musset, *La Confession d'un enfant du siècle* (Paris: Charpentier, 1867), 7–8.

27 Adam Smith, *An Inquiry into the Nature and Causes of the Wealth of Nations*, 2 vols. (Indianapolis, IN: Liberty Fund, 1981), vol. 2, 782–83, 842.

28 Friedrich Schiller, *On the Aesthetic Education of Man* (Mineola, NY: Dover Publications, 1954), 40.

29 George Sand, "Obermann," par E. P. de Senancour, in *Questions d'art et de littérature* (Paris: C. Lévy, 1878), 37.

30 "Les Femmes poètes aux XIXᵉ siècle," *Revue de Paris* (May 1835), 279.

31 Thomas Carlyle, "Memoirs of the Life of Scott," from *London and Westminster Review* (1838), in *Critical and Miscellaneous Essays* (Boston: Phillips, Sampson and Co., 1855), 522.

32 Jonathan Beecher and Richard Bienvenu, eds., *The Utopian Vision of Charles Fourier: Selected Texts on Work, Love, and Passionate Attraction* (Boston: Beacon Press, 1971), 200.

33 Robert Owen, *A New View of Society* (London: Longman, 1817), 115; Claude Henri de Saint-Simon, *De la réorganisation de la société européenne* (Paris: Adrien Égron, 1814), 112.

34 Gustave Flaubert, *The Sentimental Education*, translated by Robert Baldick (London: Penguin Books, 2004), 460.

35 Max Weber, *The Protestant Ethic and the Spirit of Capitalism*, translated by Stephen Kalberg (New York: Routledge, 2012), 123, 124.

36 Quoted in Salmi, *Nineteenth-Century Europe*, 98.

37 See Heinrich Von Treitschke, *History of German in the Nineteenth Century*, translated by Eden and Cedar Paul (Chicago: University of Chicago Press, 1975), xiv; Treitschke, *Selections from Lectures on Politics*, translated by Adam L. Gowan (London: Gowans and Gray, 1914), 9.

38 Philip D. Curtin, *The World and the West: The European Challenge and the Overseas Response in the Age of Empire* (Cambridge: Cambridge University Press, 2000), 30.

39 Frederick L. Nussbaum, *A History of the Economic Institutions of Modern Europe* (New York: Crofts & Co., 1933), 276.

40 Edward Gibbon, *The History of the Decline and Fall of the Roman Empire*, 3 vols. (London: Allen Lane, 1994), vol. 2, 511, 516.

41 From "National Life from the Standpoint of Science" (1905), quoted in Winfried Baumgart, *Imperialism: The Idea and the Reality of English and French Colonial Expansion, 1880–1914* (Oxford: Oxford University Press, 1982), 86.

42 From *Naval Development in the Century* (1902), quoted in Baumgart, *Imperialism*, 88.

43 Stéphane Audoin-Rouzeau and Annette Becker, *14–18: Understanding the Great War* (New York: Hill and Wang, 2002), 22–3.

44 José Ortega y Gasset, *Revolt of the Masses* (New York: W. W. Norton & Company, 1994), 35.

Chapter 1

1   Jean-Antoine-Nicolas de Caritat, marquis de Condorcet, *Sketch for a Historical Picture of the Progress of the Human Mind*, in *Condorcet: Selected Writings*, edited by Keith Michael Baker (1793, Indianapolis, IN: Bobbs-Merrill, 1976), 210.

2   Ibid., 210.

3   Ibid., 210–11.

4   Ibid., 211–12.

5   Ibid., 213, 216.

6   Ibid., 260, 262.

7   Jennifer Pitts, *A Turn to Empire: The Rise of Imperial Liberalism in Britain and France* (Princeton, NJ: Princeton University Press, 2005), 1–6, 168–75.

8   Condorcet, *Sketch for a Historical Picture of the Progress of the Human Mind*, 218, 221 223, 225.

9   Ibid., 228–29, 231, 234.

10 Ibid., 258.

11 And so on, ibid., Ibid., 261–65, 274, 280.

12 Wilhelm von Humboldt, *Journal parisien, 1797–1799*, translated by Elisabeth Beyer, edited by Raymond Trousson (Paris: Honoré Champion, 2013), 181, 197, 199.

13 Anthony J. LaVopa, *Fichte: The Self and the Calling of Philosophy, 1762–1799* (Cambridge: Cambridge University Press, 2001), 2, ch. 7.

14 Georg Wilhelm Friedrich Hegel, Preface to *The Phenomenology of Spirit* in *Hegel: Texts and Commentary*, edited by Walter Kaufmann (1807, New York: Doubleday, 1965), 81n20; John Edward Toews, *Hegelianism: The Path toward Dialectical Humanism, 1805–1841* (Cambridge: Cambridge University Press, 1980), 52–3.

15 Dieter Henrich, *Between Kant and Hegel: Lectures on German Idealism* (Cambridge, MA: Harvard University Press, 2003), 2, 2–3n7, 17–18.

16 Terry P. Pinkard, *Hegel's Phenomenology: The Sociality of Reason* (Cambridge: Cambridge University Press, 1994), 189.

17 Toews, *Hegelianism,* chs. 6–10, Epilogue.

18 Jan Goldstein, *The Post-Revolutionary Self: Politics and Psyche in France, 1750–1850* (Cambridge, MA: Harvard University Press, 2005), chs. 3–4.

19 Heinrich Heine, *Religion and Philosophy in Germany*, translated by J. Snodgrass (1834, Boston: Beacon, 1959), 157.

20 Alfred de Musset, "Première Lettre," in "Lettres de Dupuis et Cotonet au Directeur de la *Revue des deux mondes*," in *Oeuvres completes*, vol. 3 (1836; Paris: Gallimard, 1957), 819–36.

21 A. O. Lovejoy, "The Meaning of Romanticism for the Historian of Ideas," *Journal of the History of Ideas* 2, no. 3 (1941): 262–64.

22 Lovejoy, "The Meaning of Romanticism for the Historian of Ideas," 272–77.

23 Raymond Williams, *Culture and Society* (London: Chatto & Windus, 1959), ch. 2.

24 Simon Schaffer, "Genius in Romantic Natural Philosophy," in *Romanticism and the Sciences*, edited by Andrew Cunningham and Nicholas Jardine (Cambridge: Cambridge University Press, 1990), quotation on p. 82.

25 Carla Hesse, *Publishing and Cultural Politics in Revolutionary France, 1789–1810* (Berkeley: University of California Press, 1991), 103–04.

26 Tim Blanning, *The Romantic Revolution: A History* (New York: Modern Library, 2010), xvii.

27 Chad Wellmon, *Organizing Enlightenment: Information Overload and the Invention of the Modern Research University* (Baltimore: Johns Hopkins University Press, 2015), 5.

28 Auguste Comte, *Cours de philosophie positive*, in *Auguste Comte and Positivism: The Essential Writings*, edited by Gertrud Lenzer (1830–1842; New York: Harper & Row, 1975), 71–86, quotation on p. 72.

29 Ibid., 75–6, 80–1, 184.

30 Ibid., 76–7, 83, Bk. 6.

31 Mary Pickering, *Auguste Comte: An Intellectual Biography* (Cambridge: Cambridge University Press, 1993), 1:678, 691–93.

32 Auguste Comte, *Système de philosophie positive*, in *Auguste Comte and Positivism: The Essential Writings*, edited by Gertrud Lenzer (1851–1854; New York: Harper & Row, 1975), 317–19, ch. 6, esp. 381–84.

33 John Tresch, *The Romantic Machine: Utopian Science and Technology After Napoleon* (Chicago: University of Chicago Press, 2012).

34 John Stuart Mill, *On Liberty*, edited by Gertrude Himmelfarb (1859; London: Penguin, 1974), quotations on pp. 57 [n.p.], 120.

35 Henri Bergson, *An Introduction to Metaphysics*, translated by T. E. Hulme (1903; Indianapolis, IN: Bobbs-Merrill, 1949), 23–4, original emphasis.

36 Henri Bergson, *Time and Free Will: An Essay on the Immediate Data of Consciousness*, trans. F.L. Pogson (1889; New York: Harper Torchbook, 1960), 100–139, 166–72, quotation on p. 169.

37 Émile Zola, "The Experiemental Novel," in *The Experimental Novel and Other Essays*, trans. Bele m. Sherman (1880, New York, Cassell, 1893); Zola *L'Assommoir*, translated by Leonard Tancock (1876; Harmondsworth, UK: Penguin, 1970), quotation on p. 307.

38 Wolf Lepenies, *Between Literature and Science: The Rise of Sociology* (New York: Cambridge University Press, 1988).

39 Steven Lukes, *Emile Durkheim: His Life and Work, A Historical and Critical Study* (New York: Harper & Row, 1972), 67–8.

40 Émile Durkheim, *The Division of Labor in Society*, translated by W. D. Halls (1893; New York: Free Press, 1984), xxv.

41 Ibid., 4, 333, 338.

42 Ibid., ch. 5.

43 Ibid., 331.

44 Émile Durkheim, *The Rules of Sociological Method*, translated by S. A. Solovay and J. H. Mueller (New York: Free Press, 1964), 14, original emphasis.

45 Fiona Maclachlan, "Max Weber within the *Methodenstreit*," *Cambridge Journal of Economics* 41, no. 4 (2017): 1161–175; Fritz Ringer, *Max Weber's Methodology: The Unification of the Cultural and Social Sciences* (Cambridge, MA: Harvard University Press, 1997), ch. 4.

46 Max Weber, *The Protestant Ethic and the Spirit of Capitalism*, translated by Talcott Parsons (Mineola, NY: Dover, 2003), quotations on pp. 95, 104.

47 Maclachlan, "Max Weber within the *Methodenstreit*," 1162.

48 Paul Ricoeur, *Freud and Philosophy: An Essay in Interpretation*, translated by Denis Savage (New Haven, CT: Yale University Press, 1970), 32–6.

49 Frederic Jameson, "The Cultural Logic of Late Capitalism," in *Postmodernism, or The Cultural Logic of Late Capitalism*, 1–54 (Durham, NC: Duke University Press, 2001), 6–9.

50 Jürgen Habermas, *The Structural Transformation of the Public Sphere*, translated by Thomas Burger (Cambridge, MA: MIT Press, 1989), pts. 1–2.

51 Terry Pinkard, *Hegel: A Biography* (Cambridge: Cambridge University Press, 2000), 242; Jan Goldstein, "Moral Contagion: A Professional Ideology of Medicine and Psychiatry in Eighteenth- and Nineteenth-Century France" in *Professions and the French State*, edited by Gerald L. Geison, 181–222 (Philadelphia: University of Pennsylvania Press, 1984), 208–09.

52 Mary Jo Maynes, *Schooling in Western Europe: A Social History* (Albany: State University of New York Press, 1985), chs. 3, 8, table on p. 134.

53 John E. Craig, "The Expansion of Education," *Review of Research in Education* 9 (1981): 177, 185.

54 Maynes, *Schooling in Western Europe*, 96.

55 Thomas Albert Howard, *Protestant Theology and the Making of the German Research University* (Oxford: Oxford University Press, 2006), 172–73.

56 Wilhelm Von Humboldt, "On the Internal Structure of the University of Berlin and Its Relationship to Other Organizations," in *The Rise of the Research University*, edited by Louis Menand, Paul Reitter, and Chad Wellmon, 108–16 (Chicago: University of Chicago Press, 2017), quotation on p. 108.

57 Wellmon, *Organizing Enlightenment*, 235.

58 Charles E. McClelland, *Berlin, The Mother of All Research Universities, 1860–1918* (Lanham, MD: Lexington Books, 2017), 74–80.

59 Wellmon, *Organizing Enlightenment*, 148.

60 George Weisz, *The Emergence of the Modern Universities in France, 1893–1914* (Princeton, NJ: Princeton University Press, 1983), 62–4, 214; Henri Massis and Alfred de Tarde, *L'Esprit de la nouvelle Sorbonne* (Paris: Mercure de France, 1911), 35–6.

61 Goldstein, *The Post-Revolutionary Self*, Epilogue.

62 Terry Nichols Clark, *Prophets and Patrons: The French University and the Emergence of the Social Sciences* (Cambridge, MA: Harvard University Press, 1973), pt. 2, esp. 162–65; Lukes, *Emile Durkheim*, 358–65, quotation on 364; W. S. F. Pickering, *Durkheim's Sociology of Religion: Themes and Theories* (London: Routledge & Kegan Paul, 1984), 509–12.

63 Wellmon, *Organizing Enlightenment*, 192–201.

64 Pinkard, *Hegel: A Biography*, 456, 611–13.

65 Alan B. Spitzer, *The French Generation of 1820* (Princeton, NJ: Princeton University Press, 1987), ch. 3; Anne Martin-Fugier, *La vie élégante, ou la formation du Tout-Paris 1815–1848* (Paris: Fayard, 1990), 242–44; Goldstein, *The Post-Revolutionary Self*, 222–24.

66 Martin-Fugier, *La vie élégante*, 244.

67 Robert D. Priest, *The Gospel According to Renan: Reading, Writing, and Religion in Nineteenth-Century France* (Oxford: Oxford University Press, 2015), 60–5, quotation on 62.

68 Tresch, *The Romantic Machine*, 266–69.

69 Annie Petit, "La diffusion des saviors comme devoir positiviste," *Romantisme* 19 (1989): 7–26.

70 Ian Inkster, "The Social Context of an Educational Movement: A Revisionist Approach to English Mechanics' Institutes, 1820–1850," *Oxford Review of Education* 2, no. 3 (1976): 277–307; Gregory Claeys, "Political Economy and Popular Education: Thomas Hodgskin and the London Mechanics' Institute," in *Radicalism and Revolution in Britain 1775–1848*, edited by Michael T. Davis, 157–75 (New York: St. Martin's Press, 2000); Roger Cooter, *The Cultural Meaning of Popular Science: Phrenology and the Organization of Consent in Nineteenth-Century Britain* (Cambridge: Cambridge University Press, 1984).

71   Nicole Savy, ed., *Le Siècle des dictionnaires* (Paris: Editions de la réunion des musées nationaux, 1987), 21.

72   Kurt Mueller-Vollmer, *Transatlantic Crossings and Transformations: German-American Cultural Transfer from the 18th to the End of the 19th Century* (Frankfurt: Peter Lang, 2015), ch. 9.

73   Savy, *Le Siècle des dictionnaires*, 17–25.

74   Raymond Schwab, *La Renaissance orientale* (Paris: Plon, 1950).

75   Sheldon Pollock, "Future Philology? The Fate of a Soft Science in a Hard World," *Critical Inquiry* 35, no. 4 (2009): 931.

76   Edward Said, *Orientalism* (New York: Pantheon 1978), 142–43 for Renan.

77   Suzanne L. Marchand, *German Orientalism in an Age of Empire: Religion, Race, and Scholarship* (Cambridge: Cambridge University Press, 2009), 62–3, 125–26.

78   Quoted in Kapil Raj, *Relocating Modern Science: Circulation and the Construction of Knowledge in South Asia and Europe, 1650–1900* (New York: Palgrave Macmillan, 2007), 98.

79   Ibid., ch. 3.

80   Pollock, "Future Philology?," 938.

Chapter 2

1   For a full discussion of Locke on the self, see Jerrold Seigel, *The Idea of the Self: Thought and Experience in Western Europe since the Seventeenth Century* (Cambridge: Cambridge University Press, 2005), ch. 3. For the importance of the notion of identity to thinking about the self, see Gerald Izenberg, *Identity: The Necessity of a Modern Idea* (Philadelphia: University of Pennsylvania Press, 2016).

2   Immanuel Kant, "The Contest of Faculties," in *Kant's Political Writings*, translated by H. B. Nisbet, edited by Hans Reiss (Cambridge: Cambridge University Press, 1970), 184–87.

3   See my discussion of Fichte in *The Idea of the Self*, ch. 11, where much recent literature is cited.

4   George Amstrong Kelly, *The Humane Comedy: Constant, Tocqueville and French Liberalism* (Cambridge: Cambridge University Press, 1992), 2. For Diderot and Rousseau, see Seigel, *The Idea of the Self*. For Rousseau's own account of what he called the *morale sensitive*, see Jean-Jacques Rousseau, *Confessions*, translated by J. M. Cohen (1953; London: Penguin, 1981), 380–81. And for a perceptive critique, Jean Starobinski, *Jean-Jacques Rousseau: Transparency and Obstruction*, translated by Arthur Goldhammer, with an introduction by Robert J. Morrissey (1971; Chicago: University of Chicago Press, 1988), 213–14.

5   Samuel Smiles, *Self-Help* (London: John Murray, 1859), 16–19.

6   The first part of this quote comes from the published edition of Mill's *Autobiography*, the second from passages in the original manuscript that were excised from the published book, but restored in the version edited by Jack Stillinger (Boston: Houghton, Mifflin, 1969), see 22–3, 28–9, 34.

7   Mill, *Autobiography*, 81.

8   Ibid., 83. For more on Mill in this regard, see my discussion in *The Idea of the Self*, ch. 13.

9   Mill, *On Liberty*, edited by Currin V. Shields (Indianapolis, IN: Bobbs-Merill, 1975), 72.

10   See John Mullan, "Feelings and Novels," in *Rewriting the Self: Histories from the Renaissance to the Present*, edited by Roy Porter (London: Routledge, 1997), 119–31.

11   Mill, *On Liberty*, 73; Mill, *Autobiography*, 86–9.

12   Mill, *On Liberty*, 76.

13 See Owen's autobiography, *The Life of Robert Owen* (London: Wilson, 1857–1858), relevant passages on pp. 39, 72, 84–5.

14 See the third of Marx's "Theses on Feuerbach," in Karl Marx and Friedrich Engels, *The German Ideology* (Moscow, 1968), 85. For more detail about Owen's views in this regard, see my discussion of him in "Necessity, Freedom, and Character Formation from the Eighteenth Century to the Nineteenth," in *Character, Self, and Sociability in the Scottish Enlightenment*, edited by Thomas Ahnert and Susan Manning (New York: Palgrave Macmillan, 2011), 249–65.

15 On the German Social Democrats, see Vernon Lidtke, *The Outlawed Party: Social Democracy in Germany, 1878–90* (Princeton, NJ: Princeton University Press, 1966); Michael Mason, *The Making of Victorian Sexual Attitudes* (Oxford: Oxford University Press, 1994), 126; see also 118–23 for the larger point.

16 Jacques Billard, *De l'école à la république: Guizot et Victor Cousin* (Paris: Presses Universitaires de France, 1998), 128.

17 Johann Gottlieb Fichte, *Addresses to the German Nation*, edited and with an Introduction by George Armstrong Kelly, based on the translation by R. F. Jones and G. H. Turnbull (New York: Harper and Row, 1968), 6. For the German text, see Fichte, *Schriften zur angewandten Philosophie*, edited by Peter Lothar Oesterreich (*Werke*, II; Frankfurt: Deutscher Klassiker Verlag, 1997), 552.

18 On Durkheim, see Steven Lukes, *Emile Durkheim: His Life and Work* (New York: Penguin Press, 1972), and my discussion in *The Idea of the Self*, ch. 14, where additional literature is cited.

19 See Weber's famous lectures of 1918 "Politics as a Vocation" and "Science as a Vocation," in *From Max Weber: Essays in Sociology*, translated and edited by H. H. Gerth and C. Wright Mills (New York: Oxford University Press, 1946, and subsequent reprintings), esp. 147–49.

20 Harriet Taylor Mill, "The Enfranchisement of Women," 113 ff. and John Stuart Mill, "The Subjection of Women," 141 ff. in John Stuart Mill and Harriet Taylor Mill, *Essays on Sex Equality*, edited by Alice Rossi (Chicago: University of Chicago Press, 1970).

21 See the discussion of Mireille de Bondeli's diary in Denis Bertholet, *Le bourgeois dans tous ses états: le roman familial de la Belle Epoque* (Paris: Plon, 1987), 56–7, and my comments in *Modernity and Bourgeois Life*, 364.

22 Camille Mauclair, "La Femme devant les peintres modernes," *La Nouvelle revue*, N. S. vol. 1 (15 November 1899): 190–213. For some similar notions, see Marius-Ary Leblond, "Les peintres de la femme nouvelle," *La Revue* (formerly *La Revue des revues*) 39 (November 1, 1901): 275–90.

Chapter 3

1 Gerhard Masur, *Prophets of Yesterday: Studies in European Culture, 1890–1914* (New York: Harper Colophon, 1966), 2. Quoting this, Gerhard Masur comments, in a vein familiar from a host of other similar remarks on Western "hubris": "Who could have foreseen that this moment of extraordinary triumph was in reality a culmination that permitted no further ascent, and that the apogee one reached entailed, as in all tragic drama, a catastrophic declension."

2 Bouda Etemad, *Possessing the World: Taking the Measurements of Colonisation from the Eighteenth to the Twentieth Century* (New York: Berghahn Books, 2007), 155; Philip T. Hoffman, *Why Did Europe Conquer the World?* (Princeton, NJ: Princeton University Press, 2015), 2.

3   Krishan Kumar, *Visions of Empire: How Five Imperial Regimes Shaped the World* (Princeton, NJ: Princeton University Press, 2017).

4   Eric Hobsbawm, *The Age of Empires, 1875–1914* (London: Weidenfeld and Nicolson, 1987).

5   Krishan Kumar, *Prophecy and Progress: The Sociology of Industrial and Post-Industrial Society* (London: Allen Lane/Penguin Books, 1978).

6   Herbert Spencer, *Social Statics* (London: John Chapman 1851), 65; and see generally Robert Nisbet, *History of the Idea of Progress*, 2nd edn. (New Brunswick, NJ: Transaction Books, 2008).

7   Hew Strachan, "The Origins of the First World War," *International Affairs* 90, no. 2 (2014): 429.

8   Eric Hobsbawm, *The Age of Revolution 1789–1848* (London: Weidenfeld and Nicolson, 1962); Robert Nisbet, *The Sociological Tradition* (London: Heinemann, 1967).

9   There are some vivid accounts of these changes, focusing on the city, in H. J. Dyos and M. Wolff, eds., *The Victorian City: Images and Realities*, 2 vols. (London: Routledge and Kegan Paul, 1973). For the wider changes wrought by industrialization, see, for example, the classic account in Eric Hobsbawm's trilogy (London: Weidenfeld and Nicolson, 1962, 1975, 1987); see also Sidney Pollard, *Peaceful Conquest: The Industrialization of Europe, 1760–1970* (New York: Oxford University Press, 1981).

10 Alexis de Tocqueville, *Journeys to England and Ireland*, translated by George Lawrence and K. P. Mayer, edited by J. P. Mayer (1835, London: Faber and Faber, 1958), 107–08.

11 Frank E. Manuel, *The New World of Henri Saint-Simon* (Notre Dame, IN: University of Notre Dame Press, 1963).

12 Émile Durkheim, *Socialism*, translated by Charlotte Sattler, edited and introduced by Alvin Gouldner (New York: Collier Books, 1962); Émile Durkheim, *The Elementary Forms of Religious Life*, translated and with an introduction by Karen E. Fields (New York: The Free Press, 1995).

13 Philip Abrams, "The Sense of the Past and the Origins of Sociology," *Past and Present* 55 (1972): 22.

14 Karl Marx and Friedrich Engels, *The Communist Manifesto*, with an Introduction and Notes by Gareth Stedman Jones (London: Penguin Books, 2002), 223.

15 Max Weber, "Prefatory Remarks to Collected Essays in the Sociology of Religion," in *The Protestant Ethic and the Spirit of Capitalism, with Other Writings on the Rise of the West*, translated and introduced by Stephen Kalberg, 205–20 (New York: Oxford University Press, 1995), 208.

16 Max Weber, *The Russian Revolutions*, translated and edited by Gordon C. Wells and Peter Baehr (Ithaca, NY: Cornell University Press, 1995).

17 Max Weber, "Bureaucracy," in *From Max Weber: Essays in Sociology*, translated and edited by H. H. Gerth and C. Wright Mills (London: Routledge and Kegan Paul, 1948), 230.

18 Karl Mannheim, "Conservative Thought," in *Essays on Sociology and Social Psychology*, 74–164 (London: Routledge and Kegan Paul, 1953).

19 Émile Durkheim, *Suicide: A Study in Sociology*, translated by John A. Spaulding and George Simpson (New York: The Free Press, 1951), 249–53.

20 Sir Lewis Namier, "1848: Seed-Plot of History," in *Vanished Supremacies' Essays on European History 1812–1918* (Harmondsworth, UK: Penguin Books, 1962).

21 Krishan Kumar, "Nationalism and Revolution: Friends or Foes?," *Nations and Nationalism* 21, no. 4 (2015): 589–608.

22 Giuseppe Mazzini, "The Duties of Man," in *The Nationalism Reader*, edited by Omar Dahbour and Micheline R. Ishay, 87–97 (Atlantic Highlands, NJ: Humanities Press, 1995), 93.

23 J. W. Burrow, *The Crisis of Reason: European Thought, 1848–1914* (New Haven, CT: Yale University Press, 2000), 26–9.

24 Melvin Richter, *The Politics of Conscience: T. H. Green and His Age* (London: Weidenfeld and Nicolson, 1964); Stefan Collini, *Liberalism and Sociology: L. T. Hobhouse and Political Argument in England 1880–1914* (Cambridge: Cambridge University Press, 1979).

25 Peter Stansky, "Harcourt, Sir William George Granville Venables Vernon (1827–1904)," in *The Oxford Dictionary of National Biography* (Oxford: Oxford University Press, 2004).

26 Michael Freeden, *The New Liberalism: An Ideology of Social Reform* (Oxford: Oxford University Press, 1986).

27 Léon Poliakov, *The Aryan Myth: A History of Racist and Nationalist Ideas in Europe*, translated by Edmund Howard (New York: Barnes and Noble, 1974), 215–54; Michael Banton, *Racial Theories*, 2nd edn. (Cambridge: Cambridge University Press, 1998), 62–8.

28 Hans Kohn, *The Habsburg Empire 1804–1918: Texts and Documents* (Princeton, NJ: Van Nostrand, 1961), 119.

29 Kumar, *Visions of Empire*, 20–36.

30 Otto Bauer, *The Question of Nationalities and Social Democracy*, edited by Ephraim J. Nimni, translated by Joseph O'Donnell (1907; Minneapolis: University of Minnesota Press, 2000), 18.

31 Terry Martin, *The Affirmative Action Empire: Nations and Nationalism in the Soviet Union, 1923–1939* (Ithaca, NY: Cornell University Press, 2001).

32 Andrzej Walicki, *The Slavophile Controversy: History of a Conservative Utopia in Nineteenth-Century Russian Thought* (Oxford: Oxford University Press, 1975).

33 Russian socialists were organized in the Russian Social Democratic Party, which at its Second Congress in 1903—Lenin exploiting a temporary majority of his supporters—split into Bolsheviks ("the majority") and Mensheviks ("the minority"). The numbers were soon reversed, but the names stuck (Richard Pipes, *The Russian Revolution, 1899–1919* [London: Fontana Press, 1992], 360). A tendency followed, less excusably, by many leading scholars of recent times commenting on nineteenth-century thought, for example, Burrow, *The Crisis of Reason*. A possible framework for such an account—though there is little on social thought itself—is provided by Jürgen Osterhammel's massive "global history of the nineteenth century," Jürgen Osterhammel, *The Transformation of the World: A Global History of the Nineteenth Century*, translated by Patrick Camiller (Princeton, NJ: Princeton University Press, 2014).

34 Richard Koebner and Helmut Dan Schmidt, *Imperialism; the Story and Significance of a Political Word, 1840–1960* (Cambridge: Cambridge University Press, 1964).

35 Daniel Chernilo, "Methodological Nationalism and Its Critique," in *The Sage Handbook of Nations and Nationalism*, edited by Gerard Delanty and Krishan Kumar, 129–40 (London: Sage Publications, 2006), 129–40.

36 Frederick Quinn, *The French Overseas Empire* (Westport, CT: Praeger, 2002), 178–81.

37 Burrow, *The Crisis of Reason*.

38 James Burnham, *The Machiavellians: Defenders of Freedom* (Chicago: Henry Regnery Co., 1962).

39 Gustave Le Bon, *The Crowd: A Study of the Popular Mind* (London: Ernest Benn, 1952), 207.

40 Carl E. Schorske, *Fin-de-Siècle Vienna: Politics and Culture* (New York: Alfred A. Knopf, 1980).

Chapter 4

1 Brian E. Vick, *The Congress of Vienna: Power and Politics after Napoleon* (Cambridge, MA: Harvard University Press, 2014), ch. 6.

2 Brendon Westler, "Between Tradition and Revolution: The Curious Case of Francisco Martínez Marina, the Cádiz Constitution, and Spanish Liberalism," *Journal of the History of Ideas* 76, no. 3 (2015): 393–416; Markus J. Prutsch, *Making Sense of Constitutional Monarchism in Post-Napoleonic France and Germany* (Basingstoke, UK: Palgrave Macmillan, 2013); Richard Stites, *The Four Horsemen: Riding to Liberty in Post-Napoleonic Europe* (Oxford: Oxford University Press, 2014); Werner Daum, *Zeit der Drucker und Buchhändler: Die Produktion und Rezeption von Publizistik in der Verfassungsrevolution Neapel-Siziliens 1820/21* (Frankfurt: Peter Lang, 2005).

3 Carlo Ghisalberti, "Lo Statuto albertino e il costituzionalismo europeo della prima metà dell'Ottocento," in *Stato Nazione e Costituzione nell'Italia contemporanea*, edited by Carlo Ghisalberti (Naples: Edizioni Scientifiche Italiane, 1999), 25–49.

4 Alan S. Kahan, *Aristocratic Liberalism: The Social and Political Thought of Jacob Burckhardt, John Stuart Mill, and Alexis de Tocqueville* (New York: Oxford University Press, 1992); Maurizio Isabella, "Aristocratic Liberalism and Risorgimento: Cesare Balbo and Piedmontese Political Thought after 1848," *History of European Ideas* 39, no. 6 (2013): 835–57.

5 Gangolf Hübinger, "Hochindustrialisierung und die Kulturwerte des deutschen Liberalismus," in *Liberalismus im 19. Jahrhundert. Deutschland im europäischen Vergleich*, edited by Dieter Langewiesche (Göttingen: Vandenhoeck & Ruprecht, 1988), 193–208.

6 Elaine Hadley, *Living Liberalism: Practical Citizenship in Mid-Victorian Britain* (Chicago: University of Chicago Press, 2010), 7–9; Pieter M. Judson, *Exclusive Revolutionaries: Liberal Politics, Social Experience, and National Identity in the Austrian Empire, 1848–1914* (Ann Arbor: University of Michigan Press, 1996).

7 Vick, *Congress of Vienna*, ch. 4; Jakob Katz, *From Prejudice to Destruction: Anti-Semitism, 1700–1933* (Cambridge, MA: Harvard University Press, 1980); Michael B. Gross, *The War Against Catholicism: Liberalism and the Anti-Catholic Imagination in Nineteenth-Century Germany* (Ann Arbor: University of Michigan Press, 2004); Caroline Ford, *Creating the Nation in Provincial France: Religion and Political Identity in Brittany* (Princeton, NJ: Princeton University Press, 1993).

8 Brian Vick, "Liberalism, Nationalism, and Gender Dichotomy in Mid Nineteenth-Century Germany: The Contested Case of German Civil Law," *Journal of Modern History* 82, no. 3 (2010): 546–84; Carole Pateman, *The Sexual Contract* (Stanford, CA: Stanford University Press, 1988); Joan Landes, *Women and the Public Sphere in the Age of Enlightenment* (Ithaca, NY: Cornell University Press, 1994); Karen M. Offen, *European Feminisms, 1700–1950: A Political History* (Stanford, CA: Stanford University Press, 2000), 121 for Richer.

9 Dieter Langewiesche, "Sozialer Liberalismus in Deutschland. Herkunft und Entwicklung im 19. Jahrhundert," in *Sozialliberalismus in Europa: Herkunft und Entwicklung im 19. und frühen 20. Jahrhundert*, edited by Detlef Lehnert (Cologne: Böhlau, 2012), 35–50, 47–9.

10 Langewiesche, "Sozialer Liberalismus," 40–3.

11 Donald Winch, *Riches and Poverty: An Intellectual History of Political Economy in Britain, 1750–1834* (Cambridge: Cambridge University Press, 1996); Winch, *Wealth and Life: Essays on the Intellectual History of Political Economy in Britain, 1848–1914* (Cambridge: Cambridge University Press, 2009); Debra Satz, "Nineteenth-Century Political Economy," in *The Cambridge History of Philosophy in the Nineteenth Century (1790–1870)*, edited by Allen W. Wood and Songsuk Susan Hahn (Cambridge: Cambridge University Press, 2012), 676–98.

12 Winch, *Riches and Poverty*, chs. 11, 13; Robert J. Mayhew, *Malthus: The Life and Legacies of an Unlikely Prophet* (Cambridge, MA: Harvard University Press, 2014), chs. 3–4; A. M. C. Waterman, *Revolution, Economics and Religion: Christian Political Economy, 1798–1833* (Cambridge: Cambridge University Press, 1991).

13 Ernesto Screpanti and Stefano Zamagni, *An Outline of the History of Economic Thought*, translated by David Field and Lynn Kirby, 2nd edn. (Oxford: Oxford University Press, 2005), 91–7, 121–29.

14 Ibid., 97–100, 102–04, 107–08; Satz, "Political Economy," 687–8; Alessandro Roncaglia, *The Wealth of Ideas: A History of Economic Thought* (Cambridge: Cambridge University Press, 2005), 186–96, 209–18.

15 Emphasizing this distinction, Satz, "Political Economy."

16 Roncaglia, *Wealth of Ideas*, chs. 7–8; Elaine Freedgood, "Banishing Panic: Harriet Martineau and the Popularisation of Political Economy," *Victorian Studies* 39, no. 1 (1995): 33–53.

17 Frederik Albritton Jonsson, "Political Economy," in *Historicism and the Human Sciences in Victorian Britain*, edited by Mark Bevir (Cambridge: Cambridge University Press, 2017), 186–210.

18 Roncaglia, *Wealth of Ideas*, 164–69.

19 Winch, *Riches and poverty*, 26–7.

20 Erik Grimmer-Solem, *The Rise of Historical Economics and Social Reform in Germany 1864–1894* (Oxford: Clarendon Press, 2003), passim, 119, 149–52 for unions; for British equivalents such as John Stuart Mill's student T. E. Cliffe Leslie, see Stefan Collini, Donald Winch, and John Burrow, *That Noble Science of Politics: A Study in Nineteenth-Century Intellectual History* (Cambridge: Cambridge University Press, 1983), ch. 8.

21 Screpanti and Zamagni, *Outline*, chs. 5–6; Philip Mirowski, *More Heat than Light: Economics as Social Physics, Physics as Nature's Economics* (Cambridge: Cambridge University Press, 1989).

22 Screpanti and Zamagni, *Outline*, 170–73.

23 Ibid., 173, 198–203; Winch, *Wealth and Life*, 50–3 (Mill), ch. 10 (Marshall).

24 Grimmer-Solem, *Historical Economics*, 271–75.

25 Iain McCalman, *Radical Underworld: Prophets, Revolutionaries and Pornographers in London, 1795–1840* (Cambridge: Cambridge University Press, 1988); Jon Mee, *Print, Publicity and Popular Radicalism in the 1790s: The Laurel of Liberty* (Cambridge: Cambridge University Press, 2016); James M. Brophy, *Popular Culture and the Public Sphere in the Rhineland, 1800–1850* (Cambridge: Cambridge University Press, 2007); Gregory Claeys and Christine Lattek, "Radicalism, Republicanism and Revolutionism: From the Principles of '89 to the Origins of Modern Terrorism," in *The Cambridge History of Nineteenth-Century Political Thought*, edited by Gareth Stedman Jones and Gregory Claeys (Cambridge: Cambridge University Press, 2011), 200–253.

26 Jonathan Sperber, *Karl Marx: A Nineteenth-Century Life* (New York: Norton, 2013), chs. 4, 5; Frank E. Manuel, *The Prophets of Paris: Turgot, Condorcet, Saint-Simon, Fourier, and Comte* (New York: Harper, 1965); J. F. C. Harrison, *Quest for the New Moral World: Robert Owen and the Owenites in Britain and America* (New York: Scribner, 1969).

27 Wolfgang Schieder, "Kommunismus," in *Geschichtliche Grundbegriffe*, edited by Otto Brunner et al., 8 vols. (Stuttgart: Klett, 1972–1997), vol. 3, 455–529, 468–71; Schieder, "Sozialismus," in ibid., vol. 5, 923–96, 934–49.

28 From a vast literature, see Sperber, *Marx*; David McLellan, *Karl Marx: A Biography*, 4th edn. (Basingstoke, UK: Palgrave Macmillan, 2006); Shlomo Avineri, *The Social and Political Thought of Karl Marx* (Cambridge: Cambridge University Press, 1968).

29 Carl E. Schorske, *German Social Democracy, 1905–1917: The Development of the Great Schism* (Cambridge, MA: Harvard University Press, 1955).

30 Ruth Kinna, *Kropotkin: Reviewing the Classical Anarchist Tradition* (Edinburgh: Edinburgh University Press, 2016).

31 Matthew Levinger, *Enlightened Nationalism: The Transformation of Prussian Political Culture, 1806–1848* (New York: Oxford University Press, 2000); Robert M. Berdahl, *The Politics of the Prussian Nobility: The Development of a Conservative Ideology, 1770–1848* (Princeton, NJ: Princeton University Press, 1988); Richard Allen Lebrun, *Throne and Altar: The Political and Religious Thought of Joseph de Maistre* (Ottawa: University of Ottawa Press, 1965); Klaus Epstein, *The Genesis of German Conservatism* (Princeton, NJ: Princeton University Press, 1966).

32 Edmund Burke, *Reflections on the Revolution in France*, edited by Frank M. Turner (New Haven, CT: Yale University Press, 2003), 50.

33 Mark Philp, "Vulgar Conservatism, 1792–3," *English Historical Review* 110, no. 435 (1995): 42–69; Levinger, *Enlightened Nationalism*.

34 Matthew Roberts, "Popular Conservatism in Britain, 1832–1914," *Parliamentary History* 26, no. 3 (2007): 387–410; Zeev Sternhell, "Paul Déroulède and the Origins of Modern French Nationalism," *Journal of Contemporary History* 6, no. 4 (1971): 46–70; Geoff Eley, *Reshaping the German Right: Radical Nationalism and Political Change after Bismarck*, 2nd edn. (Ann Arbor: University of Michigan Press, 1991); Judson, *Exclusive Revolutionaries*, chs. 6–9.

35 John Stuart Mill, *On Representative Government*, in *Collected Works* XIX, 567; Jennifer Pitts, *A Turn to Empire: The Rise of Imperial Liberalism in Britain and France* (Princeton, NJ: Princeton University Press, 2005); Brian Vick, "Power, Humanitarianism and the Global Liberal Order: Abolition and the Barbary Corsairs in the Vienna Congress System," *International History Review* 40, no. 4 (2018): 939–60.

36 Samuel Moyn and Andrew Sartori, eds., *Global Intellectual History* (New York: Columbia University Press, 2013).

37 John Lynch, *Simón Bolívar: A Life* (New Haven, CT: Yale University Press, 2006), 36, 38, 245; Jonathan Harris, "Bernardino Rivadavia and Benthamite 'Discipleship,'" *Latin American Research Review* 33, no. 1 (1998): 129–49; Manuel, *Prophets*, 274; Arturo Ardao, "Assimilation and Transformation of Positivism in Latin America," *Journal of the History of Ideas* 24, no. 4 (1963): 515–22.

38 Albert Hourani, *Arabic Thought in the Liberal Age, 1798–1939*, 2nd edn. (1962; Cambridge: Cambridge University Press, 1983); Jens Hanssen and Max Weiss, eds., *Arabic Thought beyond the Liberal Age: Towards an Intellectual History of the Nahda* (Cambridge: Cambridge University Press, 2016).

39   Daniel T. Rodgers, *Atlantic Crossings: Social Politics in a Progressive Age* (Cambridge, MA: Harvard University Press, 1998), 62, 77–111; Erik Grimmer-Solem, "German Social Science, Meiji Conservatism, and the Peculiarities of Japanese History," *Journal of World History* 16, no. 2 (2005): 187–222.

40   Christopher L. Hill, "Conceptual Universalization in the Transnational Nineteenth Century," in *Global Intellectual History*, edited by Moyn and Sartori, 134–58, 141; Douglas Howland, "Translating Liberty in Nineteenth-Century Japan," *Journal of the History of Ideas* 62, no. 1 (2001): 161–81.

41   Harris, "Rivadavia," 131.

42   C. A. Bayly, *Recovering Liberties: Indian Thought in the Age of Liberalism and Empire* (Cambridge: Cambridge University Press, 2012), 131, 134, 139, 190–98.

43   Ibid., 11–13, 200–203, 132–50.

44   Ibid., 43–7, 50–60; Lynn Zastoupil, *Rammohun Roy and the Making of Victorian Britain* (Basingstoke, UK: Palgrave Macmillan, 2010).

45   Jonathan Schneer, *London 1900: The Imperial Metropolis* (New Haven, CT: Yale University Press, 1999), ch. 8; Kris Manjapra, *Age of Entanglement: German and Indian Intellectuals Across Empire* (Cambridge, MA: Harvard University Press, 2014).

46   David P. Geggus, ed., *The Impact of the Haitian Revolution in the Atlantic World* (Columbia: University of South Carolina Press, 2001), particularly the essay by Karin Schüller on German reception; Susan Buck-Morss, "Hegel and Haiti," *Critical Inquiry* 26, no. 4 (2000): 821–65; Laurent Dubois, *Avengers of the New World: The Story of the Haitian Revolution* (Cambridge, MA: Harvard University Press, 2004), 304–06; for Wedderburn, McCalman, *Radical Underworld*, ch. 3; Hannah-Rose Murray, "A 'Negro Hercules': Frederick Douglass' Celebrity in Britain," *Celebrity Studies* 7, no. 2 (2016): 264–79.

47   H. Stuart Hughes, *Consciousness and Society: The Reorientation of European Social Thought 1890–1930*, Rev. edn. (New York: Vintage, 1977); Manjapra, *Age of Entanglement*, 8–11; Walter E. Houghton, *The Victorian Frame of Mind, 1830–1870* (New Haven, CT: Yale University Press, 1957), 14–18.

Chapter 5

1   Todd H. Weir, ed., *Monism: Science, Philosophy, Religion, and the History of a Worldview* (New York: Palgrave Macmillian, 2012), 12–15.

2   Although coined by Immanuel Kant in his *Critique of Judgment* of 1790 to convey the narrow sense of our intuition of the world, the term *Weltanschauung* broadened in meaning over the course of the century. See David Naugle, *Weltanschauung: The History of a Concept* (Grand Rapids, MI: Wm. B. Eerdmans, 2002), 58ff.

3   Erazim Kohak, *The Embers and the Stars: A Philosophical Inquiry into the Moral Sense of Nature* (Chicago: University of Chicago Press, 1984), 126.

4   Pierre Simon Laplace, *A Philosophical Essay on Probabilities*, translated by F. W. Truscott and F. L. Emory, from the 6th French edn. (London: John Wiley and Sons, 1902), 4.

5   Stephen Gaukroger has argued eloquently that the mechanistic ideal was undermined in the eighteenth century both by internal problems and by the emergence of the notion of sensibility, referring to "the collapse of mechanism." Stephen Gaukroger, *The Collapse of Mechanism and the Rise of Sensibility: Science and the Shaping of Modernity, 1680–1760* (Oxford: Oxford University Press, 2010); and especially Stephen Gaukroger, *The Natural and the Human: Science and the Shaping of Modernity, 1739–1841* (Oxford: Oxford University Press, 2016). For example, he notes that Laplace was careful to say that due to their ignorance

of causes, humans must surrender the certainty associated with the ideal and accept merely probable results (Gaukroger, *The Natural and the Human*, 62). What distinguishes claims made here from those of Gaukroger, whose careful scholarship about individual research programs is pathbreaking and much appreciated, is the concern for worldview. My intent is to focus on the meaning of nature in popular culture, often expressed with respect to religion.

6 Immanuel Kant, *Metaphysical Foundations of Natural Science*, translated by Ernest Bax (London: George Bell and Sons, 1883), 140.

7 Kant's treatment of organism did have its detractors, but it also formed the foundation for what Timothy Lenoir has called the teleomechanical tradition of nineteenth-century German biological science; see Timothy Lenoir, *The Strategy of Life: Teleology and Mechanics in Nineteenth-Century German Biology* (Dodrecht: D. Reidel, 1982). For criticism of Kant's position here, see Frederick Gregory, "'Nature is an Organized Whole': J.F. Fries's Reformulation of Kant's Philosophy of Organism," in *Romanticism in Science*, edited by S. Poggi and M. Bossi, 91–101 (Dordrecht: Kluwer Academic Publishers, 1994).

8 Kant's work carried the subtitle *Essay on the Constitution and the Mechanical Origin of the Whole Universe According to Newtonian Principles.*

9 Peter Gay, *The Enlightenment: An Interpretation*, II (New York: Alfred A. Knopf, 1969), 140ff.

10 "Creation by law" appeared in the title of an 1845 hostile treatment of Robert Chambers's sensational book, *Vestiges of the Natural History of Creation* of 1844. See Thomas Monck Mason, *Creation by the Immediate Agency of God, as Opposed to Creation by Natural Law* (London: John W. Parker, 1845). It also was the title used by Alfred Russell Wallace in 1867 when he defended Darwin against criticisms by the Duke of Argyle in his book, *The Reign of Law*. See Alfred Russell Wallace, "Creation by Law," *Quarterly Journal of Science* 4 (1867): 471–88.

11 Lorraine Daston, "The Ethos of Enlightenment," in *The Sciences in Enlightened Europe*, edited by William Clark, Jan Golinski, and Simon Schaffer, 495–504 (Chicago: University of Chicago Press, 1999), 502.

12 Charles Babbage, *The Ninth Bridgewater Treatise*, 2nd edn. (London: John Murray, 1838), 226. Herschel wrote this letter in 1836, and it was publicly available the following year when Charles Babbage included it in his contribution to the natural theology series known as the Bridgewater Treatises.

13 R. G. Collingwood, *The Idea of Nature* (Oxford: Oxford University Press, 1967), 3ff. Collingwood delivered lectures on this subject during the 1930s and was revising and preparing them for publication when he died in 1943. It was left to others to see the entire series through to publication, which came about originally with Clarendon Press in 1945.

14 Ibid., 9.

15 Ibid., 10.

16 Citations from this work are taken from: Arthur O. Lovejoy, *The Great Chain of Being: A Study of the History of an Idea* (New York: Harper and Row, 1960).

17 Ibid., 292, 294.

18 Ibid., 293.

19 Michel Foucault, *The Order of Things* (New York: Pantheon Books, 1970), 127–28. The original French edition, *Les mots et le choses*, appeared in 1966.

20 The most thorough and balanced treatment of Goethe's stance over against Newton is Dennis Sepper, *Goethe contra Newton* (Cambridge: Cambridge University Press, 1988).

21 Lovejoy, *The Great Chain of Being*, chs. 9–11.

22 Frederick Beiser, *The Fate of Reason: German Philosophy from Kant to Fichte* (Cambridge, MA: Harvard University Press, 1987), 30.

23 Quoted from Jacobi's *Fliegende Blätter* by Beiser. No date is given by Beiser, nor is there a date given in the original source (F. H. Jacobi, *Werke*, vol. 6 [Leipzig: Gerhard Fleischer, 1825], 155). Jacobi was born in 1743 and died in 1819. In a brief forward to the *Fliegende Blätter* (130) the contents are identified as "casual maxims thrown out at very different times."

24 Ibid., 81–2.

25 Ibid., 46–7. There is no better nor more comprehensive treatment of the issue of nihilism in its various guises at the end of the eighteenth century than that of Beiser.

26 Lovejoy, *The Great Chain of Being*, 317.

27 Gaukroger, *The Natural and the Human*, 44–5.

28 Lovejoy, *The Great Chain of Being*, 318. Lovejoy quotes Schelling's *Philosophische Untersuchungen über das Wesen des menschlichen Freiheit* of 1809 from the 1907 edition of Schelling's Werke (edited by Oskar Weiss).

29 Ibid., 325.

30 Natural theology blossomed in the German states in the middle decades of the eighteenth century. See William Clark, "The Death of Metaphysics in Enlightened Prussia," in *The Sciences in Enlightened Europe*, edited by William Clark, Jan Golinski, and Simon Schaffer, 423–73 (Chicago: University of Chicago Press, 1999), 434. Cf. also Frederick Gregory, "Continental Europe," in *The Warfare between Science & Religion (The Idea that Wouldn't Die)*, edited by Jeff Hardin, Ronald L. Numbers, and A. Binzley (Baltimore: Johns Hopkins University Press, 2018).

31 Norbert Guterman, ed., *F.W.J. Schelling, On University Studies*, translated by Ella S. Morgan (Athens, OH: University Press, 1966), 34, 10–11.

32 Frederick Gregory, "Proto-Monism in German Philosophy, Theology, and Science, 1800–1845," in *Monism: Science, Philosophy, Religion, and the History of a Worldview*, edited by Todd H. Weir, 45–69 (New York: Palgrave Macmillan, 2012).

33 Todd H. Weir, *Secularism and Religion in Nineteenth-Century Germany: The Rise of the Fourth Confession* (Cambridge: Cambridge University Press, 2014).

34 Weir, *Secularism and Religion in Nineteenth-Century Germany*, ch. 2; Andreas Daum, *Wissenschaftspopularisierung im 19. Jahrhundert. Bürgerliche Kultur, naturwissenschaftliche Bildung und die deutsche Öffentlichkeit, 1848–1914*, 2nd edn. (Munich: R. Oldenbourg Verlag, 2002), 198–99; and Robert J. Richards, *The Romantic Conception of Life: Science and Philosophy in the Age of Goethe* (Chicago: University of Chicago Press, 2002), ch. 14.

35 Frederick Gregory, *Scientific Materialism in Nineteenth Century Germany* (Dordrecht: D. Reidel Publishing Co., 1977).

36 Ibid., 90–2. Feuerbach's review carried the title "Natural Science and the Revolution."

37 Jakob Moleschott, *Der Kreislauf des Lebens* (Mainz: Verlag Viktor von Zabern, 1855), 455. The scientific materialists' relation to Schelling's pantheistic *Naturphilosophie* is not straightforward, ranging from an outright dismissal to genuine appreciation. See Gregory *Scientific Materialism in Nineteenth Century Germany*, 178, 180–82; on their strong teleological sense, see 136–37, 181–82, 186–87.

38 For a thorough treatment of Darwin's voyage and his gradual conversion to evolution, see Janet Browne, *Charles Darwin: Voyaging* (Princeton, NJ: Princeton University Press, 1995), esp. chs. 13–19.

39 Ibid, 464–65.

40 Frederick Burkhardt et al., eds., *The Correspondence of Charles Darwin*, vol. 12 (1864; Cambridge: Cambridge University Press, 2001), xx.

41 Daum, *Wissenschaftspopularisierung im 19. Jahrhundert*, 66–7.

42 Robert J. Richards, *The Tragic Sense of Life. Ernst Haeckel and the Struggle over Evolutionary Thought* (Chicago: University of Chicago Press, 2008), 15.

43 Bernhard Kleeberg, "God-Nature Progressing: Natural Theology in German Monism," *Science in Context* 20 (2007): 537–69; and Gregory, "Continental Europe," 91–5.

44 Charles Darwin, Correspondence Project, "Letter no. 13230." Available online: http://www.darwinproject.ac.uk/DCP-LETT-13230 (accessed May 14, 2017).

45 Arnold Thackray, "Quantified Chemistry—the Newtonian Dream," in *John Dalton and the Progress of Science*, edited by D. S. L. Cardwell, 92–108 (New York: Barnes and Noble, 1968), 92.

46 Albert Einstein and Leopold Infeld, *The Evolution of Physics* (New York: Simon and Shuster, 1966), 54; see Part I: "The Rise of the Mechanical View," 3–65.

47 British chemistry was not the only example. See Frederick Gregory, "Romantic Kantianism and the End of the Newtonian Dream in Chemistry," *Archives internationales d'histoire des sciences* 34 (1984): 108–23.

48 Bruce J. Hunt, *The Maxwellians* (Ithaca, NY: Cornell University Press, 1991), 78.

49 Ludwig Büchner, *Kraft und Stoff* (Frankfurt: Meidinger Sohn, 1855), 24. The quotation of Wundt is included in a volume of Büchner's essays. See Ludwig Büchner, *Im Dienst der Wahrheit* (Giessen: Emil Roth, 1890), 56.

50 These utterances come from late in his life. See Gregory, *Scientific Materialism in Nineteenth Century Germany*, 150–51. For Kant's unknowable *Ding-an-sich* as theological, see 148.

51 Lawrence Badash, "The Completeness of Nineteenth Century Science," *Isis* 63 (1972): 52.

52 Helge S. Kragh, *Entropic Creation: Religious Context of Thermodynamics and Creation* (Burlington, VT: Ashgate Publishing, 2008), ch. 4.

Chapter 6

1 See Michael A. Meyer, *Response to Modernity: A History of the Reform Movement in Judaism* (New York: Oxford University Press, 1988); Paul Mendes-Flohr and Jehuda Reinharz, eds., *The Jew in the Modern World: A Documentary History* (New York: Oxford University Press, 1995); and Susannah Heschel, *Abraham Geiger and the Jewish Jesus* (Chicago: University of Chicago Press, 1998).

2 Jaroslov Pelikan, *Christian Doctrine and Modern Culture (Since 1700)*, vol. 5 of *The Christian Tradition: A History of Development of Doctrine* (Chicago: University of Chicago Press, 1989), 174; B. M. B. Reardon, ed., *Religious Thought in the Nineteenth Century* (New York: Cambridge University Press, 1966), 39.

3 Friedrich Schleiermacher, *On Religion: Speeches to Its Cultured Despisers*, edited by Richard Crouter (New York: Cambridge University Press, 1988), 77.

4 Ibid., 89.

5 Ibid., 136, 138.

6 Ibid., 102.

7 Karl Barth, *Protestant Theology in the Nineteenth Century: Its Background and History* (Valley Forge, PA: Judson Press, 1973), 454.

8 Pelikan, *Christian Doctrine and Modern Culture*, 172–73.

9 Schleiermacher, *On Religion*, 192.

10 François-René de Chateaubriand, *Génie du christianisme*, 2 vols. (Paris: Garnier, 1966), 2:50.

11 Hugh Honour, *Romanticism* (New York: Harper and Row, 1979), 156–91.

12 Howard Foster Lowry and Willard Thorp, eds., *An Oxford Anthology of English Poetry* (New York: Oxford University Press, 1956), 590.

13 André Vauchez, "The Cathedral," in *Realms of Memory*, II: *Traditions*, edited by Pierre Nora and Lawrence Kritzman, 37–68 (New York: Columbia University Press, 1997), 58.

14 John Toews, *Hegelianism: The Path Toward Dialectical Humanism, 1805–1841* (New York: Cambridge University Press, 1980), 141.

15 Ludwig Feuerbach, *The Essence of Christianity*, translated by George Eliot (New York: Harper and Row, 1957), xxxvi, xxxviii.

16 Ibid., 60.

17 Ibid., 33.

18 Karl Marx and Friedrich Engels, *On Religion* (New York: Schocken, 1964), 41–2.

19 Barth, *Protestant Theology in the Nineteenth Century*, 461; Albert Schweitzer, *The Quest for the Historical Jesus* (New York: Macmillan, 1961).

20 Reardon, *Religious Thought in the Nineteenth Century*, 121.

21 David Friedrich Strauss, *The Life of Jesus Critically Examined*, translated by George Eliot (New York: Macmillan, 1892), xxx.

22 Ibid., 757.

23 Ibid., 759.

24 Robert D. Priest, *The Gospel According to Renan: Reading, Writing, and Religion in Nineteenth-Century France* (New York: Oxford University Press, 2015); Ernest Renan, "Les historiens critiques de Jésus," in *Etudes d'histoire religieuse*, 116–67 (Paris: Gallimard, 1992).

25 Michael Paul Driskel, *Representing Belief: Religion, Art, and Society in Nineteenth-Century France* (University Park: Pennsylvania State University Press, 1992), 190–93, 211.

26 Ernest Renan, *The Life of Jesus* (New York: Modern Library, 1927), 383, 388.

27 Priest, *The Gospel According to Renan*, 102; Frank Paul Bowman, *Le Christ des barricades, 1789–1848* (Paris: Cerf, 1987).

28 Renan, *The Life of Jesus*, 269.

29 Ibid., 214.

30 Ibid., 226.

31 John Henry Cardinal Newman, *Apologia Pro Vita Sua and Six Sermons*, edited by Frank M. Turner (New Haven, CT: Yale University Press, 2008), 133.

32 Ibid., 289, 332.

33 Søren Kierkegaard, *Fear and Trembling and The Sickness Unto Death* (Princeton, NJ: Princeton University Press, 1954), 46.

34 Maurice Mandelbaum, *History, Man, & Reason: A Study in Nineteenth-Century Thought* (Baltimore, MD: Project Muse, 2019), 32.

35 Pelikan, *Christian Doctrine and Modern Culture*, 199–203.

36 Joseph Mazzini, *Life and Writings of Joseph Mazzini*, vol. 5 (London: Smith, Elder, 1891), 279.

37 Mark Bevir, "The West Turns Eastward: Madame Blavatsky and the Transformation of the Occult Tradition," *Journal of the American Academy of Religion* 62 (1994): 753.

38 Friedrich Nietzsche, *Nietzsche and the Death of God—Selected Writings*, translated, edited, and with an introduction by Peter Fritzsche (Boston: Bedford St. Martin's, 2007), 71–2.

39 Émile Durkheim, *The Elementary Forms of Religious Life*, translated and edited by Karin Fields (New York: Free Press, 1995), 227.

40 Ibid., xxxix.

41 Émile Durkheim, *Moral Education* (New York: Free Press, 1961), 3.

42 Émile Durkheim, *Durkheim on Religion*, edited by W. S. F. Pickering (Atlanta, GA: Scholars Press, 1994), 184–85.

43 Durkheim, *The Elementary Forms of Religious Life*, 1.

Chapter 7

1 T. S. Eliot, *The Waste Land: A Facsimile and Transcript of the Original Drafts, Including the Annotations of Ezra Pound* (London: Faber & Faber, 1971), 5.

2 Arthur Symons, *The Symbolist Movement in Literature* (New York: E. P. Dutton & Co., 1919), 302–03.

3 Émile Zola, *Mes Haines* (Paris: Achille Faure, 1866), 58.

4 T. E. Hulme, *The Collected Writings of T. E. Hulme* (London: Clarendon Press, 1994), 61.

5 Henry-D. Davray, "Art," *Mercure de France*, April 16, 1918, 717.

6 Ibid., 718.

7 Désiré Nisard, *Etudes de critique et de moeurs sur les poètes latins de la décadence*, 2 vols. (Paris: Hachette, 1849), 1:164.

8 Jean-Marie Guyau, *L'Art au point de vue sociologique* (Paris: Alcan, 1889), 354.

9 Germaine de Staël, *De l'Allemagne* (Paris: Didot Frères, 1845), 574.

10 Germaine de Staël, *Corinne ou l'Italie*, 2 vols. (Paris: Duprat-Duverger, 1822), 2:237.

11 R. L. Brett and A. R. Jones, eds., *Wordsworth and Coleridge: Lyrical Ballads* (London: Routledge Classics, 2005), 291.

12 Ibid., 307.

13 François-René de Chateaubriand, *René* in *Oeuvres complètes de Chateaubriand* (Paris: P.-H. Crabbe, 1852), 83.

14 François-René de Chateaubriand, *Mémoires d'outre-tombe*, 2 vols. (Paris: Gallimard, 1988), 2:43.

15 Benjamin Constant, *Adolphe* (Paris: A. Quantin, 1878), 74.

16 Ibid., 182.

17 Arthur Rimbaud, letter to Georges Izambard, May 13, 1871, in *Oeuvres complètes* (Paris: Gallimard, 2009), 340.

18 Stéphane Mallarmé, *Variations sur un sujet*, "Crise de vers," in *Oeuvres complètes* (Paris: Gallimard, 1945), 366.

19 Charles Baudelaire, *Petits poëmes en prose*, vol. 4 of *Oeuvres complètes de Charles Baudelaire* (Paris: Lévy Frères, 1869), 106.

20 *The Collected Letters of Samuel Taylor Coleridge*, edited by Earl Leslie Griggs, 6 vols. (Oxford: Clarendon Press, 1956–1971), 1:626.

21 *Lectures 1808–1819: On Literature*, edited by R. A. Foakes, 2 vols. (London: Routledge; Princeton: Princeton University Press, 1987), 1:540.

22 The 1806 reference is in *The Notebooks of Samuel Taylor Coleridge*, edited by Kathleen Coburn et al., 5 double vols. (London: Routledge; Princeton: Princeton University Press, 1957–2002), 2:2784, and the 1818 reference is in the *Collected Letters*, ed. Griggs, 4:885. For an excellent exploration of these notions, see Gregory Leadbetter, *Coleridge and the Daemonic Imagination* (London: Palgrave, 2011), 85. I am grateful to Dr. Leadbetter for his insights on Coleridge, which have helped me hugely.

23 For the best exploration of Mallarmé's thing/nothing etymological play, see Roger Pearson, *Unfolding Mallarmé* (Oxford: Oxford University Press, 1997).

24 The unpublished poem "Le Silence du soir" appears in a manuscript held by the Bibliothèque nationale de France. See René Journet and Guy Robert, *Contribution aux études sur Victor Hugo*, 5 vols. (Paris: Belles Lettres, 1979–1982), 4:38.

25 Translated by Patrick McGuinness. See Raffaello Fornaciari, ed., *Poesie di Giacomo Leopardi* (Florence: Barbèra, 1889), 84 (lines 8–15).

Chapter 8

1   In an academic context, the term "art history" usually refers to the history solely of visual art, but I use it here to denote the history of the arts in general, including music, literature, dance, and architecture.

2   Cited in Reinhart Koselleck, *Futures Past: On the Semantics of Historical Time*, translated by Keith Tribe (Cambridge, MA: MIT Press, 1985), 252.

3   Reinhold Brinkmann, "In the Time of the Eroica," in *Beethoven and His World*, edited by Scott Burnham and Michael P. Steinberg (Princeton, NJ: Princeton University Press, 2000), 1–26.

4   When Hegel later turned his attention to the arts, in lectures given in the 1820s (subsequently published as *Aesthetics: Lectures on Fine Art*), he proposed that the arts followed the same evolutionary idea of human progress.

5   Koselleck, *Futures Past*, 246.

6   Charles Baudelaire, "The Painter of Modern Life," in Baudelaire, *Selected Writings on Art and Literature*, translated by P. Charvet (London: Penguin, 1992), 402.

7   Arthur Rimbaud, "A Season in Hell," in *Complete Works*, translated by Paul Schmidt (New York: Harper Collins, 1975).

8   A. W. Schlegel, *Vorlesungen über schöne Literatur und Kunst*, in *Music and Aesthetics in the Eighteenth and Early-Nineteenth Centuries*, edited by Peter Le Huray and James Day (Cambridge: Cambridge University Press, 1981), 270.

9   The Mastersingers themselves exemplify the idea of the medieval guild of artists or craftsmen. The idea was taken up by the Nazarenes, the Pre-Raphaelite Brotherhood in England, and the circles that formed around key figures of the early twentieth century, such as Stefan George and Arnold Schoenberg.

10 Pinthus's title plays on that of Wagner's *Götterdämmerung* (1876), but a similar idea can be found in Karl Kraus's contemporary work, *The Last Days of Mankind* (1915–1922).

11 Jürgen Habermas, *The Philosophical Discourse of Modernity: Twelve Lectures*, translated by Friedrich Lawrence (Oxford: Blackwell, 1987), 46.

12 Richard Wagner, *Religion and Art*, translated by William Ashton Ellis (Lincoln: University of Nebraska Press, 1994), 213.

13 Walter Pater, "The School of Giorgione," in *The Renaissance* (New York: Boni, 1919), 111.

14 See, among many other studies, Anthony J. Cascardi, *The Subject of Modernity* (Cambridge: Cambridge University Press, 1992), and Charles Taylor, *Sources of the Self: The Making of the Modern Identity* (Cambridge: Cambridge University Press, 2002).

15 Georg Simmel, "The Metropolis and Mental Life," in *Simmel on Culture: Selected Writings*, edited by David Frisby and Mike Featherstone (London: Sage, 2000), 184.

16 See Julie Brown, *Bartók and the Grotesque* (Aldershot, UK: Ashgate, 2007).

17 Thomas Crow, "Classicism in Crisis: Gros to Delacroix," in *Nineteenth Century Art: A Critical History*, edited by Stephen F. Eisenman, 4th edn. (London: Thames and Hudson, 2011), 60.

18 Brian Lukacher, "Nature and History in English Romantic Landscape Painting," in *Nineteenth Century Art*, 140.

19 See James H. Johnson, *Listening in Paris: A Cultural History* (Berkeley: University of California Press, 1995).

20 Mark Evan Bonds, *Music as Thought: Listening to the Symphony in the Age of Beethoven* (Princeton, NJ: Princeton University Press, 2006), xv.

21 Arnold Hauser, *The Social History of Art*, Vol. 4: *Naturalism, Impressionism, The Film Age* (London: Routledge and Kegan Paul, 1962), 16.

22 Derek B. Scott, *Sounds of the Metropolis: The 19th-Century Popular Music Revolution in London, New York, Paris and Vienna* (New York: Oxford University Press, 2008), 19.

23 See Judith Beniston and Robert Vilain, eds., "Culture and Politics in Read Vienna," Special Issue of *Austrian Studies* 14 (2006).

24 Frances K. Pohl, "The Rhetoric of Realism," in *Nineteenth Century Art*, 260.

25 Brian Lukacher, "Nature and History in English Romantic Landscape Painting," in *Nineteenth Century Art*, 146.

26 Kenneth Clarke, *The Romantic Rebellion: Romantic versus Classic Art* (London: Fontana, 1976), 270.

27 Stephen Kern, *The Culture of Time and Space 1880–1918* (Cambridge, MA: Harvard University Press, 1983), 1.

28 Sara Danius, *The Senses of Modernism: Technology, Perception, and Aesthetics* (Ithaca, NY: Cornell University Press, 2002), 1.

29 Nicholas Slonimsky, *Music Since 1900*, 4th edn. (London: Cassell, 1972), 1298.

30 Ibid., 1299.

31 The invention of sound recording by Thomas Edison in 1877 was of equal importance but its impact was not evident until after 1900. Similarly, the first experiments in film did not become influential until after the start of the new century.

32 David Llewellyn Phillips, "Photography, Modernity, and Art," in *Nineteenth Century Art*, 287.

33 Glenn Watkins, *Pyramids at the Louvre. Music, Culture, and Collage from Stravinsky to the Postmodernists* (Cambridge, MA: Belknap Press, 1994), 1.

34 Norbert Lynton, *The Story of Modern Art* (London: Phaidon Press, 1982), 18.

35 "Natural Reality and Abstract Reality" (1920), quoted in Mark A. Cheetham, *The Rhetoric of Purity: Essentialist Theory and the Advent of Abstract Painting* (Cambridge: Cambridge University Press, 1991), 41.

36 Christopher Butler, *Early Modernism: Literature, Music and Painting in Europe 1900–1916* (Oxford: Clarendon Press, 1994), 64.

37 Clarke, *The Romantic Rebellion*, 263.

Chapter 9

1 Michael Symes, *An Account of the Embassy to the Kingdom of Ava* (London: 1800), 383, quoted in Anthony Milner, "Southeast Asian Historical Writing," in *Oxford History of Historical Writing 1800–1945*, edited by Stuart Macintyre et al., 5 vols. (New York: Oxford University Press, 2011), 540.

2 Quoted in Donald R. Kelley, *Fortunes of History: Historical Inquiry from Herder to Huizinga* (New Haven, CT: Yale University Press, 2003), 1.

3 Christophe Meiners, *Geschichte der Entstehung und Entwickelung der hohen Schulen unsers Erdtheils*, 2 vols. (Göttingen: Johann Friedrich Römer, 1804), vol. 1, 1.

4 Heinrich Von Treitschke, *Treitschke's History of Germany in the Nineteenth Century*, translated by Eden and Cedar Paul, 7 vols. (New York: McBride, Nast & Co., 1915–1919), 2:235.

5 Leopold Von Ranke, *The Secret of World History*, translated by Roger Wines (New York: Fordham University Press, 1981), 21.

6 Theodor Mommsen, *The History of Rome*, translated by William P. Dickson, 4 vols. (London: Bentley, 1868), 4:288.

7 Johann Gottfried Eichhorn, *Allgemeine Geschichte der Kultur und Litteratur des neueren Europa*, 2 vols. (Göttingen: Rosenbusch, 1796–1799), 1:vi–vii.

8 Mommsen, *The History of Rome*, 288.

9 Quoted in Karl Obermann, "Heinrich Luden," in *Die deutsche Geschichtswissenschaft von Beginn des 19. Jahrhunderts bis zur Reichseinigung von oben* (Berlin, 1969), 95.

10 Quoted in George Peabody Gooch, *History and Historians in the Nineteenth Century* (London: Longmans, Green and Co., 1928), 155.

11 Germaine de Staël, *Corinne, or Italy*, translated by Avriel H. Goldberger (New Brunswick, NJ: Rutgers University Press, 1987), 17.

12 From Thierry, *Considérations sur l'histoire de France* (1840), quoted in Ceri Crossley, *French Historians and Romanticism: Thierry, Guizot, the Saint-Simonians, Quinet, Michelet* (New York: Routledge, 1993), 49.

13 François Guizot, *History of Civilization in Europe*, translated by William Hazlitt, 3 vols. (London: Bohn, 1856–1861), 3:4, 5.

14 Augustin Thierry, *Oeuvres d'Augustin Thierry*, 6 vols. (Brussels: Gregoir and Wouters, 1839), 5:56.

15 See François Dosse, *New History in France: The Triumph of the Annales*, translated by Peter V. Conroy Jr. (Urbana: University of Illinois Press, 1994), 19.

16 Jules Michelet, *Histoire de la revolution française*, 9 vols. (Paris: C. Marpon et E. Flammarion, 1879), 7:xxvii.

17 Sir Francis Palgrave, *The Collected Historical Works*, 4 vols. (Cambridge: Cambridge University Press, 1919–1922), 1:2; Henry Hallam, *The Constitutional History of England from the Accession of Henry VII to the Death of George II*, 3 vols. (London: John Murray, 1876), 1:2.

18 John Emerich Edward Dalberg-Acton, *Selected Writings of Lord Acton*, 3 vols. (Indianapolis, IN: Liberty Classics, 1985), 3:640.

19 From "Professor Stubbs's Inaugural Lecture," *Saturday Review*, March 2, 1867, quoted in Ian Hesketh, *The Science of History in Victorian Britain: Making the Past Speak* (London: Pickering & Chatto, 2011), 48.

20 J. R. Green, *A Short History of the English People*, 4 vols. (London: MacMillan and Co., 1902–1903), 1:vi.

21 Quoted in Mauricio Tenorio Trillo, "Historical Thought in the Other America," in *A Companion to Global Historical Thought*, edited by Prasenjit Duara, Viren Murthy, and Andrew Sartirum (London: Wiley Blackwell, 2014), 278.

22 Quoted in Julie Des Jardins, *Women and the Historical Enterprise in America: Gender, Race, and the Politics of Memory* (Chapel Hill: University of North Carolina Press, 2003), 107.

23 Quoted in Des Jardins, *Women and the Historical Enterprise*, 100.

BIBLIOGRAPHY

Primary Sources

Babbage, Charles. *The Ninth Bridgewater Treatise*. 2nd edition. London: John Murray, 1838.

Baudelaire, Charles. *Oeuvres complètes*, 2 volumes. Paris: Bibliothèque de la Pléiade, 1976.

Baudelaire, Charles. *Selected Writings on Art and Literature*. Translated by P. Charvet. London: Penguin, 1992.

Bauer, Otto. *The Question of Nationalities and Social Democracy*. Edited by Ephraim J. Nimni. Translated by Joseph O'Donnell. Minneapolis: University of Minnesota Press, 2000.

Bergson, Henri. *An Introduction to Metaphysics*. Translated by T. E. Hulme. Indianapolis, IN: Bobbs-Merrill, 1949.

Bergson, Henri. *Time and Free Will: An Essay on the Immediate Data of Consciousness*. Translated by F. L. Pogson. New York: Harper Torchbook, 1960.

Büchner, Ludwig. *Kraft und Stoff*. Frankfurt: Meidinger Sohn, 1855.

Büchner, Ludwig. *Im Dienst der Wahrheit*. Giessen: Emil Roth, 1890.

Burke, Edmund. *Reflections on the Revolution in France*. Edited by Frank M. Turner. New Haven, CT: Yale University Press, 2003.

Carlyle, Thomas. "Memoirs of the Life of Scott." From *London and Westminster Review*, in *Critical and Miscellaneous Essays*. Boston: Phillips, Sampson and Co., 1855.

de Chateaubriand, François-René. *Génie du christianisme*. 2 volumes. Paris: Garnier, 1966.

de Chateaubriand, François-René. *Mémoires d'outre-tombe*. 2 volumes. Paris: Gallimard, 1988.

de Chateaubriand, François-René. *René*. In *Oeuvres complètes de Chateaubriand*. Paris: P.-H. Crabbe, 1852.

Coleridge, Samuel Taylor. *The Collected Letters of Samuel Taylor Coleridge*. Edited by Earl Leslie Griggs. 6 volumes. Oxford: Clarendon Press, 1956–1971.

Coleridge, Samuel Taylor. *Lectures 1808–1819: On Literature*. Edited by R. A. Foakes. 2 volumes. London: Routledge; Princeton: Princeton University Press, 1987.

Coleridge, Samuel Taylor. *The Notebooks of Samuel Taylor Coleridge*. Edited by Kathleen Coburn et al. 5 double volumes. London: Routledge; Princeton: Princeton University Press, 1957–2002.

Comte, Auguste. *Cours de philosophie positive*. In *Auguste Comte and Positivism: The Essential Writings*, edited by Gertrud Lenzer, 71–306. 1830–1842; New York: Harper & Row, 1975.

Comte, Auguste. *Système de philosophie positive*. In *Auguste Comte and Positivism: The Essential Writings*, edited by Gertrud Lenzer, 309–476. New York: Harper & Row, 1975.

de Condorcet, Jean-Antoine-Nicolas de Caritat, marquis. *Political Writings*. Cambridge: Cambridge University Press, 2012.

de Condorcet, Jean-Antoine-Nicolas de Caritat, marquis. *Sketch for a Historical Picture of the Progress of the Human Mind*. In *Condorcet: Selected Writings*, edited by Keith Michael Baker, 209–82. Indianapolis, IN: Bobbs-Merrill, 1976.

Constant, Benjamin. *Adolphe*. Paris: A. Quantin, 1878.

Dalberg-Acton, John Emerich Edward. *Selected Writings of Lord Acton*. 3 volumes. Indianapolis, IN: Liberty Classics, 1985.

Darwin, Charles. *The Correspondence of Charles Darwin*. Edited by Frederick Burkhardt et al. Cambridge: Cambridge University Press, 2001.

Darwin, Charles. Correspondence Project. "Letter no. 13230." Available online: http://www.darwinproject.ac.uk/DCP-LETT-13230 (accessed May 14, 2017).

Durkheim, Émile. *The Division of Labor in Society*. Translated by W. D. Halls. New York: Free Press, 1984.

Durkheim, Émile. *Durkheim on Religion*. Edited by W. S. F. Pickering. Atlanta, GA: Scholars Press, 1994.

Durkheim, Émile. *The Elementary Forms of Religious Life*. Translated with an introduction by Karen E. Fields. New York: The Free Press, 1995.

Durkheim, Émile. *Moral Education*. New York: Free Press, 1961.

Durkheim, Émile. *The Rules of Sociological Method*. Translated by S. A. Solovay and J. H. Mueller. New York: Free Press, 1964.

Durkheim, Émile. *Socialism*. Translated by Charlotte Sattler. Edited and introduced by Alvin Gouldner. New York: Collier Books, 1962.

Durkheim, Émile. *Suicide: A Study in Sociology*. Translated by John A. Spaulding and George Simpson. New York: The Free Press, 1951.

Einstein, Albert and Leopold Infeld. *The Evolution of Physics*. New York: Simon and Shuster, 1966.

Eliot, T. S. *The Waste Land: a Facsimile and Transcript of the Original Drafts, Including the Annotations of Ezra Pound*. London: Faber & Faber, 1971.

Feuerbach, Ludwig. *The Essence of Christianity*. Translated by George Eliot. New York: Harper and Row, 1957.

Fichte, Johann Gottlieb. *Addresses to the German Nation*. Edited and with an Introduction by George Armstrong Kelly. Based on the translation by R. F. Jones and G. H. Turnbull. New York: Harper and Row, 1968.

Fichte, Johann Gottlieb. *Schriften zur angewandten Philosophie*. Edited by Peter Lothar Oesterreich. Frankfurt: Deutscher Klassiker Verlag, 1997.

Flaubert, Gustave. *The Sentimental Education*. Translated by Robert Baldick. London: Penguin Books, 2004.

"France Under Louis Napoleon." *The Westminster Review* no. 70 (October 1858): 194.

Gibbon, Edward. *The History of the Decline and Fall of the Roman Empire*. 3 volumes. London: Allen Lane, 1994.

de Goncourt, Edmond. *Journal des Goncourt: Mémoires de la vie littéraire*. Paris: Bibliothèque-Charpentier, 1891.

Gosse, Edmund. *Father and Son*. Oxford: Oxford University Press, 2004.

Guizot, François. *History of Civilization in Europe*. Translated by William Hazlitt. 3 volumes. London: Bohn, 1856–1861.

Guyau, Jean-Marie. *L'Art au point de vue sociologique*. Paris: Alcan, 1889.

Hallam, Henry. *The Constitutional History of England from the Accession of Henry VII to the Death of George II*. 3 volumes. London: John Murray, 1876.

Hegel, Georg Wilhelm Friedrich. Preface to *The Phenomenology of Spirit*. In *Hegel: Texts and Commentary*, edited by Walter Kaufmann, 6–111. New York: Doubleday, 1965.

Hegel, Georg Wilhelm Friedrich. *The Phenomenology of Spirit*. Translated by A. V. Miller. Oxford: Oxford University Press, 1977.

Heine, Heinrich. *Religion and Philosophy in Germany*. Translated by J. Snodgrass. Boston: Beacon, 1959.

von Hofmannsthal, Hugo. "The Letter of Lord Chandos." In *The Whole Difference: Selected Writings of Hugo von Hofmannsthal*, edited by J. D. McClatchy, 69–79. Princeton, NJ: Princeton University Press, 2008.

von Hofmannsthal, Hugo. *The Lord Chandos Letter*. Translated by Michael Hofmann. London: Syrens, 1995.

Hulme, T. E. *The Collected Writings of T. E. Hulme*. London: Clarendon Press, 1994.

von Humboldt, Wilhelm. *Journal parisien, 1797–1799*. Translated by Elisabeth Beyer. Edited by Raymond Trousson. Paris: Honoré Champion, 2013.

von Humboldt, Wilhelm. "On the Internal Structure of the University of Berlin and Its Relationship to Other Organizations." In *The Rise of the Research University*, edited by Louis Menand, Paul Reitter, and Chad Wellmon, 108–16. Chicago: University of Chicago Press, 2017.

Jacobi, F. H. *Werke*. Volume 6. Leipzig: Gerhard Fleischer, 1825.

Javary, Auguste. *De l'idée de progrès*. Paris: Librairie Philosophique de Ladrange, 1851.

Kant, Immanuel. *Kant's Political Writings*. Translated by H. B. Nisbet. Edited by Hans Reiss. Cambridge: Cambridge University Press, 1970.

Kant, Immanuel. *Metaphysical Foundations of Natural Science*. Translated by Ernest Bax. London: George Bell and Sons, 1883.

Kierkegaard, Søren. *Fear and Trembling and The Sickness Unto Death*. Princeton, NJ: Princeton University Press, 1954.

Laplace, Pierre Simon. *A Philosophical Essay on Probabilities*. Translated by F. W. Truscott and F. L. Emory from the 6th French edition. London: John Wiley and Sons, 1902.

Leblond, Marius-Ary. "Les peintres de la femme nouvelle." *La Revue* 39 (November 1, 1901): 275–90.

Le Bon, Gustave. *The Crowd: A Study of the Popular Mind*. New York: Macmillan, 1897.

Le Bon, Gustave. *The Crowd: A Study of the Popular Mind*. London: Ernest Benn, 1952.

Leopardi, Giacomo. *Leopardi: Selected Poems*. Translated by Eamon Grennan. Princeton, NJ: Princeton University Press, 1997.

"Les Femmes poètes aux XIXe siècle." *Revue de Paris*, May 1835, 279.

Mallarmé, Stéphane. *Variations sur un sujet*, "Crise de vers." In *Oeuvres complètes*, 360–68. Paris: Gallimard, 1945.

Marx, Karl, and Friedrich Engels. *The Communist Manifesto*. With an Introduction and Notes by Gareth Stedman Jones. London: Penguin Books, 2002.

Marx, Karl, and Friedrich Engels. *The German Ideology*. Moscow, 1968.

Marx, Karl, and Friedrich Engels. *On Religion*. New York: Schocken, 1964.

Mason, Thomas Monck. *Creation by the Immediate Agency of God, as Opposed to Creation by Natural Law*. London: John W. Parker, 1845.

Massis, Henri, and Alfred de Tarde. *L'Esprit de la nouvelle Sorbonne*. Paris: Mercure de France, 1911.

Mauclair, Camille. "La Femme devant les peintres modernes." *La Nouvelle Revue* 1 (1899): 190–213.

Mazzini, Giuseppe. "The Duties of Man." In *The Nationalism Reader*, edited by Omar Dahbour and Micheline R. Ishay, 87–97. Atlantic Highlands, NJ: Humanities Press, 1995.

Mazzini, Joseph. *Life and Writings of Joseph Mazzini*. London: Smith, Elder, 1891.

Mill, John Stuart. *Autobiography*. Edited by Jack Stillinger. Boston: Houghton Mifflin, 1969.

Mill, John Stuart. *Considerations on Representative Government*, in *Essays on Politics and Government*, edited by J. M. Robson, 371–616. Toronto: University of Toronto Press, 1977. Volume 19 of *The Collected Works of John Stuart Mill*, 33 vols. Toronto: University of Toronto Press, 1963–.

Mill, John Stuart. *On Liberty*. Edited by Gertrude Himmelfarb. London: Penguin, 1974.

Mill, John Stuart. *On Liberty*. Edited by Currin V. Shields. Indianapolis, IN: Bobbs-Merill, 1975.

Mill, John Stuart. *On Liberty*. Indianapolis, IN: Hackett Publishing, 1978.

Mill, John Stuart, and Harriet Taylor Mill. *Essays on Sex Equality*. Edited by Alice Rossi. Chicago: University of Chicago Press, 1970.

Moleschott, Jakob. *Der Kreislauf des Lebens*. Mainz: Verlag Viktor von Zabern, 1855.

de Musset, Alfred. *La Confession d'un enfant du siècle*. Paris: Charpentier, 1867.

de Musset, Alfred. "Première Lettre." In "Lettres de Dupuis et Cotonet au Directeur de la *Revue des deux mondes*," in *Oeuvres completes*, vol. 3, 819–36. Paris: Gallimard, 1957.

Newman, John Henry Cardinal. *Apologia Pro Vita Sua and Six Sermons*. Edited by Frank M. Turner. New Haven, CT: Yale University Press, 2008.

Nietzsche, Friedrich. *The Birth of Tragedy and the Genealogy of Morals*. Translated by Francis Golffing. Garden City, NY: Doubleday Anchor, 1956.

Nietzsche, Friedrich. *Nietzsche and the Death of God—Selected Writings*. Translated, edited, and with an Introduction by Peter Fritzsche. Boston: Bedford St. Martin's, 2007.

Nisard, Désiré. *Etudes de critique et de moeurs sur les poètes latins de la décadence*. 2 volumes. Paris: Hachette, 1849.

Ortega Y Gasset, José. *Revolt of the Masses*. New York: W. W. Norton & Company, 1994.

Owen, Robert. *The Life of Robert Owen*. London: Wilson, 1857–1858.

Owen, Robert. *A New View of Society*. London: Longman, 1817.

Pater, Walter. "The School of Giorgione." In *The Renaissance*, 107–27. New York: Boni, 1919.

Renan, Ernest. "Les historiens critiques de Jésus." In *Etudes d'histoire religieuse*, 116–67. Paris: Gallimard, 1992.

Renan, Ernest. *The Life of Jesus*. New York: Modern Library, 1927.

Rimbaud, Arthur. *Letter to Georges Izambard*, May 13, 1871. In *Oeuvres complètes*. Paris: Gallimard, 2009.

Rimbaud, Arthur. "A Season in Hell." In *Complete Works*, translated by Paul Schmidt. New York: Harper Collins, 1975.

Rousseau, Jean-Jacques. *Confessions*. Translated by J. M. Cohen. London: Penguin, 1981.

de Saint-Simon, Claude Henri. *De la réorganisation de la société européenne*. Paris: Adrien Égron, 1814.

Sand, George. "Obermann." In *Questions d'art et de littérature*. Paris: C. Lévy, 1878.

von Schelling, Friedrich Wilhelm Joseph. *F.W.J. Schelling, On University Studies*. Edited by Norbert Guterman. Translated by Ella S. Morgan. Athens: Ohio University Press, 1966.

Schiller, Friedrich. *On the Aesthetic Education of Man*. Mineola, NY: Dover Publications, 1954.

Schlegel, A. W. *Vorlesungen über schöne Literatur und Kunst*. In *Music and Aesthetics in the Eighteenth and Early-Nineteenth Centuries*, edited by Peter Le Huray and James Day. Cambridge: Cambridge University Press, 1981.

Schlegel, Friedrich. *"Lucinde" and the Fragments*. Translated by Peter Firchow. Minneapolis: University of Minnesota Press, 1971.

Schleiermacher, Friedrich. *On Religion: Speeches to Its Cultured Despisers*. Edited by Richard
    Crouter. New York: Cambridge University Press, 1988.
Smiles, Samuel. *Self-Help*. London: John Murray, 1859.
Smith, Adam. *An Inquiry into the Nature and Causes of the Wealth of Nations*. 2 volumes.
    Indianapolis, IN: Liberty Fund, 1981.
Spencer, Herbert. *Social Statics*. London: John Chapman, 1851.
de Staël, Germaine. *Corinne, or Italy*. Translated by Avriel H. Goldberger. New Brunswick, NJ:
    Rutgers University Press, 1987.
de Staël, Germaine. *Corinne ou l'Italie*. 2 volumes. Paris: Duprat-Duverger, 1822.
de Staël, Germaine. *De l'Allemagne*. Paris: Didot Frères, 1845.
Stendhal. *Life of Henry Brulard*. Translated by John Sturrock. New York: New York Review
    Books, 2002.
Strauss, David Friedrich. *The Life of Jesus Critically Examined*. Translated by George Eliot.
    New York: Macmillan, 1892.
Symons, Arthur. *The Symbolist Movement in Literature*. New York: E. P. Dutton & Co.,
    1919.
Tocqueville, Alexis de. *Journeys to England and Ireland*. Translated by George Lawrence and K.
    P. Mayer, edited by J. P. Mayer. London: Faber and Faber, 1958.
von Treitschke, Heinrich. *History of German in the Nineteenth Century*. Translated by
    Eden and Cedar Paul. Chicago: University of Chicago Press, 1975.
von Treitschke, Heinrich. *Selections from Lectures on Politics*. Translated by Adam L. Gowan.
    London: Gowans and Gray, 1914.
Wagner, Richard. *Religion and Art*. Translated by William Ashton Ellis. Lincoln: University of
    Nebraska Press, 1994.
Wallace, Alfred Russell. "Creation by Law." *Quarterly Journal of Science* 4 (1867): 471–88.
Weber, Max. "Bureaucracy." In *From Max Weber: Essays in Sociology*, translated and edited
    by H. H. Gerth and C. Wright Mills, 196–244. London: Routledge and Kegan Paul,
    1948.
Weber, Max. *From Max Weber: Essays in Sociology*. Translated and edited by H. H. Gerth and
    C. Wright Mills. New York: Oxford University Press, 1946.
Weber, Max. *The Protestant Ethic and the Spirit of Capitalism, with Other Writings on the Rise
    of the West*, translated and introduced by Stephen Kalberg. New York: Oxford University
    Press, 1995.
Weber, Max. *The Protestant Ethic and the Spirit of Capitalism*. Translated by Talcott Parsons.
    Mineola, NY: Dover, 2003.
Weber, Max. *The Protestant Ethic and the Spirit of Capitalism*. Translated by Stephen Kalberg.
    New York: Routledge, 2012.
Weber, Max. *The Russian Revolutions*. Translated and edited by Gordon C. Wells and Peter
    Baehr. Ithaca, NY: Cornell University Press, 1995.
Wilberforce, William. *Practical View of the Prevailing Religious System of Professed Christians
    in the Higher and Middle Classes of this Country Contrasted with Real Christianity*. Dublin:
    Dugdale, 1797.
Wordsworth, William. *The Prelude: A Parallel Text*. London: Penguin Books, 1971.
Zola, Émile. *L'Assommoir*. Translated by Leonard Tancock. Harmondsworth: Penguin,
    1970.
Zola, Émile. "The Experimental Novel." In *The Experimental Novel and Other Essays*,
    translated by Belle M. Sherman, 1–54. New York: Cassell, 1893.
Zola, Émile. *Mes Haines*. Paris: Achille Faure, 1866.

Secondary Sources

Abrams, Meyer. *Natural Supernaturalism: Tradition and Revolution in Romantic Literature.* New York: Norton, 1971.

Abrams, Philip. "The Sense of the Past and the Origins of Sociology." *Past and Present 55* (1972): 18–32.

Ahnert, Thomas, and Susan Manning, eds. *Character, Self, and Sociability in the Scottish Enlightenment.* New York: Palgrave Macmillan, 2011.

Ardao, Arturo. "Assimilation and Transformation of Positivism in Latin America." *Journal of the History of Ideas* 24, no. 4 (1963): 515–22.

Audoin-Rouzeau, Stéphane, and Annette Becker. *14–18: Understanding the Great War.* New York: Hill and Wang, 2002.

Avineri, Shlomo. *The Social and Political Thought of Karl Marx.* Cambridge: Cambridge University Press, 1968.

Badash, Lawrence. "The Completeness of Nineteenth Century Science." *Isis* 63 (1972): 48–58.

Baek, Seung Jin. *The Political Economy of Neo-modernisation: Rethinking the Dynamics of Technology, Development and Inequality.* London: Palgrave Macmillan, 2018.

Banton, Michael. *Racial Theories.* 2nd edition. Cambridge: Cambridge University Press, 1998.

Baron, Beth. *The Women's Awakening in Egypt: Culture, Society, and the Press.* New Haven, CT: Yale University Press, 1994.

Barth, Karl. *Protestant Theology in the Nineteenth Century: Its Background and History.* Valley Forge, PA: Judson Press, 1973.

Baumgart, Winfried. *Imperialism: The Idea and the Reality of English and French Colonial Expansion, 1880–1914.* Oxford: Oxford University Press, 1982.

Bayly, C. A. *Recovering Liberties: Indian Thought in the Age of Liberalism and Empire.* Cambridge: Cambridge University Press, 2012.

Bebbington, David W. *Evangelicalism in Modern Britain—A History from the 1730s to the 1980s.* London: Unwin Hyman, 1989.

Becker, George Joseph, ed. *Documents of Modern Literary Realism.* Princeton, NJ: Princeton University Press, 1963.

Beecher, Jonathan, and Richard Bienvenu, eds. *The Utopian Vision of Charles Fourier: Selected Texts on Work, Love, and Passionate Attraction.* Boston: Beacon Press, 1971.

Beiser, Frederick. *The Fate of Reason: German Philosophy from Kant to Fichte.* Cambridge, MA: Harvard University Press, 1987.

Beniston, Judith, and Robert Vilain eds. "Culture and Politics in Red Vienna." Special Issue of *Austrian Studies* 14 (2006).

Berdahl, Robert M. *The Politics of the Prussian Nobility: The Development of a Conservative Ideology, 1770–1848.* Princeton, NJ: Princeton University Press, 1988.

Bertholet, Denis. *Le bourgeois dans tous ses états: le roman familial de la Belle Epoque.* Paris: Plon, 1987.

Bevir, Mark. "The West Turns Eastward: Madame Blavatsky and the Transformation of the Occult Tradition." *Journal of the American Academy of Religion* 62 (1994): 747–67.

Billard, Jacques. *De l'école à la république: Guizot et Victor Cousin.* Paris: Presses Universitaires de France, 1998.

Blanning, Tim. *The Romantic Revolution: A History.* New York: Modern Library, 2010.

Blaschke, Olaf. "Das 19. Jahrhundert: Ein Zweites Konfessionelles Zeitalter?" *Geschichte und Gesellschaft* 26 (2000): 38–70.

Bonds, Mark Evan. *Music as Thought: Listening to the Symphony in the Age of Beethoven.* Princeton, NJ: Princeton University Press, 2006.

Bowman, Frank Paul. *Le Christ des barricades, 1789–1848.* Paris: Cerf, 1987.

Bradbury, Malcolm, and James McFarlane, eds. *Modernism: 1890–1930.* New York: Penguin, 1976.

Bressani, Martin. *Architecture and the Historical Imagination: Eugène-Emmanuel Viollet-le-Duc, 1814–1879.* New York: Routledge, 2014.

Brett, R. L., and A. R. Jones, eds. *Wordsworth and Coleridge: Lyrical Ballads.* London: Routledge Classics, 2005.

Brinkmann, Reinhold. "In the Time of the Eroica." In *Beethoven and His World*, edited by Scott Burnham and Michael P. Steinberg, 1–26. Princeton, NJ: Princeton University Press, 2000.

Brophy, James M. *Popular Culture and the Public Sphere in the Rhineland, 1800–1850.* Cambridge: Cambridge University Press, 2007.

Brown, Julie. *Bartók and the Grotesque.* Aldershot, UK: Ashgate, 2007.

Browne, Janet. *Charles Darwin. Voyaging.* Princeton, NJ: Princeton University Press, 1995.

Brunner, Otto et al., eds. *Geschichtliche Grundbegriffe.* 8 volumes. Stuttgart: Klett, 1972–1997.

Buck-Morss, Susan. "Hegel and Haiti." *Critical Inquiry* 26, no. 4 (2000): 821–65.

Burleigh, Michael. *Earthly Powers: The Clash of Religion and Politics in Europe from the French Revolution to the Great War.* New York: HarperCollins, 2005.

Burnham, James. *The Machiavellians: Defenders of Freedom.* New edition. Chicago: Henry Regnery Co., 1962.

Burrow, J. W. *The Crisis of Reason: European Thought, 1848–1914.* New Haven, CT: Yale University Press, 2000.

Butler, Christopher. *Early Modernism: Literature, Music and Painting in Europe 1900–1916.* Oxford: Clarendon Press, 1994.

Cascardi, Anthony J. *The Subject of Modernity.* Cambridge: Cambridge University Press, 1992.

Chadwick, Owen. *The Secularization of the European Mind.* New York: Cambridge University Press, 1975.

Charlton, D. G. *Secular Religions in France.* London: Oxford University Press, 1963.

Cheetham, Mark A. *The Rhetoric of Purity: Essentialist Theory and the Advent of Abstract Painting.* Cambridge: Cambridge University Press, 1991.

Chernilo, Daniel. "Methodological Nationalism and Its Critique." In *The Sage Handbook of Nations and Nationalism*, edited by Gerard Delanty and Krishan Kumar, 129–40. London: Sage Publications, 2006.

Claeys, Gregory. "Political Economy and Popular Education: Thomas Hodgskin and the London Mechanics' Institute." In *Radicalism and Revolution in Britain 1775–1848*, edited by Michael T. Davis, 157–75. New York: St. Martin's Press, 2000.

Clark, Terry Nichols. *Prophets and Patrons: The French University and the Emergence of the Social Sciences.* Cambridge, MA: Harvard University Press, 1973.

Clark, William. "The Death of Metaphysics in Enlightened Prussia." In *The Sciences in Enlightened Europe*, edited by William Clark, Jan Golinski, and Simon Schaffer, 423–73. Chicago: University of Chicago Press, 1999.

Clarke, Kenneth. *The Romantic Rebellion: Romantic versus Classic Art.* London: Fontana, 1976.

Collingwood, R. G. *The Idea of Nature.* Oxford: Oxford University Press, 1967.

Collini, Stefan. *Liberalism and Sociology: L. T. Hobhouse and Political Argument in England 1880–1914.* Cambridge: Cambridge University Press, 1979.

Collini, Stefan, Donald Winch, and John Burrow. *That Noble Science of Politics: A Study in Nineteenth-Century Intellectual History*. Cambridge: Cambridge University Press, 1983.

Cooter, Roger. *The Cultural Meaning of Popular Science: Phrenology and the Organization of Consent in Nineteenth-Century Britain*. Cambridge: Cambridge University Press, 1984.

Craig, John E. "The Expansion of Education." *Review of Research in Education* 9 (1981): 151–213.

Crossley, Ceri. *French Historians and Romanticism: Thierry, Guizot, the Saint-Simonians, Quinet, Michelet*. New York: Routledge, 1993.

Crow, Thomas. "Classicism in Crisis: Gros to Delacroix." In *Nineteenth Century Art: A Critical History*, edited by Stephen F. Eisenman, 59–85. 4th edition. London: Thames and Hudson, 2011.

Curtin, Philip D. *The World and the West: The European Challenge and the Overseas Response in the Age of Empire*. Cambridge: Cambridge University Press, 2000.

Danius, Sara. *The Senses of Modernism: Technology, Perception, and Aesthetics*. Ithaca, NY: Cornell University Press, 2002.

Daston, Lorraine. "The Ethos of Enlightenment." In *The Sciences in Enlightened Europe*, edited by William Clark, Jan Golinski, and Simon Schaffer, 495–504. Chicago: University of Chicago Press, 1999.

Daum, Andreas. *Wissenschaftspopularisierung im 19. Jahrhundert. Bürgerliche Kultur, naturwissenschaftliche Bildung und die deutsche Öffentlichkeit, 1848–1914*. 2nd edition. Munich: R. Oldenbourg Verlag, 2002.

Daum, Werner. *Zeit der Drucker und Buchhändler: Die Produktion und Rezeption von Publizistik in der Verfassungsrevolution Neapel-Siziliens 1820/21*. Frankfurt: Peter Lang, 2005.

Davray, Henry-D. "Art." *Mercure de France*, April 16, 1918.

Delanty, Gerard, and Krishan Kumar, eds. *The Sage Handbook of Nations and Nationalism*. London: Sage Publications, 2006.

Deloria, Phillip J. "Historiography." In *A Companion to American Indian History*, edited by Phillip J. Deloria and Neal Salisbury, 6–24. Oxford: Wiley Blackwell, 2002.

Des Jardins, Julie. *Women and the Historical Enterprise in America: Gender, Race, and the Politics of Memory 1880–1945*. Chapel Hill: University of North Carolina Press, 2003.

Driskel, Michael Paul. *Representing Belief: Religion, Art, and Society in Nineteenth-Century France*. University Park: Pennsylvania State University Press, 1992.

Duara, Prasenjitet al., eds. *A Companion to Global Historical Thought*. Oxford: Wiley Blackwell, 2014.

Dubois, Laurent. *Avengers of the New World: The Story of the Haitian Revolution*. Cambridge, MA: Harvard University Press, 2004.

Dyos, H. J., and M. Wolff, eds. *The Victorian City: Images and Realities*. 2 volumes. London: Routledge and Kegan Paul, 1973.

Eley, Geoff. *Reshaping the German Right: Radical Nationalism and Political Change after Bismarck*. 2nd edition. Ann Arbor: University of Michigan Press, 1991.

Epstein, Klaus. *The Genesis of German Conservatism*. Princeton, NJ: Princeton University Press, 1966.

Etemad, Bouda. *Possessing the World: Taking the Measurements of Colonisation from the Eighteenth to the Twentieth Century*. New York: Berghahn Books, 2007.

Febvre, Lucien. "*Civilisation*: Evolution of a Word and a Group of Ideas." In *A New Kind of History and Other Essays*, edited by Peter Burke, 219–57. New York: Harper and Row, 1973.

Ford, Caroline. *Creating the Nation in Provincial France: Religion and Political Identity in Brittany*. Princeton, NJ: Princeton University Press, 1993.

Foucault, Michel. *The Order of Things*. New York: Pantheon Books, 1970.

Freeden, Michael. *The New Liberalism: An Ideology of Social Reform*. Oxford: Oxford University Press, 1986.

Freedgood, Elaine. "Banishing Panic: Harriet Martineau and the Popularisation of Political Economy." *Victorian Studies* 39, no. 1 (1995): 33–53.

Gallagher, John, and Ronald Robinson. "The Imperialism of Free Trade." *Economic History Review*, n.s., 6, no. 1 (1953): 1–15.

Gaukroger, Stephen. *The Collapse of Mechanism and the Rise of Sensibility: Science and the Shaping of Modernity, 1680–1760*. Oxford: Oxford University Press, 2010.

Gaukroger, Stephen. *The Natural and the Human: Science and the Shaping of Modernity, 1739–1841*. Oxford: Oxford University Press, 2016.

Gay, Peter. *The Enlightenment: An Interpretation*. New York: Alfred A. Knopf, 1969.

Geggus, David P., ed. *The Impact of the Haitian Revolution in the Atlantic World*. Columbia: University of South Carolina Press, 2001.

Ghisalberti, Carlo. "Lo Statuto albertino e il costituzionalismo europeo della prima metà dell'Ottocento." In *Stato Nazione e Costituzione nell'Italia contemporanea*, edited by Carlo Ghisalberti, 25–50. Naples: Edizioni Scientifiche Italiane, 1999.

Goldstein, Jan. "Moral Contagion: A Professional Ideology of Medicine and Psychiatry in Eighteenth- and Nineteenth-Century France." In *Professions and the French State*, edited by Gerald L. Geison, 181–222. Philadelphia: University of Pennsylvania Press, 1984.

Goldstein, Jan. *The Post-Revolutionary Self: Politics and Psyche in France, 1750–1850*. Cambridge, MA: Harvard University Press, 2005.

Gregory, Frederick. "The Conflict Thesis in Nineteenth Century Germany." In *The Warfare between Science and Religion: The Idea That Wouldn't Die*, edited by Jeff Hardin, Ronald L. Numbers, and Ronald A. Binzley, 84–102. Baltimore: Johns Hopkins University Press, 2018.

Gregory, Frederick. "'Nature is an Organized Whole': J.F. Fries's Reformulation of Kant's Philosophy of Organism." In *Romanticism in Science*, edited by S. Poggi and M.Bossi, 91–101. Dordrecht: Kluwer Academic Publishers, 1994.

Gregory, Frederick. "Proto-Monism in German Philosophy, Theology, and Science, 1800–1845." In *Monism: Science, Philosophy, Religion, and the History of a Worldview*, edited by Todd H. Weir, 45–69. New York: Palgrave Macmillan, 2012.

Gregory, Frederick. "Romantic Kantianism and the End of the Newtonian Dream in Chemistry." *Archives internationales d'histoire des sciences* 34 (1984): 108–23.

Gregory, Frederick. *Scientific Materialism in Nineteenth Century Germany*. Dordrecht: D. Reidel Publishing Co., 1977.

Gross, Michael B. *The War Against Catholicism: Liberalism and the Anti-Catholic Imagination in Nineteenth-Century Germany*. Ann Arbor: University of Michigan Press, 2004.

Grimmer-Solem, Erik. *The Rise of Historical Economics and Social Reform in Germany 1864–1894*. Oxford: Clarendon Press, 2003.

Habermas, Jürgen. *The Philosophical Discourse of Modernity: Twelve Lectures*. Translated by Friedrich Lawrence. Oxford: Blackwell, 1987.

Habermas, Jürgen. *The Structural Transformation of the Public Sphere*. Translated by Thomas Burger. Cambridge, MA: MIT Press, 1989.

Hadley, Elaine. *Living Liberalism: Practical Citizenship in Mid-Victorian Britain*. Chicago: University of Chicago Press, 2010.

Hanssen, Jens, and Max Weiss, eds. *Arabic Thought beyond the Liberal Age: Towards an Intellectual History of the Nahda*. Cambridge: Cambridge University Press, 2016.

Harris, Jonathan. "Bernardino Rivadavia and Benthamite 'Discipleship.'" *Latin American Research Review* 33, no. 1 (1998): 129–49.

Harrison, J. F. C. *Quest for the New Moral World: Robert Owen and the Owenites in Britain and America*. New York: Scribner, 1969.

Hauser, Arnold. *The Social History of Art*, Vol. 4: *Naturalism, Impressionism, The Film Age*. London: Routledge and Kegan Paul, 1962.

Hayes, Carlton J. H. *Nationalism: A Religion*. New York: Macmillan, 1960.

Henrich, Dieter. *Between Kant and Hegel: Lectures on German Idealism*. Cambridge, MA: Harvard University Press, 2003.

Heschel, Susannah. *Abraham Geiger and the Jewish Jesus*. Chicago: University of Chicago Press, 1998.

Hesketh, Ian. *The Science of History in Victorian Britain: Making the Past Speak*. London: Pickering & Chatto, 2011.

Hesse, Carla. *Publishing and Cultural Politics in Revolutionary France, 1789–1810*. Berkeley: University of California Press, 1991.

Hobsbawm, Eric. *The Age of Capital 1848–1875*. London: Weidenfeld and Nicolson, 1975.

Hobsbawm, Eric. *The Age of Empires, 1875–1914*. London: Weidenfeld and Nicolson, 1987.

Hobsbawm, Eric. *The Age of Revolution 1789–1848*. London: Weidenfeld and Nicolson, 1962.

Hoffman, Philip T. *Why Did Europe Conquer the World?* Princeton, NJ: Princeton University Press, 2015.

Honour, Hugh. *Romanticism*. New York: Harper and Row, 1979.

Houghton, Walter E. *The Victorian Frame of Mind, 1830–1870*. New Haven, CT: Yale University Press, 1957.

Hourani, Albert. *Arabic Thought in the Liberal Age, 1798–1939*. 2nd edition. Cambridge: Cambridge University Press, 1962.

Howard, Thomas Albert. *Protestant Theology and the Making of the German Research University*. Oxford: Oxford University Press, 2006.

Howland, Douglas. "Translating Liberty in Nineteenth-Century Japan." *Journal of the History of Ideas* 62, no. 1 (2001): 161–81.

Hughes, H. Stuart. *Consciousness and Society: The Reorientation of European Social Thought 1890–1930*. Revised edition. New York: Vintage, 1977.

Hunt, Bruce J. *The Maxwellians*. Ithaca, NY: Cornell University Press, 1991.

Inkster, Ian. "The Social Context of an Educational Movement: A Revisionist Approach to English Mechanics' Institutes, 1820–1850." *Oxford Review of Education* 2, no. 3 (1976): 277–307.

Isabella, Maurizio. "Aristocratic Liberalism and Risorgimento: Cesare Balbo and Piedmontese Political Thought after 1848." *History of European Ideas* 39, no. 6 (2013): 835–57.

Izenberg, Gerald. *Identity: The Necessity of a Modern Idea*. Philadelphia: University of Pennsylvania Press, 2016.

Jameson, Frederic. "The Cultural Logic of Late Capitalism." In *Postmodernism, or The Cultural Logic of Late Capitalism*, 1–54. Durham, NC: Duke University Press, 2001.

Johnson, James H. *Listening in Paris: A Cultural History*. Berkeley: University of California Press, 1995.

Jones, Gareth Stedman, and Gregory Claeys, eds. *The Cambridge History of Nineteenth-Century Political Thought*. Cambridge: Cambridge University Press, 2011.

Jonsson, Frederik Albritton. "Political Economy." In *Historicism and the Human Sciences in Victorian Britain*, edited by Mark Bevir, 186–210. Cambridge: Cambridge University Press, 2017.

Judson, Pieter M. *Exclusive Revolutionaries: Liberal Politics, Social Experience, and National Identity in the Austrian Empire, 1848–1914*. Ann Arbor: University of Michigan Press, 1996.

Kahan, Alan S. *Aristocratic Liberalism: The Social and Political Thought of Jacob Burckhardt, John Stuart Mill, and Alexis de Tocqueville*. New York: Oxford University Press, 1992.

Katz, Jakob. *From Prejudice to Destruction: Anti-Semitism, 1700–1933*. Cambridge, MA: Harvard University Press, 1980.

Kaufmann, Walter. *Nietzsche: Philosopher, Psychologist, Antichrist*. Princeton, NJ: Princeton University Press, 1974.

Kelley, Donald R. *Fortunes of History: Historical Inquiry from Herder to Huizinga*. New Haven, CT: Yale University Press, 2003.

Kelly, George Amstrong. *The Humane Comedy: Constant, Tocqueville and French Liberalism*. Cambridge: Cambridge University Press, 1992.

Ker, Ian. *John Henry Newman: A Biography*. New York: Oxford University Press, 1988.

Kern, Stephen. *The Culture of Time and Space 1880–1918*. Cambridge, MA: Harvard University Press, 1983.

Kinna, Ruth. *Kropotkin: Reviewing the Classical Anarchist Tradition*. Edinburgh: Edinburgh University Press, 2016.

Kippenberg, Hans G. *Discovering Religious History in the Modern Age*. Translated by Barbara Harshaw. Princeton, NJ: Princeton University Press, 2002.

Kleeberg, Bernhard. "God-Nature Progressing: Natural Theology in German Monism." *Science in Context* 20 (2007): 537–69.

Koebner, Richard, and Helmut Dan Schmidt. *Imperialism: The Story and Significance of a Political Word, 1840–1960*. Cambridge: Cambridge University Press, 1964.

Kohak, Erazim. *The Embers and the Stars: A Philosophical Inquiry into the Moral Sense of Nature*. Chicago: University of Chicago Press, 1984.

Kohn, Hans. *The Habsburg Empire 1804–1918: Texts and Documents*. Princeton, NJ: Van Nostrand, 1961.

Koselleck, Reinhart. *Futures Past: On the Semantics of Historical Time*. Translated by Keith Tribe. Cambridge, MA: MIT Press, 1985.

Kragh, Helge S. *Entropic Creation: Religious Context of Thermodynamics and Creation*. Burlington, VT: Ashgate Publishing, 2008.

Kselman, John, and Ronald Withrup. "Modern New Testament Criticism." In *The New Jerome Biblical Commentary*, edited by Raymond Brown, Joseph Fitzmeyer, and Roland Murphy, 1130–145. Englewood Cliffs, NJ: Prentice-Hall, 1990.

Kumar, Krishan. "Nationalism and Revolution: Friends or Foes?" *Nations and Nationalism* 21, no. 4 (2015): 589–608.

Kumar, Krishan. *Prophecy and Progress: The Sociology of Industrial and Post-Industrial Society*. London: Allen Lane/Penguin Books, 1978.

Kumar, Krishan. *Visions of Empire: How Five Imperial Regimes Shaped the World*. Princeton, NJ: Princeton University Press, 2017.

Landes, Joan. *Women and the Public Sphere in the Age of Enlightenment*. Ithaca, NY: Cornell University Press, 1994.

Langewiesche, Dieter, ed. *Liberalismus im 19. Jahrhundert. Deutschland im europäischen Vergleich*. Göttingen: Vandenhoeck & Ruprecht, 1988.

LaVopa, Anthony J. *Fichte: The Self and the Calling of Philosophy, 1762–1799*. Cambridge: Cambridge University Press, 2001.

Leadbetter, Gregory. *Coleridge and the Daemonic Imagination*. London: Palgrave, 2011.

Lebrun, Richard Allen. *Throne and Altar: The Political and Religious Thought of Joseph de Maistre*. Ottawa: University of Ottawa Press, 1965.

Lehnert, Detlef, ed. *Sozialliberalismus in Europa. Herkunft und Entwicklung im 19. und frühen 20. Jahrhundert*. Cologne: Böhlau, 2012.

Lenoir, Timothy. *The Strategy of Life: Teleology and Mechanics in Nineteenth-Century German Biology*. Dodrecht: D. Reidel, 1982.

Lepenies, Wolf. *Between Literature and Science: The Rise of Sociology*. New York: Cambridge University Press, 1988.

Levinger, Matthew. *Enlightened Nationalism: The Transformation of Prussian Political Culture, 1806–1848*. New York: Oxford University Press, 2000.

Lidtke, Vernon. *The Outlawed Party: Social Democracy in Germany, 1878–90*. Princeton, NJ: Princeton University Press, 1966.

Lilla, Mark. *The Stillborn God: Religion, Politics, and the Modern West*. New York: Knopf, 2007.

Lovejoy, A. O. "The Meaning of Romanticism for the Historian of Ideas." *Journal of the History of Ideas* 2, no. 3 (1941): 257–78.

Lovejoy, A. O. *The Great Chain of Being: A Study of the History of an Idea*. New York: Harper and Row, 1960.

Lowry, Howard Foster, and Willard Thorp, eds. *An Oxford Anthology of English Poetry*. New York: Oxford University Press, 1956.

Lukacher, Brian. "Nature and History in English Romantic Landscape Painting." In *Nineteenth Century Art*, edited by Stephen F. Eisenman, 123–45. 4th edition. London: Thames and Hudson, 2011.

Lukes, Steven. *Emile Durkheim: His Life and Work, A Historical and Critical Study*. New York: Harper & Row, 1972.

Lynch, John. *Simón Bolívar: A Life*. New Haven, CT: Yale University Press, 2006.

Lynton, Norbert. *The Story of Modern Art*. London: Phaidon Press, 1982.

Macintyre, Stuart, Juan Maiguashca, and Attila Pók, eds. *The Oxford History of Historical Writing, 1800–1945*. 5 volumes. New York: Oxford University Press, 2011.

Maclachlan, Fiona. "Max Weber within the *Methodenstreit*." *Cambridge Journal of Economics* 41, no. 4 (2017): 1161–175.

Maddison, Angus. *Phases of Capitalist Development*. Oxford: Oxford University Press, 1982.

Mandelbaum, Maurice. *History, Man, & Reason: A Study In Nineteenth-century Thought*. Baltimore, MD: Project Muse, 2019.

Manjapra, Kris. *Age of Entanglement: German and Indian Intellectuals Across Empire*. Cambridge, MA: Harvard University Press, 2014.

Mannheim, Karl. "Conservative Thought." In *Essays on Sociology and Social Psychology*, 74–164. London: Routledge and Kegan Paul, 1953.

Manuel, Frank E. *The New World of Henri Saint-Simon*. Notre Dame, IN: University of Notre Dame Press, 1963.

Manuel, Frank E. *The Prophets of Paris: Turgot, Condorcet, Saint-Simon, Fourier, and Comte*. New York: Harper, 1965.

Marchand, Suzanne L. *German Orientalism in an Age of Empire: Religion, Race, and Scholarship*. Cambridge: Cambridge University Press, 2009.

Martin, Terry. *The Affirmative Action Empire: Nations and Nationalism in the Soviet Union, 1923–1939*. Ithaca, NY: Cornell University Press, 2001.

Martin-Fugier, Anne. *La vie élégante, ou la formation du Tout-Paris 1815–1848*. Paris: Fayard, 1990.

Mason, Michael. *The Making of Victorian Sexual Attitudes*. Oxford: Oxford University Press, 1994.

Masur, Gerhard. *Prophets of Yesterday: Studies in European Culture, 1890–1914*. New York: Harper Colophon, 1966.

Mayhew, Robert J. *Malthus: The Life and Legacies of an Unlikely Prophet*. Cambridge, MA: Harvard University Press, 2014.

Maynes, Mary Jo. *Schooling in Western Europe: A Social History*. Albany: State University of New York Press, 1985.

McCalman, Iain. *Radical Underworld: Prophets, Revolutionaries and Pornographers in London, 1795–1840*. Cambridge: Cambridge University Press, 1988.

McClelland, Charles E. *Berlin, The Mother of All Research Universities, 1860–1918*. Lanham, MD: Lexington Books, 2017.

McLellan, David. *Karl Marx: A Biography*. 4th edition. Basingstoke, UK: Palgrave Macmillan, 2006.

Mee, Jon. *Print, Publicity and Popular Radicalism in the 1790s: The Laurel of Liberty*. Cambridge: Cambridge University Press, 2016.

Mellers, Wilfred. *Beethoven and the Voice of God*. New York: Oxford University Press, 1983.

Mendes-Flohr, Paul, and Jehuda Reinharz, eds. *The Jew in the Modern World: A Documentary History*. New York: Oxford University Press, 1995.

Meyer, Michael A. *Response to Modernity: A History of the Reform Movement in Judaism*. New York: Oxford University Press, 1988.

Mirowski, Philip. *More Heat than Light: Economics as Social Physics, Physics as Nature's Economics*. Cambridge: Cambridge University Press, 1989.

Moyn, Samuel, and Andrew Sartori, eds. *Global Intellectual History*. New York: Columbia University Press, 2013.

Mueller-Vollmer, Kurt. *Transatlantic Crossings and Transformations: German-American Cultural Transfer from the 18th to the End of the 19th Century*. Frankfurt: Peter Lang, 2015.

Mullan, John. "Feelings and Novels." In *Rewriting the Self: Histories from the Renaissance to the Present*, edited by Roy Porter, 119–31. London: Routledge, 1997.

Murray, Hannah-Rose. "A 'Negro Hercules': Frederick Douglass' Celebrity in Britain." *Celebrity Studies* 7, no. 2 (2016): 264–79.

Namier, Sir Lewis. "1848: Seed-Plot of History." In *Vanished Supremacies' Essays on European History 1812–1918*. Harmondsworth, UK: Penguin Books, 1962.

Naugle, David. *Weltanschauung: The History of a Concept*. Grand Rapids, MI: Wm. B. Eerdmans, 2002.

Nisbet, Robert. *History of the Idea of Progress*. 2nd edition. New Brusnwick, NJ: Transaction Books, 2008.

Nisbet, Robert. *The Sociological Tradition*. London: Heinemann, 1967.

Nochlin, Linda. *Realism*. New York: Penguin, 1991.

Numbers, Ronald. *Creation by Natural Law: Laplace's Nebular Hypothesis in American Thought*. Seattle: University of Washington Press, 1997.

Nussbaum, Frederick L. *A History of the Economic Institutions of Modern Europe*. New York: Crofts & Co., 1933.

Offen, Karen M. *European Feminisms, 1700–1950: A Political History*. Stanford, CA: Stanford University Press, 2000.

Oppenheim, Janet. *The Other World: Spiritualism and Psychical Research in England, 1850–1914*. New York: Cambridge University Press, 1988.

Osterhammel, Jürgen. *The Transformation of the World: A Global History of the Nineteenth Century*. Translated by Patrick Camiller. Princeton, NJ: Princeton University Press, 2014.

Ozouf, Mona. *Festivals and the French Revolution*. Translated by Alan Sheridan. Cambridge, MA: Harvard University Press, 1988.

Pateman, Carole. *The Sexual Contract*. Stanford, CA: Stanford University Press, 1988.

Pearson, Roger. *Unfolding Mallarmé*. Oxford: Oxford University Press, 1997.

Pelikan, Jaroslov. *Christian Doctrine and Modern Culture (Since 1700)*. Volume 5 of *The Christian Tradition: A History of Development of Doctrine*. Chicago: University of Chicago Press, 1989.

Petit, Annie. "La diffusion des saviors comme devoir positiviste." *Romantisme* 19 (1989): 7–26.

Phillips, David Llewellyn. "Photography, Modernity, and Art." In *Nineteenth Century Art*, edited by Stephen F. Eisenman, 273–308. 4th edition. London: Thames and Hudson, 2011.

Philp, Mark. "Vulgar Conservatism, 1792–3." *English Historical Review* 110, no. 435 (1995): 42–69.

Pickering, Mary. *Auguste Comte: An Intellectual Biography*. Cambridge: Cambridge University Press, 1993.

Pickering, W. S. F. *Durkheim's Sociology of Religion: Themes and Theories*. London: Routledge & Kegan Paul, 1984.

Pinkard, Terry. *Hegel: A Biography*. Cambridge: Cambridge University Press, 2000.

Pinkard, Terry. *Hegel's Phenomenology: The Sociality of Reason*. Cambridge: Cambridge University Press, 1994.

Pipes, Richard. *The Russian Revolution, 1899–1919*. London: Fontana Press, 1992.

Pitts, Jennifer. *A Turn to Empire: The Rise of Imperial Liberalism in Britain and France*. Princeton, NJ: Princeton University Press, 2005.

Pohl, Frances K. "The Rhetoric of Realism," 250–72. In *Nineteenth Century Art*, edited by Stephen F. Eisenman. 4th edition. London: Thames and Hudson, 2011.

Poliakov, Léon. *The Aryan Myth: A History of Racist and Nationalist Ideas in Europe*. Translated by Edmund Howard. New York: Barnes and Noble, 1974.

Pollard, Sidney. *Peaceful Conquest: The Industrialization of Europe, 1760–1970*. New York: Oxford University Press, 1981.

Pollock, Sheldon. "Future Philology? The Fate of a Soft Science in a Hard World." *Critical Inquiry* 35, no. 4 (2009): 931–61.

Priest, Robert D. *The Gospel According to Renan: Reading, Writing, and Religion in Nineteenth-Century France*. New York: Oxford University Press, 2015.

Prutsch, Markus J. *Making Sense of Constitutional Monarchism in Post-Napoleonic France and Germany*. Basingstoke, UK: Palgrave Macmillan, 2013.

Quinn, Frederick. *The French Overseas Empire*. Westport, CT: Praeger, 2002.

Raj, Kapil. *Relocating Modern Science: Circulation and the Construction of Knowledge in South Asia and Europe, 1650–1900*. New York: Palgrave Macmillan, 2007.

Reardon, B. M. B., ed. *Religious Thought in the Nineteenth Century*. New York: Cambridge University Press, 1966.

Richards, Robert J. *The Romantic Conception of Life: Science and Philosophy in the Age of Goethe*. Chicago: University of Chicago Press, 2002.

Richards, Robert J. *The Tragic Sense of Life: Ernst Haeckel and the Struggle over Evolutionary Thought*. Chicago: University of Chicago Press, 2008.

Richter, Melvin. *The Politics of Conscience: T.H. Green and His Age*. London: Weidenfeld and Nicolson, 1964.

Ricoeur, Paul. *Freud and Philosophy: An Essay in Interpretation*. Translated by Denis Savage. New Haven, CT: Yale University Press, 1970.

Ringer, Fritz. *Max Weber's Methodology: The Unification of the Cultural and Social Sciences*. Cambridge, MA: Harvard University Press, 1997.

Roberts, Matthew. "Popular Conservatism in Britain, 1832–1914." *Parliamentary History* 26, no. 3 (2007): 387–410.

Rodgers, Daniel T. *Atlantic Crossings: Social Politics in a Progressive Age*. Cambridge, MA: Harvard University Press, 1998.

Roncaglia, Alessandro. *The Wealth of Ideas: A History of Economic Thought*. Cambridge: Cambridge University Press, 2005.

Royce, Josiah. *The Spirit of Modern Philosophy*. New York: Norton, 1967.

Said, Edward. *Orientalism*. New York: Pantheon, 1978.

Salmi, Hannu. *Nineteenth-Century Europe: A Cultural History*. Cambridge, UK: Polity Press, 2008.

Savy, Nicole, ed. *Le Siècle des dictionnaires*. Paris: Editions de la réunion des musées nationaux, 1987.

Schaffer, Simon. "Genius in Romantic Natural Philosophy." In *Romanticism and the Sciences*, edited by Andrew Cunningham and Nicholas Jardine, 82–98. Cambridge: Cambridge University Press, 1990.

Schneer, Jonathan. *London 1900: The Imperial Metropolis*. New Haven, CT: Yale University Press, 1999.

Schorske, Carl E. *Fin-de-Siècle Vienna: Politics and Culture*. New York: Alfred A. Knopf, 1980.

Schorske, Carl E. *German Social Democracy, 1905–1917: The Development of the Great Schism*. Cambridge, MA: Harvard University Press, 1955.

Schwab, Raymond. *La Renaissance orientale*. Paris: Plon, 1950.

Schweitzer, Albert. *The Quest for the Historical Jesus*. New York: Macmillan, 1961.

Scott, Derek B. *Sounds of the Metropolis: The 19th-Century Popular Music Revolution in London, New York, Paris and Vienna*. New York: Oxford University Press, 2008.

Screpanti, Ernesto, and Stefano Zamagni. *An Outline of the History of Economic Thought*. Translated by David Field and Lynn Kirby. 2nd edition. Oxford: Oxford University Press, 2005.

Seigel, Jerrold. *The Idea of the Self: Thought and Experience in Western Europe since the Seventeenth Century*. Cambridge: Cambridge University Press, 2005.

Sepper, Dennis. *Goethe contra Newton*. Cambridge: Cambridge University Press, 1988.

Sheehan, Jonathan. *The Enlightenment Bible: Translation, Scholarship, Culture*. Princeton, NJ: Princeton University Press, 2005.

Simmel, Georg. "The Metropolis and Mental Life." In *Simmel on Culture: Selected Writings*, edited by David Frisby and Mike Featherstone. London: Sage, 2000.

Slonimsky, Nicholas. *Music Since 1900*. 4th edition. London: Cassell, 1972.

Smart, Ninian, ed. *Nineteenth-Century Religious Thought in the West*. 3 volumes. New York: Cambridge University Press, 1988.

Smith, Bonnie G. *The Gender of History: Men, Women, and Historical Practice*. Cambridge, MA: Harvard University Press, 1998.

Sperber, Jonathan. *Karl Marx: A Nineteenth-Century Life*. New York: Norton, 2013.

Spitzer, Alan B. *The French Generation of 1820*. Princeton, NJ: Princeton University Press, 1987.

Stansky, Peter. "Harcourt, Sir William George Granville Venables Vernon (1827–1904)." In *The Oxford Dictionary of National Biography*. Oxford: Oxford University Press, 2004. Online edition, accessed January 2008.

Starobinski, Jean. *Jean-Jacques Rousseau: Transparency and Obstruction*. Translated by Arthur Goldhammer, with an introduction by Robert J. Morrissey. Chicago: University of Chicago Press, 1988.

Sternhell, Zeev. "Paul Déroulède and the Origins of Modern French Nationalism." *Journal of Contemporary History* 6, no. 4 (1971): 46–70.

Stites, Richard. *The Four Horsemen: Riding to Liberty in Post-Napoleonic Europe*. Oxford: Oxford University Press, 2014.

Strachan, Hew. "The Origins of the First World War." *International Affairs* 90, no. 2 (2014): 429–39.

Taylor, Charles. *A Secular Age*. Cambridge, MA: Harvard University Press, 2007.

Taylor, Charles. *Sources of the Self: The Making of the Modern Identity*. Cambridge: Cambridge University Press, 2002.

Thackray, Arnold. "Quantified Chemistry—the Newtonian Dream." In *John Dalton and the Progress of Science*, edited by D. S. L. Cardwell, 92–108. New York: Barnes and Noble, 1968.

Toews, John Edward. *Hegelianism: The Path toward Dialectical Humanism, 1805–1841*. New York: Cambridge University Press, 1980.

Tresch, John. *The Romantic Machine: Utopian Science and Technology After Napoleon*. Chicago: University of Chicago Press, 2012.

Vauchez, André. "The Cathedral." In *Realms of Memory*, edited by Pierre Nora and Lawrence Kritzman, Vol. 2: *Traditions*, 37–68. New York: Columbia University Press, 1997.

Vick, Brian. *The Congress of Vienna: Power and Politics after Napoleon*. Cambridge, MA: Harvard University Press, 2014.

Vick, Brian. "Liberalism, Nationalism, and Gender Dichotomy in Mid Nineteenth-Century Germany: The Contested Case of German Civil Law." *Journal of Modern History* 82, no. 3 (2010): 546–84.

Vick, Brian. "Power, Humanitarianism and the Global Liberal Order: Abolition and the Barbary Corsairs in the Vienna Congress System." *International History Review* 40, no. 4 (2018): 939–60.

Vlastos, Stephen, ed. *Mirror of Modernity: Invented Traditions of Modern Japan*. Berkeley: University of California Press, 1998.

Walicki, Andrzej. *The Slavophile Controversy: History of a Conservative Utopia in Nineteenth-Century Russian Thought*. Oxford: Oxford University Press, 1975.

Waterman, A. M. C. *Revolution, Economics and Religion: Christian Political Economy, 1798–1833*. Cambridge: Cambridge University Press, 1991.

Watkins, Glenn. *Pyramids at the Louvre. Music, Culture, and Collage from Stravinsky to the Postmodernists*. Cambridge, MA: Belknap Press, 1994.

Weir, Todd H., ed. *Monism: Science, Philosophy, Religion, and the History of a Worldview*. New York: Palgrave Macmillan, 2012.

Weir, Todd H. *Secularism and Religion in Nineteenth-Century Germany: The Rise of the Fourth Confession*. Cambridge: Cambridge University Press, 2014.

Weisz, George. *The Emergence of the Modern Universities in France, 1893–1914*. Princeton, NJ: Princeton University Press, 1983.

Wellmon, Chad. *Organizing Enlightenment: Information Overload and the Invention of the Modern Research University*. Baltimore: Johns Hopkins University Press, 2015.

Westler, Brendon. "Between Tradition and Revolution: The Curious Case of Francisco Martínez Marina, the Cádiz Constitution, and Spanish Liberalism." *Journal of the History of Ideas* 76, no. 3 (2015): 393–416.

Williams, Raymond. *Culture and Society*. London: Chatto & Windus, 1959.

Williamson, Goerge S. *The Longing for Myth in Germany: Religion and Aesthetic Culture from Romanticism to Nietzsche*. Chicago: University of Chicago Press, 2004.

Winch, Donald. *Riches and Poverty: An Intellectual History of Political Economy in Britain, 1750–1834*. Cambridge: Cambridge University Press, 1996.

Winch, Donald. *Wealth and Life: Essays on the Intellectual History of Political Economy in Britain, 1848–1914*. Cambridge: Cambridge University Press, 2009.

Wood, Allen W., and Songsuk Susan Hahn, eds. *The Cambridge History of Philosophy in the Nineteenth Century (1790–1870)*. Cambridge: Cambridge University Press, 2012.

Wulf, Andrea. *The Invention of Nature: Alexander von Humbold's New World*. New York: Alfred A. Knopf, 2015.

Zastoupil, Lynn. *Rammohun Roy and the Making of Victorian Britain*. Basingstoke, UK: Palgrave Macmillan, 2010.

CONTRIBUTORS

Jan Goldstein is Norman and Edna Freehling Professor of History at the University of Chicago, USA. She is the author of *Console and Classify: The French Psychiatric Profession in the Nineteenth Century* (1987, 2nd edn. 2001), *The Post-Revolutionary Self: Politics and Psyche in France, 1750–1850* (2005), and *Hysteria Complicated by Ecstasy: The Case of Nanette Leroux* (2010). She served as President of the American Historical Association in 2014 and in 2018 was named *Chevalier dans l'Ordre des Palmes Académiques* by the French government.

Frederick Gregory is Professor of History of Science Emeritus at the University of Florida, USA. He is the author of *Nature Lost: Natural Science and the German Theological Traditions of the 19th Century* (1992), *Natural Science in Western History*, 2 vols. (2008), and most recently an essay, "Continental Europe," in the collection called *The Warfare of Science and Religion: The Idea That Wouldn't Die* (2018).

James H. Johnson is Professor of History at Boston University, USA, where he teaches courses in European Intellectual and Cultural History. He is the author of *Listening in Paris: A Cultural History* (1995) and *Venice Incognito: Masks in the Serene Republic* (2011), which have received awards from the American Historical Society, the American Philosophical Society, and the Center for Eighteenth-Century Studies. He is an active pianist and presents regular lecture-performances on music in its cultural and political contexts.

Julian Johnson is Regius Professor of Music at Royal Holloway, University of London, UK. His work explores wide-ranging questions in the history and philosophy of music, and he is the author of six books including *Out of Time: Music and the Making of Modernity* (2015) and *After Debussy: Music, Language and the Margins of Philosophy* (2020). He is a regular public speaker and broadcaster on music and, in 2017, was made a Fellow of the British Academy.

Donald R. Kelley is James Westfall Thompson Professor Emeritus of History at Rutgers University, USA. He is the author of numerous books and articles on Western historiography, European intellectual history, and the history of law. His books include *Fortunes of History: Historical Inquiry from Herder to Huizinga* (2003) and *The Descent of Ideas: The History of Intellectual History* (2002). From 1985 to 2005, he was the editor of *The Journal of the History of Ideas*.

Thomas Kselman is Professor of History Emeritus at the University of Notre Dame, USA. He is the author of *Miracles and Prophecies in Nineteenth-Century France* (1983), *Death and the Afterlife in Modern France* (1993, 2016), and *Conscience* *and Conversion: Religious Liberty in Post-Revolutionary France* (2018). He was the recipient of NEH Fellowships in 1984 and 2008 and a Guggenheim Fellowship in 1989. He served as the President of the American Catholic Historical Association in 2005.

Krishan Kumar is University Professor and William R. Kenan, Jr., Professor of Sociology at the University of Virginia, USA. His most recent book is *Visions of Empire: How Five Imperial Regimes Shaped the World* (2017), which was co-winner of the Barrington Moore Prize of the American Sociological Association for the best book in comparative historical sociology published in 2017–2018. He has just completed *Empires: A Historical and Political Sociology* (2020).

Patrick McGuinness is Professor of French and Comparative Literature at the University of Oxford, UK. He is also a poet, novelist, and critic. His academic work includes books and articles on English literary criticism, writers of the French *fin de siècle*, and the poetry of the First World War. Among the many awards he has received for his poetry and fiction are the Writers' Guild Award for Fiction and the Encore Award. He was a finalist for the Prix Médicis. In 2009, he was named *Chevalier dans l'Ordre des Palmes Académiques*.

Jerrold Seigel is Kenan Professor of History Emeritus at New York University, USA. His first field of interest was the Italian Renaissance (*Rhetoric and Philosophy in Renaissance Humanism*, 1968), but he has since devoted himself to more modern topics, beginning with *Marx's Fate: The Shape of a Life* (1975), followed by *Bohemian Paris: Culture, Politics, and the Boundaries of Bourgeois Life* (1986), *The Private Worlds of Marcel Duchamp* (1995), *The Idea of the Self* (2005), *Modernity and Bourgeois Life* (2012), and *Between Cultures: Europe and its Others in Five Exemplary Lives* (2015). He lives in New York, where he is a devoted amateur cellist.

Bonnie G. Smith is Board of Governors Distinguished Professor of History Emerita at Rutgers University, USA. She has written a wide range of books and essays on women's history and the history of gender, European history, and world history. Her books include the *Gender of History, Women's Studies: The Basics* (2nd edn., 2019) and *Europe in the Contemporary World, 1900 to the Present* (2nd edn., 2020). She has served on the boards of editors of *French Historical Studies, Feminist Studies*, and the *Journal of Women's History*.

Brian Vick is Professor of History at Emory University, USA. He is the author of essays on German liberalism, nationalism, and ideas of race, and the books *Defining Germany: The 1848 Frankfurt Parliamentarians and National Identity* (2002), and *The Congress of Vienna: Power and Politics after Napoleon* (2014), winner of the 2015 Hans Rosenberg Book Prize of the Central European History Society of the American Historical Association.

INDEX